W9-CDL-930

the
convection
oven bible

the
convection
oven bible

Linda Stephen

Robert
ROSE

The Convection Oven Bible
Text copyright© 2007 Linda Stephen
Photographs copyright© 2007 Robert Rose Inc.
Cover and text design copyright© 2007 Robert Rose Inc.

No part of this publication may be reproduced, stored in a retrieval system or transmitted, in
any form or by any means, without the prior written consent of the publisher or a licence from
The Canadian Copyright Licensing Agency (Access Copyright). For an Access Copyright
licence, visit www.accesscopyright.ca or call toll-free: 1-800-893-5777.

For complete cataloguing information, see page 290.

Disclaimer
The recipes in this book have been carefully tested by our kitchen and our tasters. To the best of
our knowledge, they are safe and nutritious for ordinary use and users. For those people with
food or other allergies, or who have special food requirements or health issues, please read the
suggested contents of each recipe carefully and determine whether or not they may create a
problem for you. All recipes are used at the risk of the consumer. Consumers should consult
their convection oven manufacturer's manual for recommended procedures and cooking times.

We cannot be responsible for any hazards, loss or damage that may occur as a result of any
recipe use.

For those with special needs, allergies, requirements or health problems, in the event of
any doubt, please contact your medical advisor prior to the use of any recipe.

Design & Production: PageWave Graphics Inc.
Photography: Mark T. Shapiro and Colin Erricson
Editorial: Shelley Tanaka
Food Styling: Kate Bush
Prop Styling: Charlene Erricson

Cover image: Toffee Chocolate Crunch Cheesecake (page 259)

We acknowledge the financial support of the Government of Canada through the Book
Publishing Industry Development Program (BPIDP) for our publishing activities.

Published by Robert Rose Inc.
120 Eglinton Avenue East, Suite 800
Toronto, Ontario, Canada M4P 1E2
Tel: (416) 322-6552   Fax: (416) 322-6936

Printed in Canada
1 2 3 4 5 6 7 8 9 CP 15 14 13 12 11 10 09 08 07

For my grandnieces —
Jenna (already a keen baker)
and Amy (who just wants to eat).
May they become happy cooks.

Contents

Acknowledgments

THANKS GO TO a wonderful group of friends and professionals for their generous time, information and patience.

- Jane at Mabe Canada Inc.; Kitchen Designer Division of Tasco Distributors; Whirlpool Canada; Brian MacIntosh of MacIntosh's General Store; the Beef Information Centre; Charles Bruce Thompson of Ontario Pork; home economist Barb Holland; the Food Safety Information Society (FSIS); the Canadian Appliance Manufacturers Association (CAMA).

- Bob Dees, Marian Jarkovich, Arden Boehm and the team at Robert Rose Inc. — Andrew Smith, Joseph Gisini, Kevin Cockburn and, especially, Daniella Zanchetta at PageWave Graphics; Mark Shapiro, Colin Erricson, Kate Bush and Charlene Erricson; Jennifer MacKenzie and Teresa Makarewicz.

- Recipe testers Rhonda Caplan, Kathy Livingston and Josée Menard.

- For sharing recipes and advice — Cathy Angus, Marion Davidson, Mitchell Davis, Evelyn Hall, Greta Holmes, Joe O'Grady, Carol Quirk, Susan Richardson, Brenda Stanford, Clarke and Susan Stephen, Bonnie Stern, Shelley Tanaka.

- Bill Vronsky, for extreme computer assistance and tolerance.

- My cooking students past and present, who continue to enrich me with their cooking and travel experiences.

- My mother, Doris Stephen, and my family — Clarke, Susan, Harry, Kathy, Craig, Jennifer, Chad and Elle-Mai.

- My editor, Shelley Tanaka, for her calm, quiet voice and for telling me that everything was fine, "but maybe we will just make this change."

Introduction

CONVECTION OVENS HAVE been a mainstay in restaurant and hotel kitchens, bakeries and pizza parlors for many years because of their speed, even browning and even cooking. During my chef training and years working in professional kitchens, I was always impressed with these commercial convection ovens — the roasts of beef that chefs would make and hold to perfect degrees of doneness; the golden and crusty baguettes, flaky croissants and crisp pastries that the pastry chefs produced; the trays of bacon that could be cooked up so quickly for sandwiches.

Although I grew up on a farm where most of the cooking was done on a woodstove, when I had an opportunity to build my own kitchen, I knew I wanted a convection oven. I would load up my semi-commercial convection oven with breads, pies and cookies (I could bake sixteen dozen cookies at a time) before heading off to the local Saturday morning market to sell my wares. My oven could also cook and roast large quantities of fish, vegetables and meat for catering functions. (At our annual Rotary Club fundraising dinner, we would grill four hundred filets mignons and then finish them to absolute perfection in a commercial convection oven — a technique that can also be used at home.)

As with many kitchen appliances adapted from industry for the home market, convection ovens have become increasingly popular and mainstream. And as technology improves, manufacturers are offering additional features that enhance the ovens' versatility even more. The Canadian Appliance Manufacturers Association (CAMA) projects that convection will continue to grow in popularity because of the improved cooking speed and consistent results that a conventional oven cannot provide.

Today I mostly use a domestic convection oven for teaching and for cooking for family and friends. I also love my convection toaster oven when I am cooking small quantities or small family meals.

Having worked with a variety of convection ovens, I am hooked on them all, and I now take them for granted. So I am always surprised when someone tells me that they have never used theirs. Many new and renovated kitchens come equipped with convection ovens, but often people don't know what to do with them. Yet this oven is easy to use, and you will instantly notice the difference in your cooking — both in time and in the finished result.

The recipes in this book have been developed to make the most of the convection oven and highlight its versatility. You can cook several batches of muffins and cookies at once without worrying about uneven cooking or the bottoms burning (I package the extras for giveaways, donations or freezing). Poultry and meats become brown and crisp on the outside while sealing in the juices. Gratins and casseroles cook quickly, with crisp, golden toppings.

Pizzas, breads and pies bake evenly, and meringues dry perfectly. Angel food cakes — my childhood specialty — cook to perfection in the convection oven. Even steaks can be as brown and juicy as any grilled on an outdoor barbecue — just sear them quickly on the stovetop and finish them in the convection oven.

You can also cook entire meals in the oven. Look for Easy Oven Meal menus throughout this book for suggestions on how to cook a main course, side dish and dessert at the same time, using energy, and your time, efficiently.

So make the most of your convection oven and cook something. You will quickly become familiar and comfortable with the features and potential of your oven — and you will never roast a chicken the same way again.

Convection Ovens: How They Work

CONVECTION OVENS DIFFER from standard conventional ovens in that they usually have a third heating element and a fan that provide continuous and consistent circulation of hot air while food is cooking. (In some countries, convection ovens are known as fan ovens.) Because of this there is even heat and even browning, and most foods can be cooked at a lower temperature and/or for a shorter time (with larger roasts and poultry, the conventional cooking time can be reduced by 25 to 30 percent).

A true convection oven (also known as "European convection" because it was first popularized in Europe) has a fan as well as a third element at the rear of the oven. Some ovens only have a fan that blows around the hot air, but true convection ovens pick up heat from all three elements, eliminating hotter and cooler spots throughout the oven, so the temperature is consistent, and the heated air surrounds and penetrates food from every angle, sealing in natural moisture and flavors. Some manufacturers have trademarked specific names to identify their ovens as being true convection, as well as adding features that are specific to their brand. Element usage may vary depending on the make of your oven. **Always consult your manufacturer's manual before using your oven.**

Getting to Know Your Convection Oven

USING YOUR CONVECTION oven is not difficult, but changing your routine may be. The best way to learn about your oven is to start using it. Make something that you usually cook (e.g., roast chicken, cookies, muffins), either from this cookbook or your own recipe (just make the simple temperature and/or time adjustment as described on page 17). Do not start out with some exotic recipe that you would not normally make. Keep it simple and familiar. As you become more comfortable, you will easily make the change from standard to convection cooking.

Features, Settings and Options

THESE ARE JUST some of the features, settings and options available on convection ovens. The terminology varies with each manufacturer, so always consult the manual for your specific oven.

Multiple Racks

In the convection oven, multiple racks and rack settings can be used, which means several batches of cookies or several different dishes can be cooked at the same time. At maximum capacity, the oven can be filled from top to bottom as long as you leave 1 to 2 inches (2.5 to 5 cm) between dishes, and between dishes and the oven walls. In many convection ovens, a filtering system traps food smells, so flavors are not transferred from one dish to another, and you can even cook fish and a dessert at the same time.

Most convection ovens come with three racks with four to six possible positions for these racks. In general, the top of the food should be in the center of the oven. This can be adjusted when other things are cooking in the oven at the same time, but try to stagger dishes to allow air to circulate more freely. (Some convection ovens even have partial oven racks for side dishes, with the "tall" food — usually a roast or poultry — on the bottom rack.) Always position the racks before preheating.

For convection broiling, food is generally positioned about 4 inches (10 cm) from the broiler element, but watch carefully, as the broil function works quickly. Some manufacturers also offer ovens with a hidden radiant element on the bottom so that pizza and bread can be baked directly on the heat source. Your manual will outline the various rack positions for your particular model.

Convection Roast

On the convection roast setting, usually the bottom (bake) and/or top (broil) elements alternately cycle on and off to maintain the oven temperature, while the rear element and fan are constant. This setting is generally used for roasting meats and poultry as well as for some pastries.

Meats and poultry sear and brown early on convection roast, because the circulating hot air renders fat from the meat, sealing the surface. Poultry develops a golden brown and crispy skin, sealing in the juices to keep breast meat from drying out as the thigh meat continues to cook. Large tender roasts such as prime rib, striploin and tenderloin roast beautifully, and even a lean, slightly less tender cut such as eye of round will roast well, provided it is not overcooked.

Steaks or chops that are started on the stovetop and briefly finished on convection roast at a high temperature are moist and succulent (this is a restaurant technique used by many chefs). You can also preheat certain grill pans in the convection oven and cook steaks and chops completely in the oven, turning them once — a great substitute for barbecuing during the winter months, or for those who live in apartments where barbecuing is not permitted.

Less tender roasts, such as blade, chuck, cross rib, etc., are best cooked covered, with liquid, at a lower oven temperature. When food is covered, the advantages of convection cooking disappear, but I still use the convection function for covered dishes if I am cooking another part of the meal at the same temperature and time.

Although it is generally recommended that you cook chicken breasts and fish fillets on convection bake, they can also be cooked successfully at a high temperature on convection roast, but they cook very quickly and require close supervision.

In some recipes, meat and poultry are started in the oven at a high temperature to brown and quickly seal in juices; then the temperature is reduced for the balance of the cooking time. If this is the technique you have always used for roasting, then just continue, making the recommended temperature and time adjustments to your usual recipe (page 17).

In this book, poultry and stuffing are always cooked separately. Because of the shorter cooking time in the convection oven, the poultry may be cooked before the stuffing reaches a safe temperature.

To roast in the convection oven, place the roast or poultry on the lightly greased rack set over the broiler pan. These usually come with the oven, but you can also make your own by setting a cake rack or roasting rack in a baking pan or rimmed baking sheet. Ideally, for more even browning, the meat should be elevated above the sides of the pan, so air can circulate around the entire piece. For easier cleanup, tightly line the broiler pan or baking sheet with foil.

To roast meats and poultry to a safe temperature, use the recommended temperatures outlined in the chart on page 14. The roasting times given in the recipes in this book are guidelines (cooking times may differ slightly depending on the oven and the size and shape of roasts). Keep in mind that meats continue to cook after they have been removed from the heat, so they can be taken out of the oven just before they reach the suggested temperature. Most recipes recommend tenting a large piece

Meat Thermometers and Oven Probes

There are several kinds of meat thermometers, from digital and instant-read to fork and pop-up indicators. Some thermometers stay in the food while it cooks; others do not. Always wash the thermometer in hot soapy water after use.

To use a meat thermometer, insert it into the thickest part of the roast beef, pork, veal or lamb, not touching bone, fat or gristle. To check whole poultry, insert the thermometer into the thickest part of the thigh between the drumstick and the breast.

To use the oven probe that comes with the oven, follow the manufacturer's directions. When the oven probe has reached the selected temperature, the oven automatically shuts off. The oven probe works very well, but you can continue to use your usual thermometer as well until you are comfortable with the oven probe. The oven probe is only recommended for use in the bake, convection bake and convection roast settings — not for broiling or bread proofing.

Recommended Safe Temperatures for Doneness

Beef and Lamb	140°F (60°C) rare to medium-rare 160°F (70°C) medium 170°F (75°C) well done
Pork	160°F (70°C) medium
Ground Beef and Pork	170°F (75°C) well done
Ham (ready to eat and fully cooked)	140°F (60°C)
Whole Chicken and Turkey (unstuffed)*	180°F (82°C)
Turkey Breast	170°F (75°C)
Ground Chicken and Turkey	175°F (80°C)

* Do not stuff whole poultry to be cooked in the convection oven. Because of the shorter cooking time, the meat may be cooked before the stuffing reaches a safe temperature.

For further information about safe cooking temperatures, check www.canfightbac.org and www.fsis.usda.gov/Food_Safety_Education/index.asp.

of meat loosely with foil and letting it stand for 10 to 15 minutes before carving. This allows the juices to retract and makes carving easier. When timing your meal service, be sure to incorporate resting time.

When roasting whole poultry (turkey, chicken, duck, etc.), the best way to check for doneness is with a meat thermometer or oven probe. Do not undercook poultry expecting the temperature to rise on standing. Cook it to the recommended temperature and then tent loosely before carving.

The recipes in this book start with a preheated oven, though not all manufacturers suggest preheating when roasting larger pieces of meat and whole turkeys and chickens, so consult your manual.

The convection roast setting can also be used for other dishes. Oven roasting vegetables and fruits, for example, enhances their natural sweetness and brings out a richness without a lot of added fat or seasonings. Vegetables and a fruit dessert can often be roasted alongside the main course, for a complete meal (see Oven Meals, page 20).

A superior result is also achieved when you cook pastries and pies (savory and sweet) on the convection roast setting. (When you start to use the convection roast setting for pies and tarts, check them 15 minutes before the time recommended in your original recipe.) Some casseroles and assembled dishes can be cooked on convection roast, too.

If your convection oven does not have a convection roast setting, just use the regular convection setting, though the cooking time may be slightly longer than the time suggested in the recipe.

Convection Bake

In convection baking, the rear element and fan operate (and in some models the bottom element also operates). In some brands the oven is preheated by the top and bottom elements, but once the target temperature is reached, the rear element goes on, while the bottom element cycles on and off to maintain the heat. Always preheat the oven when you are using the convection bake function.

The convection bake setting is used for most baking (pastry is the exception, although some manufacturers suggest the convection bake setting for pastry, too), such as cakes, muffins, cookies, loaf cakes, quickbreads, yeast breads, soufflés, desserts, casseroles and other items requiring gentler cooking than roasting.

When making cookies, cupcakes, biscuits and muffins, three racks can be used, which means several batches can be baked at one time. This also works for storebought cookie dough (follow the package instructions, but reduce the oven temperature by 25°F/13°C). Ideally, use rimless baking sheets for cookies to allow the air to circulate.

Cakes, loaf cakes and biscuits that contain sugar, milk and eggs brown nicely and quickly in the convection oven, yet they retain their moisture and freshness (often giving them a good shelf life when they are properly stored). With multiple racks, more than one cake or loaf can be baked at the same time, but stagger the pans for the best air circulation. Up to six single-layer cakes and four to six loaf cakes can be baked at one time.

Outstanding results are also achieved when yeast breads are baked in the convection oven. The time and temperature will depend on the ingredients in the bread. When heavier flours and rich ingredients such as eggs, milk and sugar are included, it is important that the baking time is long enough for the heat to penetrate to the center. Several loaves (four to six, depending on their height) can be baked at one time; stagger the pans for efficient air circulation. Baking rolls on several racks is a great time saver, since up to three dozen can be baked at once.

Fish and poultry pieces are often cooked on convection bake, although some cooks like the result produced by the convection roast setting. Make a note on your recipes once you find the ideal setting.

Soufflés rise beautifully on the convection bake setting (but do not keep opening the oven door). Assembled dishes and casseroles are also usually baked on this setting, though occasionally the convection roast setting can be used. Again, check your owner's manual.

Convection Broil

In convection broiling, the top element heats while the fan circulates the hot air. This feature may vary in different makes of ovens. Most convection broilers are preset (450°F to 500°F/230°C to 260°C), but these temperatures can be changed depending on the size and thickness of the food being broiled.

Preheat the broiler, and broil with the oven door closed. In convection broiling, the fan shuts off when the door is opened. It will come back on when the door is closed.

Adjust the rack position before preheating the broiler. Most recipes in this book call for the top of the food to be placed about 4 inches (10 cm) from the heat source, but in general, the thicker the food, the farther it is placed from the heat. Broiling time will depend on the rack position and broiler temperature.

When broiling meat, trim off any excess fat to prevent splattering. Try to turn foods only once for even cooking.

If your oven does not have a convection broil setting, simply use the standard broiler. (When using the standard broiler, often the door is kept slightly ajar, but check the manual.) The cooking time may be slightly longer if you are using a standard broiler.

Most convection ovens come with a broiler pan and/or a broiler grid or searing grill and a wire/roasting rack.

Other Settings and Features

As convection ovens become more popular, manufacturers keep improving and adding settings and features. It's like buying a car, computer or sewing machine; it depends on how many bells and whistles you need and want.

Most home models combine a standard oven with convection options. In addition to the basic convection settings (convection roast, convection bake and broil/convection broil), other options might include functions that allow the oven to self-clean, keep food hot after it is cooked, prepare food for the Sabbath, proof bread (let it rise), convert time and temperature, and any number of other features. Some models include a bake stone (for pizzas) and a rotisserie. Some are so highly computerized that they practically think and cook for you — you punch in what you are cooking and the oven

automatically sets the temperature and cooking time, depending on your dish size and roast size. Some will even tell you how many baking sheets to use for cookies, etc.

Always read the manufacturer's manual, and purchase your oven from a business where you can obtain further information if necessary (ideally a place where you can actually speak to a sales representative or technician if follow-up is required).

Convection Toaster Ovens

Convection toaster ovens bake, broil and toast. As with large convection ovens, hot air is circulated around the food while it cooks. Smaller than standard floor or wall ovens, convection toaster ovens sit on a heatproof counter surface, taking up minimal space, so they are ideal for cottages, chalets and recreational vehicles. (Check your manual for suggestions about counter placement, use and care.) They are less expensive than large kitchen stove/ovens, but more expensive than standard toaster ovens. They can serve as the only oven for students and singles, occasional cooks or retirees with small kitchens. They can also serve as a second oven when you are preparing smaller quantities of food or when you need extra oven space.

Most convection toaster ovens have both standard and convection functions. Most offer toaster and broiler options. The ovens are usually equipped with an oven rack and a combination broiler rack with oven pan (also called a drip tray or bake pan). The oven pan doubles as a baking sheet.

Use caution when lining a pan or dish with parchment paper in the convection toaster oven. Do not let the paper extend beyond the pan edges, as grease can accumulate, causing flareups. Most manufacturers do not recommend using foil in the convection toaster oven.

To convert recipes designed for a standard oven, use the same temperature; the cooking time may be slightly shorter (check 5 to 20 minutes before the end of the cooking time, depending on the item being cooked). If you are cooking a convection oven recipe (such as the ones in this book) in a convection toaster oven, increase the temperature by 25°F (13°C) (e.g., if the recipe calls for a temperature of 325°F/160°C in the regular convection oven, increase the temperature to 350°F/180°C if you are making the same dish in the convection toaster oven).

Select baking pans and casserole dishes that fit easily in your convection toaster oven, leaving at least 1 inch (2.5 cm) between the dish and the oven wall to allow air to circulate. Use shallow-sided baking pans for even heat distribution. (Make sure your pan fits in the oven before you start making the recipe!)

The toaster oven recipes in this book (pages 267 to 289) highlight the oven's versatility — from appetizers and main courses to desserts. Meals can easily be rounded out with a simple salad, steamed vegetable and a potato or rice dish.

If you want to make your favorite recipes in the convection toaster oven, the most important consideration will be container size. You may need to adjust quantities and yields to adapt recipes to the smaller oven.

Converting and Adapting Recipes

MANY CONVECTION OVENS now include a feature that automatically converts the temperature and/or time of your standard oven recipes to convection cook. Basically, you enter the temperature and time of your original recipe and the oven does the math, usually reducing the oven temperature and/or reducing the time.

For example, if your recipe cooks at 375°F (190°C) for 30 minutes in a standard oven, the temperature will be reduced by 25°F (13°C) to 350°F (180°C) for the convection oven, and the time will probably be the same. This feature varies from brand to brand, so check your manual.

Some manuals suggest decreasing the standard oven cooking time while maintaining the oven temperature (for example, cooking times for fresh pies and pastries start with a 10 percent reduction). Generally, the longer a food cooks, the more the cooking time will be reduced.

If your oven does not have the automatic conversion feature, the following guidelines can be used:

• For convection baking, reduce the oven temperature by 25°F (13°C). For example, if a cake is to bake at 350°F (180°C) in a standard oven, reduce the temperature to 325°F (160°C) in the convection oven.

The cooking time may be the same or reduced slightly. Start checking about 5 to 8 minutes before the end of the cooking time. Make a note of the new temperature and time on your recipe for future reference.

- When baking cookies, reduce the oven temperature by 25°F (13°C) and reduce the baking time by 2 to 3 minutes. (The big time saving comes with being able to bake at least three trays of cookies at once.)

- To convection bake cake mixes, brownie mixes, pudding mixes, prepared cookie dough, etc., reduce the oven temperature by 25°F (13°C) and bake for approximately the same time, but always check 5 minutes before the end of the suggested cooking time.

- To convection roast large cuts of meat and poultry, reduce the temperature by 25°F to 50°F (13°C to 25°C) and roast for about the same amount of time. Or, roast at the same temperature given in the standard recipe and reduce the roasting time by 20 to 30 percent. With either method, check for doneness before the end of the suggested cooking time using a meat thermometer or oven probe.

- When convection roasting smaller foods such as chicken pieces, steaks, vegetables and fruits, maintain the suggested standard oven temperature and reduce the time by 25 percent. Do not stray far from the oven. Remember, this cooking method is quick.

- When baking pastries on convection roast, reduce the oven temperature by 25°F (13°C) and start checking 15 minutes before the end of the suggested cooking time. Timing will depend on the pastry type and filling (for example, some apples require a longer cooking time, depending on the variety).

- When cooking assembled dishes such as some casseroles, reduce the oven temperature by 25°F (13°C) and start checking 5 minutes before the end of the suggested cooking time. Food in a shallow dish will cook faster than food cooked in a deeper dish.

Cookware and Containers

CONVECTION COOKING WORKS best when air is allowed to circulate freely throughout the oven. Using the correct cookware and containers will help to produce the best results.

- For cookies, rolls, biscuits, free-form flatbreads and pizzas, shiny rimless cookie sheets produce the best results, though baking sheets with very low sides will also work. Lining baking sheets with parchment paper or using reusable nonstick baking mats makes cleanup easy. If you are using insulated baking sheets, the cooking time may need to be increased.

- Metal baking pans conduct heat well. Dark metal absorbs heat, which is conducive to browning, while shiny metal reflects heat, producing a lighter finish. Use metal pans if possible for pies, loaves, squares, muffins, cakes and breads. Nonstick baking mats and pans come in various sizes and shapes and can also be used.

- Glass or ceramic dishes do not conduct heat as well as metal, so there will be less browning and crisping on the sides and bottom (which is desirable for dishes like casseroles). Use these pans for some cakes, fruit desserts, casseroles, one-dish meals, gratins and soufflés.

- Foods requiring some containment, such as roasted vegetables, appetizers, chicken pieces, fish, etc., are best cooked on baking sheets with shallow sides to encourage air circulation and browning.

- For roasting, most ovens come with a broiler pan, a wire rack and sometimes a searing pan or perforated tray. By elevating the meat on a rack over the pan, air circulates around the item. Roasting pans with high sides block the heat flow.

- Unless it is recommended in the recipe, do not cover food with lids or foil. This defeats the advantage of convection cooking. However, if other foods are being convection cooked at the same time, you can cook covered dishes in the convection oven to make the most of the oven's space.

- Many recipes call for parchment (baking) paper, available in supermarkets and kitchen shops. Parchment paper is nonstick and heatproof and is used to line loaf pans, cake pans, cookie sheets and baking pans. It prevents food from sticking and cuts down on the need for additional fat (though sometimes the pan is lightly greased first to help the paper stick to the pan). It can sometimes be reused.

- Foil is suggested for lining pans when food juices may run and caramelize. Do not let the foil block heat conduction or touch elements. Sometimes both foil and parchment paper are called for — the foil to keep juices from burning onto the pan, and the parchment paper to prevent food from sticking.

Oven Meals

TO MAKE THE MOST of your convection oven, you can cook more than one item at a time. This saves time and energy (yours as well as the oven's). The multiple racks allow several dishes to be cooked simultaneously, and the constant circulation of air produces even heat throughout the oven.

Throughout this book you'll find menus for Easy Oven Meals. They usually include a main dish, starch, vegetable and dessert, and most dishes cook in the oven together. The menus are simple to prepare, and they are accompanied by a work schedule that tells you how to prepare the meal efficiently.

These menus are just examples; there are any number of mix and match recipes in this book that use the same convection setting and temperature, so you can easily create your own menus. The recipe introductions also frequently include suggestions for side dishes or desserts that can be cooked alongside the main course.

Tips for Cooking Complete Meals in the Oven

- Select recipes that use the same convection setting and temperature. Not all dishes will cook for the same amount of time, with some being tested, added or removed at various times, but open the oven door as infrequently as possible.

- Stagger dishes and allow at least 1 to 2 inches (2.5 to 5 cm) around pans for the best air circulation.

- Timing may increase slightly when the oven is full. Add extra cooking time if necessary.

- Some convection ovens include a "whole meal" setting that presets the temperature and time according to a set menu included in the manual. Check your manual for menus and cooking times and temperatures.

General Tips

- Read the manufacturer's use and care manual before using your oven.
- Do not store items in the oven.
- Use dry pot holders (wet pot holders or oven mitts conduct heat and can cause steam burns).
- To keep the oven heat at a consistent temperature, use the interior light and oven window to check cooking progress instead of frequently opening the oven door, which lowers the temperature.
- Check for doneness a bit before the suggested cooking time until you get used to your oven and how it cooks.
- Open the door slowly to allow hot air or steam to escape before reaching in.
- For best results, position food in the center of the oven, leaving space around pans, trays and oven walls to allow air to circulate. Stagger the placement of pans in the oven where possible.

Food Safety

- Wash your hands for 20 seconds before starting to cook and after coughing, sneezing, using the restroom and touching pets.
- Keep work surfaces, cutting boards and counter surfaces clean. Sanitize them with a mild chlorine bleach solution (especially when working with meats, poultry and seafood). Mix 1 tsp (5 mL) bleach with 3 cups (750 mL) water and store the solution in a well-labeled spray bottle.
- Use two cutting boards: one for raw meat, poultry and fish; one for cooked foods, fresh vegetables and fruits.
- Keep cold foods cold, below 40°F (4°C).
- Keep hot foods hot, above 140°F (60°C).
- Keep raw meat, poultry and seafood separate from one another, other foods and cooked foods. Use clean utensils and dishes when switching from raw to cooked foods.
- Defrost meat, poultry and fish completely under refrigeration and keep in the refrigerator until cooking.
- Marinate foods in the refrigerator. Boil any remaining marinade for 7 minutes. Do not reuse raw marinades.
- Use a meat thermometer to check the internal temperature of foods.
- Refrigerate leftovers as quickly as possible. Cooling to room temperature on the counter invites bacteria growth. Use leftovers quickly.

About These Recipes

- The recipes in this book were tested in a variety of ovens — some with just a single convection feature; others featuring convection bake, convection roast and convection broil. Always check your oven manual before cooking and make sure your oven temperature is calibrated correctly (manuals have directions for this). Make notes on your recipes regarding setting, temperature and cooking time. All ovens are not exactly the same.

- The following were used unless otherwise specified: regular table salt, freshly ground black pepper, salted butter, 2 percent milk and yogurt, homemade or canned stock (canned broth diluted according to package instructions).

- Always taste and adjust seasonings at the end of the cooking time.

- Certain recipes can be prepared to a point, covered and refrigerated. For good finishing results, it is recommended that the dish stand for up to 30 minutes at room temperature (68° to 70°F/20° to 21°C) before final baking or reheating to take off some refrigerator chill.

Appetizers and Soups

Airplane Snacks

When I accompanied a tour group to Thailand, I prepared goody bags that contained bottled water, small spritz bottles (for cooling down), towelettes, note pads and these treats to eat on the plane. Some snacks almost made it to Thailand.

Roasted chickpeas can be found in bulk food stores.

Make Ahead
Snacks can be prepared two weeks in advance. For traveling, pack in small plastic bags or storage containers.

2 cups	wheat square cereal	500 mL
2 cups	toasted o-shaped cereal	500 mL
1 cup	pretzel sticks	250 mL
1 cup	roasted chickpeas	250 mL
1 cup	roasted peanuts or cashews	250 mL
1 cup	whole almonds or pecan halves	250 mL
1/2 cup	unsalted sunflower seeds	125 mL
1/2 cup	maple syrup or corn syrup	125 mL
1 tbsp	Worcestershire sauce	15 mL
1 1/2 tsp	curry powder	7 mL
1 tsp	garlic salt or garlic powder	5 mL
1/2 tsp	dried thyme leaves	2 mL
1/2 tsp	salt	2 mL
1/4 tsp	cayenne pepper	1 mL
1/4 tsp	black pepper	1 mL
1 cup	golden raisins	250 mL
1 cup	dried cranberries	250 mL

1. In a large bowl, combine cereals, pretzel sticks, chickpeas, peanuts, almonds and sunflower seeds.

2. In a small saucepan, combine maple syrup, Worcestershire, curry powder, garlic salt, thyme, salt, cayenne and pepper. Heat over medium heat until warm. Pour over cereal and nuts. Toss well.

3. Spoon mixture onto two parchment-lined baking sheets. Convection bake in a preheated 225°F (110°C) oven for 30 to 35 minutes, or until golden and dry. Stir occasionally during toasting.

4. Let mixture cool and transfer to a bowl. Stir in raisins and cranberries. Store in an airtight container at room temperature.

Savory Toasted Pumpkin Seeds

2 cups	green pumpkin seeds	500 mL
2 tsp	lime juice	10 mL
1 tsp	Worcestershire sauce	5 mL
½ tsp	smoked paprika (page 279)	2 mL
½ tsp	dried oregano leaves	2 mL
½ tsp	coarse salt	2 mL

1. In a bowl, combine pumpkin seeds, lime juice, Worcestershire, paprika, oregano and salt. Spread on a parchment-lined baking sheet.
2. Convection bake in a preheated 350°F (180°C) oven for 6 minutes, or until lightly browned. Stir once during cooking. (When seeds start to pop it means they are almost done.)

Makes about 2 cups (500 mL)

Pumpkin seeds are also called pepitas. For a spicy version, add a few shakes of cayenne pepper or chipotle chili pepper (page 54). Serve them as little snacks either with nuts or as an alternative, or sprinkle them on salads.

Make Ahead
Toast pumpkin seeds, cool and freeze in an airtight container for up to three weeks.

Roasted Olives

2 tbsp	olive oil	25 mL
2 cups	assorted olives, drained	500 mL
4	cloves garlic, peeled and smashed	4
1 tbsp	fresh rosemary sprigs	15 mL
2 tsp	fresh thyme leaves	10 mL
¼ tsp	hot pepper flakes	1 mL
¼ tsp	coarse salt	1 mL

1. In a small baking dish, combine oil, olives, garlic, rosemary, thyme, pepper flakes and salt.
2. Convection roast in preheated 375°F (190°C) oven for 10 to 15 minutes, or until warmed through.

Makes 4 to 6 servings

Supermarkets now offer a wide assortment of packaged and loose olives. Good olives are satisfying eaten as they are, but for a fuller flavor, combine them with a few seasonings and pop them in the convection oven.

Double-roasted Peanuts

**Makes 3 cups
(750 mL)**

Serve these with pre-dinner drinks or as a snack. Other nuts such as almonds, cashews or pecans can also be used. If you are using salted peanuts, omit the salt in the recipe.

Make Ahead

Nuts can be roasted and frozen in an airtight container for up to three weeks.

3 cups	dry roasted peanuts	750 mL
4 tsp	olive oil	20 mL
3 tbsp	grated Parmesan cheese	45 mL
¼ tsp	smoked paprika (page 279)	1 mL
¼ tsp	coarse salt	1 mL

1. Spread peanuts on a parchment-lined baking sheet. Pour oil over nuts, stirring to coat.
2. Convection roast in a preheated 325°F (160°C) oven for 6 to 8 minutes, or until warm.
3. Sprinkle nuts with cheese, paprika and salt. Cool slightly before serving.

Apricot Prosciutto Wraps

Makes 20 pieces

This last-minute appetizer is elegant enough for entertaining. For variety you can use dried prunes, dates or figs instead of apricots. Guests often don't realize how much they enjoy dried fruit until they try this salty-sweet combination.

20	dried apricots	20
½ cup	orange juice or apple juice	125 mL
½ tsp	dried rosemary leaves	2 mL
6 to 7	thin slices prosciutto, cut lengthwise in 3 or 4 strips	6 to 7

1. In a small saucepan, combine apricots, orange juice and rosemary. Bring to a boil. Cover and remove from heat. Let stand for 20 minutes, or until apricots have softened. Stir occasionally.
2. Wrap each apricot with a prosciutto strip (use toothpicks if you wish). Place on a parchment-lined baking sheet. Convection bake in a preheated 400°F (200°C) oven for 6 to 8 minutes, or until prosciutto is slightly crisp. Serve warm.

Pepper Salsa with Feta

4	red bell peppers, seeded and cut in ½-inch (1 cm) pieces	4
1	red onion, cut in ½-inch (1 cm) pieces	1
3	cloves garlic, peeled and sliced	3
3 tbsp	olive oil	45 mL
½ tsp	salt	2 mL
¼ tsp	black pepper	1 mL
2 tbsp	balsamic or red wine vinegar	25 mL
2 tbsp	chopped fresh basil or parsley	25 mL
¾ cup	crumbled feta cheese	175 mL

1. Combine red peppers, onion, garlic, oil, salt and pepper on a parchment-lined baking sheet. Toss and spread out slightly.

2. Convection roast in a preheated 375°F (190°C) oven for 25 minutes, stirring a couple of times during cooking. Cool to room temperature.

3. Toss peppers with vinegar and sprinkle with basil and feta.

Makes about 3 cups (750 mL)

Make this roasted salsa when peppers are at their peak. It is easy to make three batches at once using all three racks in the convection oven. Use red peppers or a mixture of red, yellow and orange. Serve as part of an antipasto tray or use as a topping for toasted bread, as a condiment with roasted meats or toss with cooked pasta.

Make Ahead

Peppers and onion can be cooked and cooled, then covered and refrigerated for up to two days or packaged and frozen for up to two months. Before serving, bring to room temperature and toss with vinegar, basil and feta.

Artichoke and Crab Dip

**Makes about
3 cups (750 mL)**

This is a variation of a popular dip. Serve it with vegetables, tortilla chips or pita crisps. Leftovers make a good sandwich filling or a topping for baked potatoes.

Make Ahead
Dip can be assembled, covered and refrigerated for up to eight hours before baking.

1	14-oz (398 mL) can artichoke hearts, drained	1
¾ cup	drained crabmeat (4-oz/120 g can)	175 mL
8 oz	cream cheese, softened	250 g
½ cup	tomato salsa	125 mL
2	green onions, coarsely chopped	2
2 tbsp	packed fresh cilantro leaves	25 mL
¼ cup	grated Parmesan cheese, divided	50 mL

1. In a food processor, coarsely chop artichoke hearts.

2. Add crab, cream cheese, salsa, green onions, cilantro and 2 tbsp (25 mL) Parmesan. Process until combined, scraping down sides of work bowl. Spoon into a shallow 8-inch (2 L) baking dish. Sprinkle with remaining Parmesan.

3. Convection bake in a preheated 350°F (180°C) oven for 20 minutes, or until hot and bubbling around edges. Let stand for 10 to 15 minutes before serving.

Pita Crisps
Cut six 7-inch (18 cm) pitas into 8 wedges each. Arrange on parchment-lined baking sheets and brush with ⅓ cup (75 mL) olive oil. Sprinkle with 1 tbsp (15 mL) dried oregano leaves (or other dried herb mix) and 1 tbsp (15 mL) coarse salt.

Convection bake in a preheated 325°F (160°C) oven for 12 to 15 minutes, or until golden and crisp. Serve warm or cool, but cool completely before storing. Cooled crisps can be packaged tightly and kept at room temperature for up to three days or frozen for up to two weeks. Makes 48 pieces.

Butternut Squash Spread

1	butternut squash (about 2 lbs/1 kg)	1
2 tbsp	red pepper jelly or sweet Asian chili sauce	25 mL
1 tbsp	lemon juice	15 mL
1 tsp	olive oil	5 mL
½ tsp	salt	2 mL
¼ tsp	ground cumin	1 mL
¼ tsp	black pepper	1 mL

1. Cut squash in half lengthwise and remove seeds. Place cut side down on a parchment-lined baking sheet.

2. Convection roast in a preheated 350°F (180°C) oven for 45 to 50 minutes, or until tender when pierced with tip of a sharp knife. Let cool until easy to handle.

3. Scoop squash pulp into a bowl. Add jelly, lemon juice, oil, salt, cumin and pepper. Mash or puree until smooth. Taste and adjust seasonings if necessary.

Variation
Roasted Garlic and Butternut Squash Spread: Add 1 head roasted garlic (page 214) with oil and seasonings.

Makes about 2 cups (500 mL)

Most roasted vegetables can be transformed into a spread or dip and served with raw vegetables, crackers or pita crisps (page 28). These spreads are a great way to serve vegetables and many, like this one, can also be served as a condiment with roasted meat, poultry or fish.

A combination of sweet potatoes and parsnips can replace the squash.

Make Ahead
Spread can be prepared, covered and refrigerated a day ahead. Bring to room temperature before serving.

Eggplant Olive Tapenade

This spread combines
the flavors of eggplant
caviar (a mixture of
roasted eggplant,
tomatoes and
seasonings) and
tapenade (a savory
Provençal spread of
black olives, anchovies
and capers). Serve with
thinly sliced bread,
raw vegetables or
as a condiment with
roast chicken or lamb.
Sometimes I spoon
the mixture into small
hollowed-out tomatoes
to serve as part of a
buffet. For a vegetarian
version, simply omit
the anchovies.

Make Ahead
The tapenade can be
prepared, covered and
refrigerated up to one
day ahead.

1	large eggplant (about 1¼ lbs/625 g)	1
¾ cup	pitted black or green olives	175 mL
2	cloves garlic, chopped	2
2	anchovy fillets, chopped	2
2 tbsp	capers	25 mL
2 tsp	chopped fresh thyme, or ½ tsp (2 mL) dried	10 mL
¼ cup	olive oil	50 mL
¼ tsp	black pepper	1 mL
2 tbsp	chopped fresh basil or parsley	25 mL

1. Pierce eggplant with a fork. Place on a foil-lined baking
   sheet and convection bake in a preheated 400°F (200°C)
   oven for 40 to 45 minutes, or until eggplant is soft and
   starting to collapse.

2. When eggplant is cool enough to handle, cut in half.
   Scoop out pulp.

3. Place olives, garlic, anchovies and capers in a food
   processor. Process until coarsely chopped. Add eggplant
   pulp and thyme. Process until blended but not pureed.

4. Add olive oil and pepper. Pulse to combine.

5. Spoon into a serving bowl and garnish with chopped
   basil.

Tomato and Olive Tart

½	14-oz (397 g) package frozen puff pastry, defrosted	½
2 tsp	Dijon mustard	10 mL
1 cup	grated Gruyère cheese	250 mL
9	thin tomato slices	9
⅓ cup	pitted black olives, coarsely chopped	75 mL
2 tsp	chopped fresh thyme, or ¼ tsp (1 mL) dried	10 mL
2 tsp	olive oil	10 mL

1. On a lightly floured surface, roll pastry into a 10-inch (25 cm) square and place on a parchment-lined baking sheet. With a sharp knife, score pastry about ½ inch (1 cm) from edge. Prick pastry with a fork to help prevent steam bubbles.

2. Spread pastry with mustard and sprinkle with cheese. Arrange tomatoes over cheese. Sprinkle with olives and thyme and drizzle with oil.

3. Convection roast in a preheated 375°F (190°C) oven for 22 to 25 minutes, or until pastry is golden and cheese has melted. Let stand for 10 minutes before cutting and serving.

Puff Pastry

Puff pastry is sold in supermarkets in at least two forms. Frozen blocks of pastry usually come in 14-oz (397 g) packages and are scored in the middle, so half can be used at a time (wrap the remaining half well).

Frozen prerolled pastry is usually packaged in two sheets that have already been rolled into 10-inch (25 cm) squares on parchment paper. One roll can be used and the remaining kept frozen.

Both versions can be defrosted in the refrigerator for several hours or at room temperature for 2 to 3 hours. For easiest handling, pastry should be cold when you use it.

Frozen and prerolled frozen pastry can be used interchangeably, though you may have to shape the prerolled pastry to conform to the measurements called for in the recipe.

Makes 4 to 6 servings

French bakeries and markets often sell pizza-like tarts like this one, available by the piece.

For a different flavor, use smoked provolone or mozzarella cheese instead of Gruyère. Setting the oven on convection roast results in a crisper pastry.

This recipe can easily be doubled.

Make Ahead

Tart can be assembled, covered and refrigerated up to four hours before cooking, but if tomatoes are really juicy, place them on baked tart just before cooking. Tart is also very good served at room temperature.

Cottage Crostini

Makes about 25 pieces

Cottage cooking tends to be uncomplicated, yet these are tasty enough for entertaining any time. Although the recipe uses minced garlic, a head of mashed roasted garlic (page 214) is an excellent substitute.

For an even quicker preparation, chop whole pitted olives in the food processor and then blend in the remaining topping ingredients.

1 cup	mayonnaise	250 mL
2	cloves garlic, minced	2
½ cup	grated Parmesan cheese	125 mL
½ cup	chopped pitted green olives	125 mL
2 tbsp	chopped chives or parsley	25 mL
1	baguette, cut in ½-inch (1 cm) slices	1

1. In a bowl, combine mayonnaise, garlic, cheese, olives and chives.
2. Spread mayonnaise mixture on bread slices. Arrange slices mayonnaise side up on one or two parchment-lined baking sheets.
3. Convection bake in a preheated 375°F (190°C) oven for 8 minutes, or until light golden and hot. Cool slightly before serving.

Tomato Basil Pizzettes

Makes 4 mini pizzas

These mini pizzas are quick to assemble as a snack or light lunch with a salad. Use a variety of tomatoes when they are in season — try the yellow varieties and even halved cherry tomatoes.

4	6-inch (15 cm) flour tortillas	4
1½ cups	grated mozzarella cheese	375 mL
1	large tomato, cored and thinly sliced	1
6	fresh basil leaves, finely shredded	6
2 tbsp	grated Parmesan cheese	25 mL
2 tbsp	olive oil	25 mL

1. Arrange tortillas on a baking sheet. Spread mozzarella evenly over tortillas and arrange tomatoes over cheese. Sprinkle with basil and Parmesan. Drizzle with oil.
2. Convection bake in a preheated 400°F (200°C) oven for 6 to 8 minutes, or until cheese is bubbling. Serve pizzas whole or cut in quarters.

Camembert Pesto Phyllo Cups

2	sheets phyllo pastry	2
4 tsp	olive oil, divided	20 mL
6 oz	Camembert, cut in ½-inch (1 cm) pieces (about 24 pieces)	175 g
¼ cup	pesto	50 mL

1. Place a sheet of phyllo pastry on a flat surface. Brush with 2 tsp (10 mL) olive oil. Top with remaining sheet of phyllo and brush with remaining 2 tsp (10 mL) oil.

2. Using a ruler and sharp knife, cut phyllo into 48 2-inch (5 cm) squares (cut 8 squares along long side and 6 squares down width).

3. Press half the squares into 24 mini muffin cups. Press remaining phyllo squares on top of first squares at an angle.

4. Convection bake or roast in a preheated 300°F (150°C) oven for 6 minutes, or until golden. Remove from oven and let sit for 5 minutes.

5. Place a piece of cheese in each cup. Top with ½ tsp (2 mL) pesto. Return to oven for 5 to 6 minutes, or until cheese has melted. Serve warm.

Makes 24 cups

Phyllo pastry bakes to golden perfection in the convection oven. Vary the filling by using other cheeses such as Brie, mozzarella or Cambozola.

Make Ahead
Bake phyllo cups, remove from pans, cool and freeze in an airtight container for up to two weeks. To reheat, return to muffin pans or simply place on a baking sheet and continue with Step 5.

Prosciutto Pinwheels

**Makes about
3 dozen**

Once these pinwheels
are assembled and
chilled, it is quick work
to slice and bake them
together using three
racks in the convection
oven.

Make Ahead
Pinwheels can be baked,
cooled and packaged in
airtight containers and
frozen for up to three
weeks. Place frozen
pinwheels on parchment-
lined baking sheets and
convection bake in a
preheated 350°F (180°C)
oven for 8 to 10 minutes,
or until hot and crispy.

1	14-oz (397 g) package frozen puff pastry, defrosted and halved	1
4 oz	prosciutto, thinly sliced	125 g
3 tbsp	chopped sun-dried tomatoes (oil-packed)	45 mL
1 cup	grated Swiss cheese	250 mL
1	egg white, beaten	1

1. On a lightly floured surface, roll each piece of pastry into a 12- by 7-inch (30 by 18 cm) rectangle. Top pastry with prosciutto, tomatoes and cheese, leaving a 1-inch (2.5 cm) border along one long edge of each piece of pastry. Brush border with egg white.

2. Roll up each piece of pastry lengthwise like a jelly roll, and seal along egg white-brushed border. Wrap each roll in plastic wrap and refrigerate until pastry has chilled completely and is firm (about 3 hours), or freeze for 30 minutes.

3. Before baking, using a serrated knife, cut rolls into $1/2$-inch (1 cm) slices. Place cut side down, about $1^1/2$ inches (4 cm) apart, on parchment-lined baking sheets.

4. Convection roast in a preheated 375°F (190°C) oven for 15 to 18 minutes, or until golden and crisp. Serve warm.

Chicken Satay Quesadillas

6	9-inch (23 cm) flour tortillas	6
¾ cup	peanut sauce	175 mL
2 cups	grated mozzarella or Gruyère cheese	500 mL
2 cups	diced cooked chicken	500 mL
3	green onions, finely chopped	3
¼ cup	chopped fresh cilantro	50 mL

1. Place tortillas on a flat surface. Spread half of each tortilla with peanut sauce. Sprinkle with cheese, chicken, green onions and cilantro. Fold tortillas in half and press firmly.

2. Arrange tortillas on two parchment-lined baking sheets. Convection bake in a preheated 400°F (200°C) oven for 6 to 7 minutes, or until cheese melts and quesadillas are heated through. Let stand for 4 minutes, then cut each tortilla into 4 wedges.

> ### Peanut Sauce
> In a small skillet, heat 2 tbsp (25 mL) vegetable oil over medium heat. Add 2 tbsp (25 mL) chopped gingerroot, 2 chopped cloves garlic and 4 chopped green onions. Cook for 2 minutes until softened.
>
> In a food processor or blender, combine cooled ginger mixture, ½ cup (125 mL) peanut butter, ½ cup (125 mL) coconut milk, ¼ cup (50 mL) chopped fresh cilantro, 2 tbsp (25 mL) soy sauce, 2 tbsp (25 mL) lime juice, 1 tbsp (15 mL) fish sauce, 1 tbsp (15 mL) brown sugar and ½ tsp (2 mL) hot chili sauce. Blend until smooth. Makes about 1½ cups (375 mL).

Makes 24 pieces

When I was a caterer, the most popular appetizers were mini chicken satays and quesadillas, so for this recipe I have combined the two. Leftover cooked turkey also works well. Serve these as appetizers or for lunch accompanied by sliced cucumber, carrots and sweet Asian chili sauce — a sweet, spicy condiment available in Asian groceries and most supermarkets.

If you are using storebought peanut sauce, select one that is not too runny (it should be almost the consistency of mayonnaise).

Ham and Cheese Quesadillas

**Makes 18 to
24 pieces**

An updated version
of the grilled ham
and cheese sandwich,
these quesadillas can
be served as a light
main course or as an
appetizer. Serve them
with sour cream and
salsa.

Make Ahead
Prepare and bake
quesadillas, wrap and
freeze for up to two weeks.
To reheat directly from
frozen state, convection
bake in a preheated
350°F (180°C) oven for
10 to 12 minutes, or
until hot.

¾ cup	grated Cheddar cheese	175 mL
½ cup	chili sauce or tomato salsa	125 mL
2 tsp	coarse-grain or Russian-style mustard	10 mL
6	6-inch (15 cm) flour tortillas	6
3	large slices Black Forest ham	3

1. In a bowl, combine cheese, chili sauce and mustard.

2. Arrange three tortillas on a flat surface. Spread half of cheese mixture evenly over tortillas, leaving a 1-inch (2.5 cm) border around edges.

3. Top cheese with ham slices and spread evenly with remaining cheese. Top with remaining tortillas. Press down slightly.

4. Arrange quesadillas on a parchment-lined baking sheet. Convection bake in a preheated 400°F (200°C) oven for 10 minutes, or until cheese melts and quesadillas are heated through. Cool for 5 minutes before cutting each quesadilla into 6 to 8 wedges.

> **Variation**
> *Black Bean and Cheese Quesadillas:* Combine 1 cup (250 mL) canned black beans (rinsed and drained), ¼ cup (50 mL) chopped fresh cilantro and ¼ tsp (1 mL) ground cumin. Replace ham with bean mixture.

Salsa Nachos

1 cup	tomato salsa	250 mL
¼ cup	diced canned green chilies, or 2 fresh jalapeños, seeded and finely chopped	50 mL
¼ cup	chopped green onion	50 mL
4 cups	tortilla chips	1 L
2 cups	grated Monterey Jack or Cheddar cheese, divided	500 mL
2 tbsp	chopped fresh cilantro	25 mL
¼ cup	sour cream	50 mL

Makes 4 to 6 servings

A favorite snack for all ages. For a less spicy version, use a mild salsa and reduce the green chilies. Some canned green chilies are not spicy; the jalapeños are. Serve with a side dish of guacamole.

1. In a small bowl, combine salsa, chilies and green onion.

2. Spread tortilla chips over a 13- by 9-inch (3 L) baking dish. Sprinkle chips with 1 cup (250 mL) cheese. Spoon salsa over cheese and top with remaining 1 cup (250 mL) cheese.

3. Convection bake in a preheated 425°F (220°C) oven for 3 to 4 minutes, or until cheese is bubbly. Top with cilantro and dollops of sour cream.

Avocados
A ripe avocado should yield gently to finger pressure. If the avocado is not quite ripe, leave it at room temperature, checking each day. Just before serving, halve the avocado and twist slightly. Remove the pit, then peel and slice the pulp.

Guacamole
Scoop flesh of 2 ripe avocados into a bowl and mash coarsely. Add 2 finely chopped green onions, 2 tbsp (25 mL) lime juice or lemon juice, ½ tsp (2 mL) chili powder, ⅓ cup (75 mL) tomato salsa, 1 minced clove garlic and 3 tbsp (45 mL) chopped fresh cilantro. Mix thoroughly. Makes about 1½ cups (375 mL).

Surf 'n' Turf Skewers

Makes 6 skewers

A popular main course combination can be scaled down to make an appealing appetizer. For a more elegant presentation, remove the shrimp and beef from the skewers and arrange over a bed of shredded lettuce. These are great at an outdoor barbecue party, but I usually remove the tails from the shrimp so guests aren't tempted to dispose of them on the lawn or in the flower pots!

¼ cup	olive oil	50 mL
3 tbsp	lemon juice	45 mL
1 tbsp	Montreal steak spice	15 mL
2	cloves garlic, minced	2
18	large shrimp, peeled and deveined	18
1 lb	beef tenderloin, cut in ¾-inch (2 cm) cubes (about 24)	500 g

Cocktail Sauce

½ cup	ketchup	125 mL
2 tbsp	horseradish	25 mL
1 tbsp	lemon juice	15 mL
½ tsp	Worcestershire sauce	2 mL
2 tbsp	chopped fresh basil or parsley	25 mL

1. In a small bowl, combine oil, lemon juice, steak spice and garlic.
2. Place shrimp and beef in two separate dishes. Pour marinade evenly over both and toss to coat. Refrigerate for 20 minutes.
3. Thread meat and shrimp onto skewers (4 pieces of beef and 3 shrimp per skewer). Arrange on a lightly greased rack set over broiler pan. Place about 4 inches (10 cm) from heat and convection broil under preheated broiler for 6 to 8 minutes, turning halfway through, until shrimp are pink and cooked through and beef is pink in center.
4. To prepare sauce, combine ketchup, horseradish, lemon juice, Worcestershire and basil. Arrange skewers on a serving platter and pass with sauce.

Crusty-topped Mussels

36	cooked mussels	36
2	cloves garlic, peeled	2
¼ cup	packed fresh basil leaves or parsley	50 mL
¼ cup	pine nuts, toasted	50 mL
¾ cup	fresh bread crumbs	175 mL
2 tbsp	grated Parmesan cheese	25 mL
3 tbsp	olive oil	45 mL

1. Remove top shells from mussels and discard. Loosen mussels from bottom shells and replace on shells. Arrange on a parchment-lined baking sheet.

2. Add garlic, basil and pine nuts to a food processor and chop finely. Transfer to a bowl and combine with bread crumbs, cheese and oil. (If mixture seems dry, add a bit more oil.) Cover each mussel with some topping.

3. Convection bake in a preheated 425°F (220°C) oven for 5 to 6 minutes, or until topping is golden and mussels are hot.

Cooking Fresh Mussels
In a large saucepan, combine mussels (cook more than you need in case some mussels do not open) with ½ cup (125 mL) dry white wine and ¼ cup (50 mL) water. Cover and bring to a boil over high heat. Reduce heat and cook, covered, for 4 to 5 minutes, or just until mussels open. Remove from heat and discard any mussels that do not open. Let cool for a few minutes.

Makes 3 dozen

Cooked mussels topped with a toasted bread-crumb mixture make an easy appetizer, especially when everything can be prepared ahead before being finished in the convection oven. Frozen cooked mussels on the half shell are available in supermarkets; defrost them before using.

Make Ahead
Mussels can be assembled with topping, covered and refrigerated for up to six hours before baking.

Parmesan Cheese Puffs

Makes about 3 dozen

These tender little puffs (also called gougère) use the same basic pastry that is used for cream puffs and eclairs. Baked in the convection oven, they become golden nuggets that can be served plain or split and filled with herbed cream cheese and/or a slice of smoked salmon, ham or turkey.

Make Ahead

Cool puffs completely on a rack. Package and refrigerate for up to two days, or freeze for up to two weeks. To reheat, place cold or frozen pastries on a baking sheet and convection bake in a preheated 325°F (160°C) oven for 10 to 15 minutes, or until hot.

1 cup	water	250 mL
½ cup	butter, cut in pieces	125 mL
½ tsp	salt	2 mL
1 cup	all-purpose flour	250 mL
4	eggs	4
½ cup	grated Parmesan cheese	125 mL
½ tsp	black pepper	2 mL

1. In a saucepan, combine water, butter and salt. Gradually bring to a boil, stirring.

2. Remove saucepan from heat and stir in flour. Return to medium heat and cook, stirring, for about 2 minutes, or until mixture dries out slightly. Transfer to a large bowl and let cool for 5 minutes.

3. Beat in eggs one at a time, mixing thoroughly after each addition. (Do this by hand or with a mixer.) Stir in cheese and pepper.

4. Spoon or pipe mixture onto parchment-lined baking sheets (1-inch/2.5 cm mounds about 1½ inches/4 cm apart). Convection bake in a preheated 375°F (190°C) oven for 25 to 30 minutes, or until puffed and golden.

Orange Chicken Tidbits

3 tbsp	orange juice concentrate	45 mL
2 tbsp	soy sauce	25 mL
2 tbsp	brown sugar	25 mL
1 tbsp	grated gingerroot	15 mL
2	cloves garlic, minced	2
1½ lbs	boneless, skinless chicken breasts (about 4), cut in bite-sized pieces	750 g

1. In a large bowl, combine orange juice concentrate, soy sauce, brown sugar, ginger and garlic.

2. Add chicken to marinade and combine. If you have time, cover and refrigerate for 30 minutes.

3. Arrange chicken on a parchment-lined baking sheet. Convection bake in a preheated 400°F (200°C) oven for 8 to 10 minutes, or until chicken is no longer pink, stirring once during baking. Serve with toothpicks.

Makes 8 to 10 servings

In this recipe, small pieces of chicken are marinated in an orange ginger sauce and served plain or with peanut sauce (page 35) or sweet Asian chili sauce. (For an Indian flavor, serve with storebought tandoori, tikka or masala sauce mixed with ¼ cup/50 mL unflavored yogurt.)

For an attractive presentation, serve the dipping sauce in a hollowed-out orange.

Make Ahead
Cook chicken, cover and refrigerate for eight hours or overnight. Serve cold as an appetizer or add to a salad.

Southwestern Wings

**Makes 4 to
5 servings**

A must for chicken-wing fans. If you are serving a crowd, double or triple the recipe. Cooking the wings in the convection oven on a wire rack makes them crispy all over.

Serve the wings with salsa, a dip or sour cream sprinkled with cilantro.

3 lbs	chicken wings	1.5 kg
¼ cup	cornmeal	50 mL
2 tbsp	all-purpose flour	25 mL
2 tsp	chili powder	10 mL
1 tsp	ground cumin	5 mL
1 tsp	garlic powder	5 mL
1 tsp	salt	5 mL
½ tsp	dried thyme leaves	2 mL
½ tsp	cayenne pepper	2 mL

1. Trim off wing tips (freeze tips and reserve to make stock). Cut each wing into two pieces at the joint.

2. In a large bowl, combine cornmeal, flour, chili powder, cumin, garlic powder, salt, thyme and cayenne. Toss wings in mixture to coat. Arrange wings "good" side up on a wire rack placed over a foil-lined baking sheet.

3. Convection bake in a preheated 400°F (200°C) oven for 35 to 40 minutes, or until wings are cooked through, crisp and golden.

> **Savory Dip**
> In a bowl, combine ½ cup (125 mL) mayonnaise, 2 tbsp (25 mL) finely chopped green onion, 2 tbsp (25 mL) finely chopped dill pickle, 1 tbsp (15 mL) chopped capers, 1 tbsp (15 mL) lemon juice, 1 tsp (5 mL) coarse-grain mustard, ½ tsp (2 mL) dried tarragon leaves, ¼ tsp (1 mL) salt and ¼ tsp (1 mL) black pepper. Makes about ¾ cup (175 mL).

Asparagus and Leek Soup

2 lbs	asparagus, trimmed, cut in 1-inch (2.5 cm) pieces	1 kg
1	leek, white and light-green part, cut in 1-inch (2.5 cm) pieces	1
2 tbsp	olive oil	25 mL
½ tsp	salt	2 mL
¼ tsp	black pepper	1 mL
4 cups	chicken or vegetable stock	1 L
2 tbsp	chopped fresh dillweed	25 mL
1 tbsp	chopped fresh chives, or some chive flowers	15 mL

Makes 4 to 5 servings

This soup says spring, but it can be made year round. For a thinner soup, add stock. For a richer soup, stir in ½ cup (125 mL) whipping cream. The soup can also be served cold, but it may need to be thinned after chilling. Other possible garnishes include diced smoked salmon or cooked ham or a small amount of crumbled goat cheese.

1. Combine asparagus, leek, oil, salt and pepper on a parchment-lined baking sheet. Convection roast in a preheated 375°F (190°C) oven for 10 to 12 minutes, or until asparagus is just tender but still green. (Timing will depend on thickness of asparagus, but don't overcook.)

2. Meanwhile, in a large saucepan, heat stock to a boil. Add roasted asparagus and leeks. Return to a boil, reduce heat and simmer for 4 minutes.

3. Puree soup until smooth. Stir in dill. Taste and adjust seasonings if necessary. Garnish with chives or chive flowers.

Variation
Asparagus and Pea Soup: Add 1 cup (250 mL) green peas to asparagus and leek. Add an extra ½ cup (125 mL) stock.

Squash and Parsnip Soup

Makes 5 servings

Roasting the vegetables gives this soup a rich flavor without adding cream. Sweet potatoes could be substituted for the squash. For variety, use blue cheese, goat cheese or Cheddar as a garnish.

Make Ahead

Soup can be prepared, covered and refrigerated for up to two days or frozen for up to two months. Onion garnish can be prepared ahead, covered and refrigerated for up to two days.

1	butternut squash (about 2 lbs/1 kg)	1
4	parsnips (about 1 lb/500 g total)	4
2 tbsp	olive oil	25 mL
1	onion, peeled and cut in 8 pieces	1
2 tsp	chopped fresh sage, or 1/2 tsp (2 mL) dried	10 mL
5 cups	vegetable or chicken stock	1.25 L
1/2 tsp	salt	2 mL
1/4 tsp	black pepper	1 mL
Garnish		
2 tbsp	olive oil	25 mL
1	onion, thinly sliced	1
	Salt and black pepper to taste	

1. Peel squash and remove seeds. Peel parsnips. Cut squash and parsnips into $1/2$-inch (1 cm) pieces. Arrange in a 13- by 9-inch (3 L) baking dish. Drizzle with oil and toss.

2. Convection bake or roast in a preheated 375°F (190°C) oven for 25 minutes. Stir in onion and sage. Continue to roast for 20 to 30 minutes, or until vegetables are tender. Stir a few times during roasting. Remove from oven and let sit for 10 minutes.

3. In a large saucepan, combine stock, roasted vegetables, salt and pepper and bring to a boil. Reduce heat and simmer for 10 minutes. Puree soup until smooth.

4. Meanwhile, for garnish, heat oil in a medium skillet over medium-high heat. Add sliced onion and cook, stirring often, for 5 to 10 minutes, or until caramelized. Season with salt and pepper. Spoon onions over soup.

Roasted Tomato and Garlic Soup

2 lbs	tomatoes, cored and halved (about 6 medium)	1 kg
2	onions, peeled and cut in 8 pieces	2
6	whole cloves garlic, peeled and halved	6
2 tbsp	olive oil	25 mL
½ tsp	salt	2 mL
¼ tsp	black pepper	1 mL
3 cups	vegetable or chicken stock	750 mL

1. In a 13- by 9-inch (3 L) baking dish, combine tomatoes, onions, garlic and olive oil. Sprinkle with salt and pepper. Convection bake or roast in a preheated 375°F (190°C) oven for 35 minutes. Stir occasionally. Let tomatoes cool slightly and slip off skins.

2. In a large saucepan, combine stock and roasted vegetables. Bring to a boil over high heat. Reduce heat to medium and simmer for 10 minutes, until slightly thickened. Puree soup until smooth. Taste and adjust seasonings if necessary.

Makes 5 to 6 servings

When tomatoes are plentiful, make several batches of this versatile soup to freeze. Choose the ripest tomatoes. You can also serve this chilled, with a squeeze of lime juice, diced cucumber, red pepper or avocado. For a hot, creamy soup, add ½ cup (125 mL) whipping cream and heat before serving. Additional garnishes might be chopped fresh dillweed, basil or pesto.

Make Ahead

Soup can be cooked, covered and refrigerated for up to two days or frozen for up to two months.

Ratatouille Soup

**Makes 6 to
8 servings**

All the vegetables
found in the traditional
Provençal vegetable
dish are combined in
this delightful summer
soup. Roasting the
vegetables brings out
their full flavor. You can
peel the eggplant if
you wish, but it is not
necessary. Puree the
soup if desired.

Garnish with a
spoonful of pesto or
shredded fresh basil.
Serve with Goat
Cheese Toasts.

1	eggplant (about 1 lb/500 g), cut in ½-inch (1 cm) pieces	1
2	zucchini (about 8 oz/250 g each), cut in ½-inch (1 cm) pieces	2
3 tbsp	olive oil, divided	45 mL
2	red bell peppers, seeded and cut in ½-inch (1 cm) pieces	2
3	tomatoes, chopped	3
1	onion, chopped	1
3	cloves garlic, peeled and thinly sliced	3
¾ tsp	herbes de Provence or dried thyme leaves	4 mL
1 tsp	salt	5 mL
¼ tsp	black pepper	1 mL
6 cups	vegetable or chicken stock	1.5 L

1. Line two baking sheets with foil (for easy cleanup, as these vegetables give off lots of juice) and parchment paper (some vegetables have a tendency to stick). On one sheet combine eggplant, zucchini and 1½ tbsp (20 mL) oil. On second sheet combine red peppers, tomatoes, onion, garlic, herbs, salt, pepper and remaining oil.

2. Convection roast in a preheated 400°F (200°C) oven for 25 to 30 minutes, or until vegetables are just tender. Stir vegetables a couple of times during roasting.

3. Meanwhile, in a large saucepan, bring stock to a boil. Add roasted vegetables and juices. Cook for 6 minutes.

> **Goat Cheese Toasts**
> Spread 4 oz (125 g) softened goat cheese over 12 baguette slices (about ½ inch/1 cm thick). Place bread, cheese side up, on a parchment-lined baking sheet. Convection roast in preheated 400°F (200°C) oven for 2 to 3 minutes, or until hot. Makes 12 toasts.

Fish and Seafood

Maple-glazed Salmon

Makes 6 servings

I came up with this simple recipe when faced with an extra piece of salmon and little preparation time. It is a great choice for a quick cottage meal or to serve cold on a buffet.

You can also use trout, salmon trout or Arctic char in this recipe.

¼ cup	maple syrup	50 mL
4 tsp	coarse-grain mustard	20 mL
4 tsp	soy sauce	20 mL
1	2-lb (1 kg) salmon fillet, skin removed	1

1. In a small bowl, combine maple syrup, mustard and soy sauce.
2. Arrange salmon on a foil- and parchment-lined baking sheet (for easy cleanup). Spoon glaze over fish.
3. Convection bake in a preheated 400°F (200°C) oven for 8 to 10 minutes, or until flesh just flakes easily with a fork. Do not overcook. Transfer fish to a serving platter using large lifters.

Hoisin Orange Salmon

Makes 6 servings

Quick, easy, full-flavored dishes are a welcome addition to any cook's repertoire. Look for hoisin sauce in the Asian section of the supermarket. Refrigerate it after opening. Other fish choices might be halibut or monkfish.

Serve with a cucumber salad (page 59).

3 tbsp	hoisin sauce	45 mL
2 tbsp	orange juice concentrate	25 mL
2 tsp	sesame oil	10 mL
2 tsp	finely chopped gingerroot	10 mL
6	6-oz (175 g) salmon fillets, skin removed	6
6	orange slices	6

1. In a small bowl, combine hoisin, orange juice concentrate, sesame oil and ginger.
2. Arrange salmon on a parchment-lined baking sheet. Spoon glaze over salmon, turning fillets to coat completely.
3. Convection bake in a preheated 400°F (200°C) oven for 8 to 10 minutes, or until fish flakes easily when tested with a fork. Garnish with orange slices.

Nut-crusted Salmon with Pineapple Sauce

6	6-oz (175 g) salmon fillets, skin removed	6
2 tbsp	olive oil	25 mL
½ tsp	salt	2 mL
½ tsp	ground ginger	2 mL
1 cup	chopped macadamia nuts	250 mL

Pineapple Sauce

⅓ cup	mayonnaise	75 mL
⅓ cup	unflavored yogurt	75 mL
1 cup	finely chopped pineapple	250 mL
1 tbsp	chopped mango chutney or ginger marmalade	15 mL
½ tsp	curry powder	2 mL
2 tbsp	chopped chives	25 mL
1 tbsp	shredded fresh mint	15 mL

1. Arrange salmon fillets on a parchment-lined baking sheet. Rub both sides with oil, salt and ginger. Pat chopped nuts onto tops and sides of fillets.

2. Convection bake in a preheated 400°F (200°C) oven for 8 to 10 minutes, or until crust is golden. (Place baking sheet in center of oven and watch closely, as nuts tend to color quickly.) To test fish for doneness, carefully peek into thickest part of fish using tip of a sharp knife, trying not to disturb coating.

3. Meanwhile, to prepare sauce, in a bowl, combine mayonnaise, yogurt, pineapple, chutney, curry powder, chives and mint. Serve fish with sauce.

Makes 6 servings

Baked in the convection oven, the macadamia nuts form a delicious topping for this tropically inspired dish. Other fish such as snapper or tilapia can be substituted. Use unsalted macadamia nuts if available, or rub salted macadamias in a tea towel to remove excess salt.

To chop the nuts in a food processor, use the pulse button and watch carefully so the nuts do not become too fine and turn into a paste. Blanched almonds can be substituted for the macadamias.

Drain any excess liquid from the yogurt before adding it to the mayonnaise. (Even a peach- or orange-flavored yogurt can be used.) Use fresh or well-drained canned pineapple.

Make Ahead

Sauce can be made ahead and refrigerated for up to six hours before serving.

Salmon Wellington

Makes 4 servings

This take-off on Beef Wellington is elegant, easy to assemble and quick to cook, so it works for either a special weeknight meal or for entertaining — prepare the Easy Oven Meal (page 51) and add a simple appetizer such as cantaloupe wedges with prosciutto slices.

2 tbsp	Russian-style mustard	25 mL
2 tbsp	chopped fresh tarragon or dillweed	25 mL
1 tbsp	horseradish	15 mL
4	6-oz (175 g) salmon fillets, skin removed	4
1	14-oz (397 g) package frozen puff pastry, defrosted and halved	1
1	egg, beaten	1

Horseradish Sauce

¾ cup	sour cream	175 mL
1 tbsp	horseradish	15 mL

1. In a small bowl, combine mustard, tarragon and horseradish.

2. Place salmon in a shallow dish. Rub mustard mixture into fillets and marinate while rolling pastry.

3. On a lightly floured surface, roll each piece of pastry into a 16- by 6-inch (40 by 15 cm) rectangle. Cut each rectangle crosswise into 4 pieces (for 8 pieces in total).

4. Place a salmon fillet in center of 4 pastry pieces. Brush pastry edges with beaten egg. Top with remaining pastry pieces, stretching pastry slightly to cover salmon and pressing sides all around to seal. Place packages on a parchment-lined baking sheet. Cut four diagonal slashes in top of each package. Brush with beaten egg.

5. Convection roast in a preheated 375°F (190°C) oven for 18 to 20 minutes, or until pastry is golden and puffed and salmon is cooked.

6. Meanwhile, in a small bowl, combine sour cream and horseradish. Serve salmon with sauce.

Mom's Salmon Loaf

2	7½-oz (213 g) cans salmon, with juices	2
2	eggs	2
¾ cup	fresh bread crumbs	175 mL
½ cup	mayonnaise	125 mL
⅓ cup	chopped sweet pickle	75 mL
¼ cup	chopped celery	50 mL
2 tbsp	lemon juice	25 mL
¼ tsp	salt	1 mL
¼ tsp	black pepper	1 mL

1. In a large bowl, break up salmon and mash bones. Add eggs, bread crumbs, mayonnaise, pickle, celery, lemon juice, salt and pepper. Mix together thoroughly. Spoon into a parchment-lined or greased 8- by 4-inch (1.5 L) loaf pan.

2. Convection bake in a preheated 325°F (160°C) oven for 35 to 40 minutes, or until center is firm and top is golden. If cooking salmon loaf for later use, let rest in pan for 25 minutes before turning out (loosen edges with knife but for sure results, line pan with parchment paper). If serving hot, let stand for 5 minutes before slicing.

EASY OVEN MEAL

Friday Night Dinner for 4

Salmon Wellington (page 50)
Roasted Fennel and Asparagus (page 146)
Ruby Fruit with Ice Cream (page 251)

- Assemble fruit, salmon and vegetables.
- Preheat oven.
- Place fennel and dessert in oven and roast for 5 minutes.
- Place salmon in oven and roast all three items for 18 to 20 minutes, or until salmon is cooked, fruit is softened and vegetables are tender.
- Meanwhile, prepare sauce for salmon. Slice avocado.
- Toss cooked vegetables with vinegar and avocado.
- Let dessert cool while you serve the main course.

Makes 4 to 5 servings

In a weekly column that I wrote for the local newspaper, I included this recipe in an article called "Post Holiday Simplicity" that appeared the first week after New Year's, when everyone had overdosed on holiday foods. Serve it cold as part of a salad dinner or hot with baked potatoes (page 91) or rice.

Make Ahead

Salmon loaf can be cooked, unmolded, covered and refrigerated up to a day ahead. Serve cold.

Oven Fish and Chips

An easy way to make homemade fish and chips without deep-frying. As a general rule, fish fillets are cooked on convection bake so they cook gently, but in this recipe they are cooked on convection roast so the potatoes become golden. Serve with lemon wedges, tartar sauce (page 56) and cherry tomatoes roasted at the same time.

Chips

4	large Yukon Gold or baking potatoes, scrubbed and dried	4
2 tbsp	olive oil	25 mL
¾ tsp	salt	4 mL
¼ tsp	black pepper	1 mL

Fish

1¼ cups	dry bread crumbs	300 mL
1 tbsp	olive oil	15 mL
½ tsp	dried savory or thyme leaves	2 mL
½ tsp	salt	2 mL
4	6-oz (175 g) fish fillets (halibut, cod, pickerel, haddock, etc.), skin removed	4

1. Cut each potato into 8 to 10 wedges. On a parchment-lined baking sheet, toss potatoes with oil, salt and pepper and spread out in a single layer. Convection roast in a preheated 425°F (220°C) oven for 25 minutes.

2. Meanwhile, to prepare fish, in a shallow dish, combine bread crumbs, oil, savory and salt. Roll fillets in bread crumb mixture to coat and arrange on a separate parchment-lined baking sheet.

3. Place fish in oven with potatoes and convection roast both dishes for 10 to 12 minutes, or until potatoes are tender and fish is cooked and crispy (total cooking time for potatoes will be about 35 minutes). Turn fillets halfway through cooking time.

> **Roasted Cherry Tomatoes**
> In a medium bowl, combine 2 cups (500 mL) cherry tomatoes with 1 tbsp (15 mL) olive oil, ½ tsp (2 mL) granulated sugar, ¼ tsp (1 mL) salt and ¼ tsp (1 mL) pepper. Place in an 8-inch (2 L) square baking dish and convection bake in a preheated 425°F (220°C) oven for 6 to 8 minutes, or until just starting to soften. Makes 4 to 5 servings.

Parmesan-topped Fish Fillets

⅓ cup	mayonnaise	75 mL
⅓ cup	grated Parmesan cheese	75 mL
2 tbsp	chopped fresh dillweed, or 1 tsp (5 mL) dried	25 mL
1 tbsp	lemon juice	15 mL
½ tsp	black pepper	2 mL
4	6-oz (175 g) white-fleshed fish fillets, about ¾ inch (2 cm) thick	4
½ cup	dry bread crumbs	125 mL

1. In a bowl, combine mayonnaise, Parmesan, dill, lemon juice and pepper.

2. Arrange fish fillets on a parchment-lined baking sheet. Spread mayonnaise mixture evenly over fillets. Top with bread crumbs.

3. Convection bake in a preheated 400°F (200°C) oven for 8 to 10 minutes, or until fish flakes easily with a fork.

Bread Crumbs

For fresh bread crumbs, cut bread into chunks and process in food processor until crumbs form. For finer crumbs, process until no large chunks remain. Freeze extra bread crumbs in freezer bags.

For dry bread crumbs, place fresh bread crumbs on a baking sheet and convection bake in a preheated 275°F (135°C) oven for 10 to 15 minutes, or until dry. Turn off oven and leave crumbs in oven for 15 minutes. Cool at room temperature. Be sure crumbs are completely dry before storing. Dry bread crumbs can be stored in an airtight container at room temperature.

Panko bread crumbs are a good storebought substitute for homemade fresh or dry bread crumbs. They are large rice-shaped, dry white breadcrumbs and are often used in restaurants to give food a light, crunchy finish. They are now available in specialty food shops and some supermarkets.

Makes 4 servings

The mayonnaise topping is almost like a tartar sauce, providing flavor, moisture and a surface for the bread crumbs to cling to. Using several racks in the convection oven, this recipe could easily be cooked in quantity for a group.

For a fish sandwich, serve the fillets on rolls with lettuce and sliced tomatoes or a cabbage salad (page 97).

Make Ahead
Fish can be cooked ahead and served cold in a sandwich.

Lemon and Dill Fish Kabobs

Makes 6 servings

You could also use chicken or vegetables such as zucchini and cherry tomatoes in this recipe. If you are using metal skewers, warn guests that they will be hot. Salmon and red peppers make an attractive combination, but yellow or green peppers can also be used. Serve with a rice pilaf or steamed new potatoes.

⅓ cup	lemon juice	75 mL
¼ cup	chopped fresh dillweed	50 mL
2 tbsp	olive oil	25 mL
1 tbsp	Russian-style mustard	15 mL
½ tsp	salt	2 mL
¼ tsp	black pepper	1 mL
2 lbs	salmon, halibut or cod, cut in 1-inch (2.5 cm) pieces	1 kg
1	large red bell pepper, seeded and cut in 1-inch (2.5 cm) pieces	1

1. In a large non-metallic bowl, combine lemon juice, dill, olive oil, mustard, salt and pepper.

2. Add fish to marinade and toss gently to coat. Marinate for 10 minutes.

3. Thread fish and pepper pieces onto six 6- to 8-inch (15 to 20 cm) skewers. Arrange on a lightly greased broiler pan. Spoon over any remaining marinade.

4. Place fish about 4 inches (10 cm) from heat and convection broil under a preheated broiler for 4 minutes. Turn and cook for 4 to 5 minutes longer, or until fish flakes easily with a fork.

Chipotles

Chipotle peppers are smoked jalapeño peppers in adobo sauce. They are much hotter than regular jalapeños and are sold in cans at specialty food shops and some supermarkets. When you buy a can, puree the peppers and sauce together and freeze in small portions. The puree can be packaged in resealable freezer bags with the air squeezed out. Flatten the package to store and break off a piece of puree as you need it.

Also available in stores now is chipotle sauce (sometimes called Mexican hot sauce). It is very smooth and can be used as a condiment like ketchup or as a substitute for pureed chipotles.

Powdered chipotle chili pepper is made from dried smoked jalapeño peppers. It is very hot and can be used like cayenne pepper.

Fish Taco Wraps
with Spicy Fruit Salsa

Spicy Fruit Salsa

1 cup	diced cantaloupe or honeydew melon	250 mL
1 cup	diced pineapple	250 mL
1 tbsp	chopped jalapeño pepper	15 mL
2	green onions, chopped	2
2 tbsp	chopped fresh cilantro or mint	25 mL
2 tbsp	lime or lemon juice	25 mL
2 tsp	liquid honey or maple syrup	10 mL

Fish and Wraps

2 tbsp	olive oil	25 mL
½ tsp	chipotle puree (page 54) or hot pepper sauce, or ¼ tsp (1 mL) chipotle chili pepper	2 mL
½ tsp	salt	2 mL
4	6-oz (175 g) fish fillets, about ½ inch (1 cm) thick	4
4	large flour tortillas	4
1½ cups	shredded lettuce or arugula	375 mL
8	lime wedges	8

1. To prepare salsa, in a bowl, combine cantaloupe, pineapple, jalapeño, green onions, cilantro, lime juice and honey.

2. To prepare fish, in a measuring cup or small bowl, combine oil, chipotle puree and salt.

3. Arrange fish on a lightly greased baking sheet and brush with chipotle mixture.

4. Place fish about 4 inches (10 cm) from heat and convection broil under a preheated broiler for 5 to 7 minutes, or until fish flakes easily with a fork (watch carefully to make sure fish does not overcook).

5. To serve, let guests assemble their own wraps with tortillas, shredded lettuce, fish, salsa and a squeeze of lime juice.

Makes 4 servings

Use catfish, halibut, cod, flounder, grouper or pickerel. Although crispy taco shells can be used, they tend to be a bit crumbly; flour tortillas (try spinach or vegetable tortillas) make an ideal package.

You can also serve this with guacamole (page 37), or other salsas. Use fresh or well-drained canned pineapple.

Make Ahead

Salsa can be prepared ahead and refrigerated for up to five hours. Fish can also be cooked ahead and refrigerated until serving time.

Red Snapper with Tartar Sauce

Makes 4 servings

The convection oven gives this gratin a crisp, golden topping, without overcooking the fish. You can substitute tilapia, grouper or trout for the red snapper. The tartar sauce can be served with any type of fish or used in sandwiches or potato salads.

Make Ahead

Tartar sauce can be made, covered and refrigerated up to one day ahead.

Tartar Sauce

¾ cup	mayonnaise	175 mL
2	green onions, finely chopped	2
¼ cup	chopped sweet or dill pickle	50 mL
2 tbsp	chopped fresh parsley	25 mL
1 tbsp	capers, chopped	15 mL
1 tbsp	lemon juice	15 mL
¼ tsp	salt	1 mL
¼ tsp	black pepper	1 mL

Red Snapper

4	6-oz (175 g) red snapper fillets	4
2 tbsp	olive oil, divided	25 mL
1 tbsp	lemon juice	15 mL
¼ tsp	salt	1 mL
¼ tsp	black pepper	1 mL
1 cup	fresh bread crumbs	250 mL
¼ cup	chopped fresh dillweed	50 mL
¼ cup	grated Parmesan cheese	50 mL
2 tbsp	chopped fresh basil	25 mL

1. To prepare sauce, in a bowl, combine mayonnaise, green onions, pickle, parsley, capers, lemon juice, salt and pepper.

2. Arrange snapper in a shallow baking dish just large enough to hold fish in a single layer.

3. In a small bowl or measuring cup, combine 1 tbsp (15 mL) olive oil, lemon juice, salt and pepper. Pour marinade over fish, turning to coat fillets.

4. In a separate bowl, combine bread crumbs, dill, Parmesan, basil and remaining oil. Sprinkle over fish and pat on.

5. Convection bake in a preheated 400°F (200°C) oven for 10 to 12 minutes, or until fish flakes easily with a fork and crumbs are golden. Serve with tartar sauce.

Tilapia Mexicana

1 tbsp	olive oil, divided	15 mL
1 lb	tilapia fillets	500 g
¼ tsp	salt	1 mL
¼ tsp	black pepper	1 mL

Marinade

½ cup	lime juice	125 mL
⅓ cup	orange juice	75 mL
3 tbsp	olive oil	45 mL
2 tsp	grated orange zest	10 mL
¼ tsp	hot pepper flakes	1 mL
½ tsp	salt	2 mL
¼ tsp	black pepper	1 mL
1	small red onion, thinly sliced	1

Garnish

1	red bell pepper, seeded and thinly sliced	1
1	orange, peeled and sliced	1
1	avocado, peeled and sliced	1
2 tbsp	chopped fresh cilantro or parsley	25 mL

Makes 4 servings

Tilapia is a mild and delicate fish that is readily available at supermarkets and fish shops. (You could also use red snapper or halibut in this recipe.)
  This salad-like dish is similar to ceviche (where the fish is "cooked" in lime juice), but here the fish is baked before marinating. Serve with bread or warm flour tortillas.

1. Brush a 13- by 9-inch (3 L) baking dish with 1 tsp (5 mL) olive oil. Arrange fish in dish in a single layer, overlapping slightly if necessary. Drizzle with remaining 2 tsp (10 mL) oil. Season with salt and pepper. Convection bake in a preheated 350°F (180°C) oven for 8 minutes, or until just cooked. Let sit at room temperature for 20 minutes.

2. Meanwhile, to make marinade, in a small saucepan, combine lime juice, orange juice, olive oil, orange zest, pepper flakes, salt and pepper. Add onion slices. Bring to a boil and cook for 4 minutes. Remove from heat for 10 minutes, then pour over cooked fish.

3. Arrange red pepper and orange slices over fish. Cover and refrigerate for 2 to 4 hours, or until cool. Garnish with avocado and cilantro before serving.

Fish Fillets with Warm Balsamic Dressing

Makes 6 servings

When time closes in on the cook, just pop these fillets in the convection oven and let them cook while you prepare the dressing. Serve with roasted asparagus (page 117). Cook the asparagus at the same temperature as the fish and reduce the cooking time to 8 minutes, or until the asparagus is just tender (the timing will depend on the thickness of the stalks).

Fish

6	6-oz (175 g) fish fillets, about ¾ inch (2 cm) thick	6
1 tbsp	olive oil	15 mL
½ tsp	salt	2 mL
¼ tsp	black pepper	1 mL

Warm Balsamic Dressing

¼ cup	orange juice	50 mL
¼ cup	balsamic vinegar	50 mL
2 tbsp	olive oil	25 mL
2	green onions, chopped	2
2 tbsp	chopped fresh mint or basil	25 mL
2 tsp	grated orange zest	10 mL
½ tsp	salt	2 mL

1. Arrange fish on a parchment-lined baking sheet. Rub or brush with oil. Sprinkle with salt and pepper.

2. Convection bake in a preheated 400°F (200°C) oven for 8 to 10 minutes, or until fish flakes easily when tested with a fork.

3. Meanwhile, to prepare dressing, in a small saucepan, combine orange juice, vinegar, oil, green onions, mint, orange zest and salt. Warm over low heat. Do not boil.

4. Serve fish with dressing spooned over top.

Testing Fish for Doneness

Fish is cooked when the flesh has turned opaque and flakes easily when the thickest part of the fish is tested with a fork. If the fish has been cooked in a coating such as nuts or bread crumbs, use the tip of a sharp knife to carefully peek into the thickest part, trying not to disturb the coating too much. The flesh should separate and flake. In any case, always try not to overcook fish.

Sweet and Sour Cod

⅓ cup	chicken or vegetable stock, or water	75 mL
⅓ cup	ketchup	75 mL
3 tbsp	rice vinegar or white vinegar	45 mL
1 tbsp	granulated sugar	15 mL
1 tbsp	soy sauce	15 mL
2 tsp	olive oil	10 mL
1 tsp	sesame oil	5 mL
1 tbsp	cornstarch	15 mL
4	6-oz (175 g) pieces cod, skin removed	4
1	green onion, chopped	1

1. In a saucepan, combine stock, ketchup, vinegar, sugar, soy sauce, olive oil, sesame oil and cornstarch. Bring to a boil over medium heat and cook, stirring, for 1 minute, or until sauce thickens.

2. Arrange fish in a single layer in a lightly greased shallow baking dish. Pour sauce over fish.

3. Convection bake in a preheated 400°F (200°C) oven for 12 minutes, or until fish flakes easily when tested with a fork. Sprinkle fish with chopped green onion.

> ### Cucumber Salad
> In a large bowl, combine 1 thinly sliced cucumber, 2 chopped green onions, 3 tbsp (45 mL) rice vinegar, 1 tsp (5 mL) granulated sugar and a pinch of salt. Let stand at room temperature for 20 minutes, tossing occasionally. Makes about 2 cups (500 mL).

Makes 4 servings

Another quick and easy fish recipe. For a light meal, serve it with a cucumber salad and rice.

Make Ahead
Sauce can be cooked, covered and refrigerated up to two days ahead.

Baked Cod with Pistou

Makes 4 servings

Pistou is basically the Provençal version of pesto, without the pine nuts. If you have pesto on hand, it can be used instead.

Make Ahead
Assemble dish completely. Cover and refrigerate for up to four hours before baking.

½ cup	packed fresh basil leaves	125 mL
1	clove garlic, chopped	1
3 tbsp	olive oil	45 mL
2 tbsp	grated Parmesan cheese	25 mL
½ tsp	salt	2 mL
¼ tsp	black pepper	1 mL
1 lb	cod, cut in 4 pieces	500 g
1	large tomato, cored and sliced	1

1. To prepare pistou, place basil, garlic, olive oil, cheese, salt and pepper in a food processor. Blend until smooth.
2. Arrange cod pieces in one layer on a parchment-lined baking sheet. Spoon pistou evenly over fish. Turn fish to coat in pistou. Place tomato slices on fish.
3. Convection bake in a preheated 400°F (200°C) oven for 10 to 12 minutes, or until fish just flakes with a fork.

Lemon Halibut with Capers

Makes 4 servings

Simple does it. With just a few ingredients and great fish, this is perfect for weeknight cooking.

4	6-oz (175 g) halibut steaks or fillets, about 1 inch (2.5 cm) thick	4
2 tbsp	lemon juice	25 mL
2 tbsp	olive oil	25 mL
1 tbsp	chopped fresh rosemary, or ½ tsp (2 mL) dried	15 mL
½ tsp	salt	2 mL
¼ tsp	black pepper	1 mL
2 tbsp	capers	25 mL

1. Arrange fillets on a parchment-lined baking sheet. Drizzle lemon juice and oil over fish. Sprinkle with rosemary, salt and pepper and rub mixture into fish.
2. Convection bake in a preheated 400°F (200°C) oven for 10 to 12 minutes, or until fish flakes easily when tested with a fork. Garnish with capers.

Fish Fillets with Miso Dressing

Miso Dressing

2 tbsp	light miso	25 mL
2 tbsp	rice vinegar	25 mL
2 tbsp	pineapple juice or orange juice	25 mL
1	clove garlic, minced	1
1 tsp	liquid honey or granulated sugar	5 mL
2 tbsp	vegetable oil	25 mL
1 tbsp	sesame oil	15 mL

Fish

6	6-oz (175 g) salmon or halibut fillets	6
1 tsp	grated lemon zest	5 mL
1 tbsp	sesame oil	15 mL
6	fresh pineapple slices	6
1 tbsp	toasted or black sesame seeds (optional)	15 mL
3	green onions, sliced on the diagonal	3

1. To prepare dressing, in a small bowl, whisk together miso, vinegar, pineapple juice, garlic, honey, vegetable oil and sesame oil.

2. Arrange fillets on a parchment-lined baking sheet. In a small bowl or cup, combine lemon zest and sesame oil. Spoon over fish. Roll fish to coat.

3. Arrange pineapple slices on a separate parchment-lined baking sheet. Convection bake fish and pineapple in a preheated 400°F (200°C) oven for 6 to 8 minutes, or until fish is opaque and flakes easily when tested with a fork.

4. To serve, place pineapple slices on individual serving plates. Place fish just slightly overlapping pineapple. Spoon dressing over fish. Garnish with sesame seeds, if using, and green onions.

Makes 6 servings

Miso, a fermented soybean paste, can be light or dark. The light- or medium-colored is the mildest and most popular. Found in Asian or health food stores in the refrigerated section, it is an everyday ingredient in Japanese cooking. Once opened, store miso tightly covered in the refrigerator.

This dish can also be served in smaller portions as a starter.

Make Ahead

Dressing can be prepared, covered and refrigerated up to two days ahead. For summer entertaining, cook the fish and pineapple up to a half hour in advance and serve at room temperature.

Grouper with Thai Curry Sauce

Makes 6 servings

Now that Thai ingredients are so readily available, the wonderful tastes of Thailand are easy to replicate at home.

Any white fish or even salmon can be used in this recipe. Serve with rice and sugar snap peas (page 146) baked at the same time as the fish. The sauce is also good with roast chicken or roasted tofu.

Fish

2 tbsp	oyster sauce, hoisin or soy sauce	25 mL
1 tbsp	lime or lemon juice	15 mL
1 tsp	granulated sugar	5 mL
6	6-oz (175 g) grouper fillets or other white fish	6

Thai Curry Sauce

1 tbsp	vegetable oil	15 mL
1	onion, finely chopped	1
2	cloves garlic, chopped	2
1 tbsp	chopped gingerroot	15 mL
1 tbsp	Thai curry paste (red or green)	15 mL
1 cup	coconut milk	250 mL
1 tbsp	fish sauce or soy sauce	15 mL
1 tbsp	lime or lemon juice	15 mL
2 tbsp	chopped fresh cilantro	25 mL

1. To prepare fish, in a small bowl, combine oyster sauce, lime juice and sugar.

2. Arrange fish on a parchment-lined baking sheet. Brush lightly with oyster sauce mixture. Convection bake in a preheated 400°F (200°C) oven for 15 minutes, or until fish flakes easily with a fork.

3. Meanwhile, to prepare sauce, in a saucepan, heat oil over medium heat. Add onion, garlic and ginger and cook for 3 minutes, or until softened but not brown. Add curry paste and cook for 30 seconds. Add coconut milk, fish sauce and lime juice. Bring to a boil, reduce heat and keep warm.

4. Top fish with curry sauce and sprinkle with cilantro.

Fish Cakes

1 lb	cooked fish (salmon, cod, crabmeat or a combination), flaked (about 2½ cups/625 mL)	500 g
2 cups	cooked mashed potatoes	500 mL
1	egg	1
½ cup	chopped celery	125 mL
¼ cup	chopped green onion	50 mL
¼ cup	mayonnaise	50 mL
2 tbsp	lemon juice	25 mL
2 tbsp	chopped fresh dillweed	25 mL
1 tsp	Dijon mustard	5 mL
¾ tsp	salt	4 mL
½ tsp	black pepper	2 mL
2 tbsp	melted butter or olive oil	25 mL

Makes 6 servings

Sometimes I even cook extra fish and potatoes, just so I can make these. Rather than being fried, these lower-fat fish cakes bake beautifully in the convection oven. Serve them as a starter (shape into smaller cakes), as a burger on a bun or as a main course with a spinach salad and tartar sauce (page 56).

1. In a large bowl, combine fish, potatoes, egg, celery, green onion, mayonnaise, lemon juice, dill, mustard, salt and pepper. Mix thoroughly.

2. With dampened hands, shape mixture into 8 to 10 cakes. Arrange on a parchment-lined baking sheet or lightly greased broiler pan. Brush cakes with melted butter.

3. Convection bake in a preheated 400°F (200°C) oven for 20 to 22 minutes, or until cakes are golden brown.

> **Quick Spinach Salad**
> In a bowl, combine 6 cups (1.5 L) baby spinach leaves and 2 peeled and sectioned oranges. To make dressing, combine 4 tsp (20 mL) orange juice, 1 tbsp (15 mL) rice vinegar and 2 tsp (10 mL) sesame oil. Toss spinach and oranges with dressing. Sprinkle with 1 tbsp (15 mL) sesame seeds. Makes 4 to 6 servings.

Shrimp with Tomato and Feta

**Makes 4 to
5 servings**

Create your own Mediterranean holiday at home by serving this dish as an appetizer or main course (serve with rice or lots of crusty bread). The Greek version would use ouzo (a licorice-flavored liqueur) in place of the wine.

Make Ahead

Tomato sauce can be prepared, covered and refrigerated up to one day earlier. Reheat sauce on stove before adding shrimp.

2 tbsp	olive oil	25 mL
2	onions, chopped	2
2	cloves garlic, finely chopped	2
1	28-oz (796 mL) can plum tomatoes, drained and chopped	1
½ cup	dry white wine	125 mL
¼ cup	chopped fresh parsley	50 mL
1 tbsp	chopped fresh oregano or basil, or 1 tsp (5 mL) dried	15 mL
¼ tsp	salt	1 mL
¼ tsp	black pepper	1 mL
1 lb	shrimp, peeled, deveined and patted dry	500 g
1 cup	crumbled feta cheese	250 mL

1. In a large skillet, heat oil over medium-high heat. Add onions and garlic. Cook, stirring occasionally, for 4 minutes, or until softened but not colored. Add tomatoes, wine, parsley, oregano, salt and pepper. Cook until thickened but not too dry, about 8 minutes.

2. Remove from heat and add shrimp. Spoon into an 8-inch (2 L) square baking dish. Sprinkle feta over shrimp.

3. Convection bake in a preheated 325°F (160°C) oven for 22 to 25 minutes, or just until shrimp is pink. Let stand for a few minutes before serving.

Tomato and Olive Tart (page 31)
Overleaf: Mom's Salmon Loaf (page 51)

Josée's Party Shrimp

1½ lbs	large shrimp, peeled and deveined	750 g
1 tbsp	olive oil	15 mL
2 tsp	curry powder	10 mL
1 tsp	salt	5 mL
½ tsp	black pepper	2 mL
⅓ cup	chopped mango chutney	75 mL
2 tbsp	mayonnaise, sour cream or unflavored yogurt	25 mL
2 tbsp	chopped fresh mint	25 mL
2 tbsp	chopped fresh cilantro or basil	25 mL

Makes 4 to 6 servings

My dear friend Josée is an avid gardener who specializes in creative container planting. Every month she gets together with her horticultural friends for lunch. Everyone brings a dish and copies of their recipe for all the members. Josée served this at one of these lunches. She cooked the shrimp in her convection oven just before guests arrived and served them at room temperature.

1. In a bowl, combine shrimp, oil, curry powder, salt and pepper. Toss to coat shrimp thoroughly.

2. Arrange shrimp on a parchment-lined baking sheet. Convection bake in a preheated 450°F (230°C) oven for 5 to 7 minutes, or until shrimp are pink and just cooked. Stir once during baking.

3. Meanwhile, in a bowl, combine chutney, mayonnaise, mint and cilantro. Drizzle over cooked shrimp and toss to coat. Serve hot, cold or at room temperature.

Variation

Shrimp and Mango Cocktail: Line 8 small sherbet glasses with shredded lettuce. Omit mayonnaise-chutney sauce.

In a bowl, combine cooked shrimp with 1 chopped mango, 1 cup (250 mL) chopped cucumber, 2 tsp (10 mL) sweet Asian chili sauce and 1 tsp (5 mL) sesame oil. Spoon into lettuce-lined glasses and sprinkle with 1 tbsp (15 mL) chopped peanuts. Makes 8 appetizer servings.

Overleaf: Grouper with Thai Curry Sauce (page 62)
Chicken Souvlaki with Tzatziki (page 73) and
    Summer Peppers (page 163)

Scallop and Pepper Skewers

If your scallops are very large, cut each one into halves or quarters. For color contrast use yellow, orange or red peppers instead of green. Serve over rice.

½ cup	orange juice	125 mL
2 tbsp	olive oil	25 mL
2 tbsp	chopped fresh tarragon	25 mL
2 tsp	Russian-style mustard	10 mL
1 lb	scallops, trimmed	500 g
1	green bell pepper, seeded and cut in 1-inch (2.5 cm) pieces	1

1. In a large bowl, whisk together orange juice, oil, tarragon and mustard.
2. Add scallops and green pepper and toss gently to coat.
3. Thread scallops and pepper pieces, alternately, on 6- to 8-inch (15 to 20 cm) skewers. Arrange on lightly greased rack set over broiler pan and spoon over any remaining marinade.
4. Place scallops about 4 inches (10 cm) from heat and convection broil under a preheated broiler for 8 to 10 minutes, turning once, until scallops are opaque.

> **Variation**
> *Scallops and Shrimp with Orange Sauce:* Toss a combination of scallops and shrimp with orange mixture (omit peppers if you wish). Place in a lightly greased shallow baking dish. Convection bake in a preheated 400°F (200°C) preheated oven for 8 to 10 minutes, until shrimp are pink and scallops are opaque. Serve over cooked rice. Makes 4 to 6 servings.

Poultry

Roast Chicken with Herbed Potatoes and Onions

Makes 4 to 6 servings

In the convection oven, a plain chicken roasts to an even, golden brown with crispy skin. The circulating hot air seals the surface, so more juices are retained, resulting in a chicken that is moist and tender. Roasting onions and potatoes at the same time is an efficient way to prepare a meal. Serve with a green vegetable and salad.

If your potatoes are large, cut them in half.

1	3½ -lb (1.75 kg) chicken, patted dry	1
¾ tsp	salt, divided	4 mL
½ tsp	black pepper, divided	2 mL
1 tbsp	olive oil or butter, melted	15 mL
¼ tsp	paprika	1 mL

Herbed Potatoes and Onions

2 lbs	baby potatoes (about 22 to 24)	500 g
2	onions, cut in large chunks	2
2 tbsp	olive oil	25 mL
1 tbsp	chopped fresh herbs (e.g., parsley, thyme and rosemary)	15 mL
1 tsp	salt	5 mL

1. Season inside of chicken with ½ tsp (2 mL) salt and ¼ tsp (1 mL) pepper. Tuck wing tips under back and tie legs together loosely. Place breast side up on a lightly greased rack set over foil-lined broiler pan (for easy cleanup). Brush chicken with oil and sprinkle with remaining salt, pepper and paprika.

2. Convection roast in a preheated 400°F (200°C) oven for 25 minutes. Reduce heat to 325°F (160°C) and continue to roast for 25 to 30 minutes, or until juices run clear or a meat thermometer registers 180°F (82°C) when inserted into inner thigh.

3. Meanwhile, to prepare vegetables, in a bowl, combine potatoes, onions, oil, herbs and salt. Spread over a parchment-lined baking sheet. (Onions will brown more quickly so try to tuck them underneath potatoes.)

4. Place vegetables on lower rack of oven 15 minutes after chicken goes in. Continue to roast with chicken until potatoes and onions are golden and tender.

5. Remove chicken from oven and tent loosely with foil. Keep vegetables warm in turned-off oven while chicken rests for 10 minutes. Carve chicken and serve with vegetables.

Pesto-stuffed Roast Chicken

1	3½ -lb (1.75 kg) chicken, patted dry	1
¾ tsp	salt, divided	4 mL
¼ tsp	black pepper	1 mL
¼ cup	pesto	50 mL
1 tbsp	olive oil	15 mL

Makes 5 to 6 servings

Nothing beats a plain roast chicken cooked to perfection in the convection oven — unless it is this chicken seasoned under the skin with pesto. Serve with polenta slices, (page 188).

1. Season inside of chicken with ½ tsp (2 mL) salt and pepper.
2. Loosen breast skin from neck and tail ends. Spread pesto over breast and top part of thighs between meat and skin. Secure skin with toothpicks or small metal skewers.
3. Place chicken on a lightly greased rack set over foil-lined broiler pan. Rub chicken with oil and sprinkle with remaining ¼ tsp (1 mL) salt. Convection roast in a preheated 400°F (200°C) oven for 25 minutes. Reduce heat to 325°F (160°C) and roast for 25 to 30 minutes, or until juices run clear or a meat thermometer registers 180°F (82°C) when inserted into inner thigh.
4. Remove chicken from oven and tent loosely with foil. Let stand for 10 minutes before carving.

Pesto

In a food processor, combine 1 cup (250 mL) packed fresh basil leaves, ¼ cup (50 mL) toasted pine nuts, 2 peeled cloves garlic, ¼ tsp (1 mL) salt and ¼ tsp (1 mL) black pepper. Pulse until finely chopped.

With machine running, pour ⅓ cup (75 mL) olive oil through feed tube. Blend in ⅓ cup (75 mL) grated Parmesan cheese, scraping down sides of bowl. Makes about 1 cup (250 mL).

Brined Roast Chicken

My students always used to talk about brining their chicken, turkey or pork roasts and chops (see To Brine or Not to Brine, page 113). Not being a fan of either extra steps or change, I was not convinced. Finally I gave in and was very pleased with the result — a moist, flavorful chicken that browns to a beautiful mahogany color when roasted in the convection oven.

Remember to plan ahead to allow time for brining, and make sure you have enough refrigerator space and a suitable container.

Make Ahead

This chicken is also great served cold. Carve after chilling.

¾ cup	coarse salt, or ½ cup (125 mL) table salt	175 mL
½ cup	brown sugar	125 mL
14 cups	cold water	3.5 L
4 cups	apple juice or cider	1 L
2 tbsp	black peppercorns	25 mL
2	bay leaves	2
1 tsp	cumin seeds	5 mL
1	3½ - to 4-lb (1.75 to 2 kg) chicken	1

1. In a bowl or bucket large enough that chicken can be completely immersed in brine, dissolve salt and brown sugar in water and apple juice. Add peppercorns, bay leaves and cumin.

2. Immerse chicken in liquid and refrigerate for several hours or up to 24 hours.

3. Remove chicken from brine and discard brine. Pat chicken very dry inside and out. Arrange breast side up on a lightly greased rack set over foil-lined broiler pan. Convection roast in a preheated 350°F (180°C) oven for 55 to 60 minutes, or until juices run clear and a meat thermometer registers 180°F (82°C) when inserted into inner thigh.

4. Remove chicken from oven and tent loosely with foil. Let stand for 10 minutes before carving.

Flat Roast Chicken

2 tbsp	Dijon mustard	25 mL
1 tbsp	soy sauce	15 mL
2	cloves garlic, finely chopped	2
2 tsp	chopped fresh rosemary, or ½ tsp (2 mL) dried	10 mL
¼ tsp	black pepper	1 mL
1	3-lb (1.5 kg) chicken, patted dry	1

1. In a small bowl, combine mustard, soy sauce, garlic, rosemary and pepper.

2. With kitchen shears or a sharp knife, cut carefully along both sides of backbone. Remove backbone. Cut off wing tips (freeze backbone and wing tips for stock). Spread chicken open and press firmly to flatten.

3. Spoon mustard mixture over both sides of chicken. Arrange chicken, skin side up, on a foil- and parchment-lined baking sheet (this will make cleanup easier).

4. Convection roast in a preheated 325°F (160°C) oven for 55 to 60 minutes, or until juices run clear and a meat thermometer registers 180°F (82°C) when inserted into thigh. (If chicken is browning too quickly, cover loosely with foil, tucking edges under chicken, during last half of roasting time.) Transfer to a carving board or serving platter and cut into serving pieces.

Makes 4 to 6 servings

I learned how to cook whole chicken flattened under foil-wrapped bricks from Carlo Middione, a great Italian restaurateur in San Francisco, but you can prepare a similar version in the convection oven. Serve with baked beets (page 119) and garlic mashed potatoes.

Crispy Chicken with Cranberry Pear Relish

Makes 6 servings

Dipping chicken breasts in the yogurt mixture helps the bread crumbs to cling. Convection cooking seals in the juices and produces a crisp exterior and moist, tender chicken. Prepare this lower-fat, flavorful dish to serve with mashed turnips (page 152). The cranberry pear relish can also be served with roast turkey, baked ham and chicken sandwiches.

Make Ahead
Relish can be prepared, covered and refrigerated for up to three days.

Cranberry Pear Relish

2	pears, peeled, cored and diced	2
1	small onion, chopped	1
1½ cups	fresh or frozen cranberries	375 mL
1 cup	apple juice or orange juice	250 mL
1 tbsp	granulated sugar (optional)	15 mL
2 tbsp	chopped fresh basil or mint	25 mL

Crispy Chicken

¾ cup	unflavored yogurt or buttermilk	175 mL
¼ cup	chopped fresh basil, or 2 tsp (10 mL) dried	50 mL
1 tbsp	horseradish	15 mL
2 cups	fresh bread crumbs	500 mL
⅓ cup	grated Parmesan cheese	75 mL
¼ tsp	salt	1 mL
¼ tsp	black pepper	1 mL
6	6-oz (175 g) boneless, skinless chicken breasts	6

1. To prepare relish, in a medium saucepan, combine pears, onion, cranberries, apple juice and sugar, if using. Bring to a boil over high heat. Reduce heat to medium-low and simmer, uncovered, for 15 minutes, or until pears are tender. Stir occasionally. Pour into a bowl and let cool to room temperature. Stir in basil.

2. To prepare chicken, combine yogurt, basil and horseradish in a shallow dish. Combine bread crumbs, cheese, salt and pepper in another dish.

3. Pat chicken pieces dry. Dip chicken into yogurt mixture to coat. Roll chicken in bread crumbs, turning to coat and patting in crumbs. Place on a parchment-lined or lightly greased baking sheet.

4. Convection bake in a preheated 350°F (180°C) oven for 25 to 30 minutes, or until juices run clear and chicken is no longer pink inside. Serve with relish.

Chicken Souvlaki with Tzatziki

2 tbsp	olive oil	25 mL
2 tbsp	dry white wine or chicken stock	25 mL
2 tbsp	lemon juice	25 mL
1	clove garlic, minced	1
1 tsp	dried oregano leaves	5 mL
1 tsp	grated lemon zest	5 mL
¼ tsp	salt	1 mL
¼ tsp	black pepper	1 mL
3	bay leaves	3
1 lb	boneless, skinless chicken breasts, cut in 1-inch (2.5 cm) pieces	500 g

Tzatziki

1 cup	unflavored yogurt	250 mL
½	English cucumber, grated	½
½ tsp	salt	2 mL
2	cloves garlic, minced	2
1 tbsp	chopped fresh dillweed	15 mL
1 tbsp	chopped fresh mint	15 mL
1 tbsp	lemon juice	15 mL
	Salt and black pepper to taste	

Makes 4 servings

Anyone who has visited Greece and spent leisurely hours in the open-air taverns and restaurants may be transported back with this recipe. Traditionally grilled over charcoal cookers, souvlaki can also be cooked quickly under the broiler. Serve tzatziki as a refreshing side dish or as a spread with warmed pita. Slice fresh tomatoes and lemon wedges to serve alongside, too.

Make Ahead

Tzatziki can be made and refrigerated, covered, up to six hours ahead.

1. To prepare chicken, combine olive oil, wine, lemon juice, garlic, oregano, lemon zest, salt, pepper, bay leaves and chicken in a large bowl. Stir thoroughly. Cover and refrigerate for 1 to 8 hours.

2. To prepare tzatziki, line a sieve or strainer with cheesecloth or a clean dish towel. Spoon yogurt into sieve. Let drain, refrigerated, for 1 hour.

3. Meanwhile, combine cucumber with salt and place in a strainer. Drain for 30 minutes. Pat cucumber dry.

4. Combine drained yogurt, cucumber, garlic, dill, mint and lemon juice. Taste and season with salt and pepper.

5. To cook souvlaki, thread chicken onto skewers. Arrange on a lightly greased broiler rack. Place 4 inches (10 cm) from heat and convection broil under preheated broiler for 4 minutes. Turn and broil for 4 to 6 minutes longer, or until pinkness disappears. Serve with tzatziki.

Broiled Cilantro Garlic Chicken Breasts

Makes 4 servings

This may sound like a lot of garlic and cilantro, but the result is a tangy, moist chicken. In Thailand, I had this served from a hibachi, but it also cooks extremely well in the convection oven. You can also use the marinade on thick slices of extra-firm tofu, but reduce the cooking time by at least half. Serve with sliced tomato and cucumber. This chicken is also good chilled and thinly sliced. Add to a salad with diced mango.

4	6-oz (175 g) boneless, skinless chicken breasts	4
4	cloves garlic, peeled	4
2	shallots or 1 small onion, peeled	2
1 cup	loosely packed fresh cilantro leaves	250 mL
¼ cup	lemon juice or lime juice	50 mL
1 tbsp	granulated sugar	15 mL
1 tbsp	fish sauce or soy sauce	15 mL
1 tsp	black pepper	5 mL

1. Place one chicken breast between sheets of parchment paper or plastic wrap (I cut open a plastic bag). With a meat pounder or rolling pin, flatten chicken until about ½ inch (1 cm) thick. Place in a shallow glass or ceramic dish. Repeat with remaining chicken breasts.

2. In a food processor or blender, finely chop garlic, shallots and cilantro. Blend in lemon juice, sugar, fish sauce and pepper. Pour over chicken, turning to coat on all sides. Cover and refrigerate for 1 to 12 hours.

3. To cook, arrange chicken breasts with marinade on a lightly greased broiler pan. Place under a preheated broiler about 4 inches (10 cm) from heat. Convection broil for 4 minutes. Turn and broil for 4 to 6 minutes longer, or until chicken is no longer pink inside. Do not overcook or chicken will be dry.

Cilantro

Also known as fresh coriander or Chinese parsley, cilantro is a fresh herb used in Asian, Mexican and Indian cooking. All parts of the herb can be used (some recipes even call for the roots). Wash well and dry in vegetable spinner or towel. Store refrigerated in plastic bags or covered containers.

Fresh parsley can be substituted for those not fond of cilantro's distinctive flavor.

Mediterranean Chicken Breasts

2 cups	cherry or grape tomatoes	500 mL
2	6-oz (170 mL) jars marinated artichoke hearts, drained	2
1	fennel bulb, trimmed and cut in ½-inch (1 cm) pieces	1
1	onion, cut in ½-inch (1 cm) pieces	1
3	cloves garlic, peeled and sliced	3
1 tbsp	capers	15 mL
6	6-oz (175 g) boneless, skinless chicken breasts	6
¼ cup	olive oil	50 mL
3 tbsp	balsamic vinegar	45 mL
2 tsp	chopped fresh thyme, or ½ tsp (2 mL) dried	10 mL
½ tsp	salt	2 mL
¼ tsp	black pepper	1 mL
½ cup	pitted black or green olives	125 mL
¼ cup	shredded fresh basil	50 mL

Makes 6 servings

Although there is a long list of ingredients, this is basically a mixture of vegetables and chicken topped with a vinaigrette and roasted — another great oven meal that can be accompanied by Rosemary Garlic Fougasse (page 203) and any roasted fruit.

1. On a foil- and parchment-lined baking sheet, spread tomatoes, artichokes, fennel, onion, garlic and capers. Arrange chicken over vegetables.

2. In a small bowl or measuring cup, whisk together oil, vinegar, thyme, salt and pepper. Drizzle dressing over chicken and vegetables.

3. Convection roast in a preheated 400°F (200°C) oven for 25 to 30 minutes, or until vegetables are tender, chicken is cooked through and juices run clear when pierced with a fork. Top with olives and basil.

Lemon Ginger Chicken Breasts

Makes 6 servings

Lemon juice and fresh gingerroot add a tangy touch to simple roasted chicken breasts. Cook the Asian Vegetable Medley (page 147) at the same time and serve with rice. Use any leftovers in a salad or wrap.

¼ cup	lemon juice	50 mL
¼ cup	butter, melted, or olive oil	50 mL
2 tbsp	finely chopped gingerroot	25 mL
2	cloves garlic, finely chopped	2
2 tsp	grated lemon zest	10 mL
½ tsp	salt	2 mL
¼ tsp	hot pepper flakes (optional)	1 mL
6	6-oz (175 g) boneless, skinless chicken breasts	6

1. In a bowl, combine lemon juice, melted butter, ginger, garlic, lemon zest, salt and hot pepper flakes, if using.

2. In a large shallow dish, arrange chicken breasts in a single layer. Pour lemon mixture over top and turn chicken breasts to coat. Refrigerate for 30 minutes or up to 6 hours.

3. Arrange chicken in a single layer on a lightly greased foil-lined baking dish. Pour marinade over chicken.

4. Convection roast in a preheated 425°F (220°C) oven for 20 minutes, or until chicken is cooked through and juices run clear. Serve chicken with juices.

Cooked Rice
Rinse 2 cups (500 mL) long-grain white rice under cold water until water is almost clear. Drain. Place in a saucepan with 3¼ cups (800 mL) cold water. Bring to a boil, uncovered. Reduce heat to low, cover and cook for 12 to 15 minutes, or until rice is tender. Remove from heat and let stand for 5 minutes. Fluff with a fork. Makes 6 servings.

Honey Garlic Chicken Wings

2 lbs	chicken wings	1 kg
¼ cup	liquid honey	50 mL
¼ cup	soy sauce	50 mL
3 tbsp	ketchup	45 mL
2 tbsp	black bean sauce or hoisin sauce	25 mL
2 tbsp	lemon juice or white vinegar	25 mL
3	cloves garlic, minced	3
¼ tsp	ground ginger	1 mL

1. Cut wing tips off chicken (freeze to make stock). Cut each chicken wing into two pieces at the joint.

2. In a large bowl, combine honey, soy sauce, ketchup, black bean sauce, lemon juice, garlic and ginger. Add chicken wings. Stir to coat wings with marinade. Cover and refrigerate for 4 hours or overnight.

3. Arrange chicken wings with marinade on a foil- and parchment-lined baking sheet.

4. Convection bake in a preheated 375°F (190°C) oven for 20 to 25 minutes, turning halfway through cooking.

Makes 2 to 3 servings

Both kids and adults love these wings. Have moist towelettes on hand for greasy fingers. For a casual gathering serve these along with other finger food such as nachos (page 37) and quesadillas (pages 35 and 36). If you are not a wing fan, or if you prefer a lower-fat version, use thin boneless, skinless chicken breasts and bake for 20 to 25 minutes, or until the chicken is no longer pink inside. Cover the chicken loosely with foil if it browns too much.

Roasted Drumsticks and Vegetables

Makes 4 to 5 servings

Weekday family dinners need easy-to-prepare dishes like this one. The chicken and vegetables are cooked together, and you only have to add a salad for a complete meal.

8	chicken drumsticks	8
2	onions, peeled and quartered	2
6	cloves garlic, peeled	6
4	medium new potatoes, quartered (about 1½ lbs/750 g total)	4
4	parsnips, peeled and halved	4
2	red bell peppers, seeded and cut in eighths	2
2 tbsp	olive oil	25 mL
1 tsp	dried thyme leaves	5 mL
¾ tsp	salt	4 mL
½ tsp	black pepper	2 mL

1. Arrange drumsticks, onions, garlic, potatoes, parsnips and peppers in a single layer on a foil-lined baking sheet.

2. Drizzle oil over chicken and vegetables. Sprinkle with thyme, salt and pepper. Turn to coat.

3. Convection roast in a preheated 325°F (160°C) oven for 60 to 70 minutes, or until vegetables are tender and chicken is golden. Turn twice during cooking time.

Chicken with Lots of Garlic

1	onion, chopped	1
20	cloves garlic, peeled	20
1 tsp	dried tarragon leaves	5 mL
1 tbsp	olive oil	15 mL
1	3½-lb (1.75 kg) chicken, cut in serving pieces	1
½ tsp	salt	2 mL
¼ tsp	black pepper	1 mL
½ cup	dry white wine	125 mL
½ cup	chicken stock	125 mL
¼ cup	chopped fresh parsley	50 mL

Makes 4 to 5 servings

A quick convection-oven version of the famous Chicken with Forty Cloves of Garlic. Because the garlic is roasted, the resulting sauce is sweet and not at all overpowering. This is good just with crusty bread and a salad. During tomato season, serve it with sliced tomatoes topped with shredded basil.

1. Spread onion, garlic and tarragon over center of a foil- and parchment-lined baking sheet. Drizzle with oil and stir to coat. Arrange chicken pieces skin side up over vegetables so garlic is covered. Sprinkle with salt and pepper. Pour wine and stock over chicken.

2. Convection roast in a preheated 375°F (190°C) oven for 35 to 40 minutes, or until juices run clear. Baste chicken once during roasting.

3. Remove chicken to a serving platter. Coarsely mash garlic and onions with a fork and spoon mixture over chicken. Garnish with parsley.

Caribbean Chicken Thighs with Buttermilk Cornbread

Makes 4 servings

Boneless, skinless chicken thighs are the way to please dark meat lovers. As a bonus, the cornbread is cooked at the same time (there will probably be extra cornbread). Serve with Pineapple Salsa and a green vegetable.

Jalapeño peppers vary in hotness. Taste a very small piece and judge the amount accordingly.

Make Ahead

Cornbread can be baked, cooled, left whole or cut into pieces, covered and refrigerated for up to two days or wrapped well and frozen for up to three weeks.

2	green onions, cut in 1-inch (2.5 cm) pieces	2
2	cloves garlic, peeled	2
1	small jalapeño pepper, seeded	1
2 tbsp	olive oil	25 mL
2 tsp	granulated sugar	10 mL
½ tsp	dried thyme leaves	2 mL
½ tsp	ground allspice	2 mL
½ tsp	ground cinnamon	2 mL
½ tsp	salt	2 mL
¼ tsp	black pepper	1 mL
¼ tsp	ground nutmeg	1 mL
½ cup	coconut milk	125 mL
8	boneless, skinless chicken thighs	8

Buttermilk Cornbread

1 cup	all-purpose flour	250 mL
¾ cup	cornmeal	175 mL
¼ cup	granulated sugar	50 mL
1½ tsp	baking powder	7 mL
½ tsp	baking soda	2 mL
½ tsp	salt	2 mL
2	eggs	2
1¼ cups	buttermilk	300 mL
¼ cup	olive or vegetable oil	50 mL

1. In a food processor or blender, combine green onions, garlic, jalapeño, oil, sugar, thyme, allspice, cinnamon, salt, pepper, nutmeg and coconut milk. Puree to form a paste.

2. Arrange chicken thighs in a shallow dish in a single layer. Cover with sauce and toss to coat. Cover and refrigerate for 4 hours or overnight.

3. Arrange chicken thighs in a single layer on a foil- and parchment-lined baking sheet. Discard marinade.

4. To prepare cornbread, in a large bowl, combine flour, cornmeal, sugar, baking powder, baking soda and salt.

5. In a separate bowl, beat together eggs, buttermilk and oil. Add to dry ingredients and stir just until combined. Transfer batter to a lightly greased and parchment-lined 9-inch (2.5 L) square baking dish.

6. Convection roast both chicken and cornbread in a preheated 375°F (190°C) oven for 22 to 25 minutes, or until a cake tester inserted in center of cornbread comes out clean and chicken juices run clear. Cool cornbread for 5 minutes before cutting into serving pieces.

Pineapple Salsa
In a bowl, combine $\frac{1}{2}$ diced fresh pineapple, 1 seeded and chopped green bell pepper, 2 tbsp (25 mL) chopped fresh cilantro, 2 tbsp (25 mL) orange juice and $\frac{1}{2}$ tsp (2 mL) hot pepper sauce. Makes about 2 cups (500 mL).

Chicken Pot Pie

Makes 6 servings

An all-time favorite. The drop biscuit batter makes a speedy topping. Of course, turkey can also be used or, in a pinch, cooked deli chicken.

Make Ahead
Sauce can be prepared up to the end of Step 2 and refrigerated a day before assembling dish.

3 tbsp	butter	45 mL
1	onion, chopped	1
1 cup	chopped celery	250 mL
1 cup	diced carrots	250 mL
1½ cups	sliced mushrooms	375 mL
¼ cup	all-purpose flour	50 mL
2½ cups	chicken stock	625 mL
½ tsp	dried thyme leaves	2 mL
½ tsp	salt	2 mL
½ tsp	black pepper	2 mL
2½ cups	diced cooked chicken	625 mL
1 cup	peas	250 mL
2 tbsp	chopped fresh parsley	25 mL

Topping

1½ cups	all-purpose flour	375 mL
2 tsp	baking powder	10 mL
½ tsp	salt	2 mL
¼ tsp	dried thyme leaves	1 mL
⅓ cup	cold butter, cut in cubes	75 mL
¾ cup	milk	175 mL
2 tbsp	grated Parmesan cheese	25 mL

1. In a large saucepan, melt butter over medium-high heat. Add onion, celery and carrots. Cook, stirring, for 4 minutes. Add mushrooms and cook for 4 minutes.

2. Add flour and cook, stirring, for 2 minutes. Add stock, thyme, salt and pepper. Bring to a boil and cook for 4 minutes.

3. Stir in chicken, peas and parsley and spoon into a lightly greased 8-cup (2 L) casserole.

4. For topping, in a large bowl, combine flour, baking powder, salt and thyme. Cut in butter until it is in tiny bits. Add milk, mixing until dough is slightly sticky.

5. Drop batter by spoonfuls over chicken and sprinkle with Parmesan. Convection bake in a preheated 375°F (190°C) oven for 25 to 30 minutes, or until top is golden and topping is cooked in center.

Chicken Meatballs with Roasted Tomato Salsa

Chicken Meatballs

1½ lbs	ground chicken	750 g
½ cup	fresh bread crumbs	125 mL
¼ cup	grated Parmesan cheese	50 mL
¼ cup	ketchup	50 mL
1	egg	1
½ tsp	dried oregano leaves	2 mL
½ tsp	salt	2 mL
¼ tsp	black pepper	1 mL

Roasted Tomato Salsa

8	plum tomatoes, cut in ½-inch (1 cm) pieces	8
1	red onion, cut in ½-inch (1 cm) pieces	1
1	red bell pepper, seeded and cut in ½-inch (1 cm) pieces	1
1	jalapeño pepper, seeded and chopped	1
3	cloves garlic, peeled and sliced	3
2 tbsp	olive oil	25 mL
2 tsp	chipotle puree (page 54)	10 mL
¾ tsp	salt	4 mL
½ tsp	ground cumin	2 mL

Makes 6 servings

Convection roasting meatballs and salsa at a high temperature makes a quick weeknight meal. The salsa can also be tossed with cooked pasta, shredded basil and Parmesan for an easy pasta dish.

1. In a large bowl, combine chicken, bread crumbs and Parmesan. Mix in ketchup, egg, oregano, salt and pepper. Shape into meatballs (2 tbsp/25 mL each) and arrange on a foil-lined and greased baking sheet.

2. For salsa, arrange tomatoes, onion, red pepper, jalapeño and garlic on a separate foil-lined and greased baking sheet.

3. In a small bowl, combine oil, chipotle, salt and cumin. Pour over vegetables and stir together.

4. Convection roast vegetables and meatballs in a preheated 400°F (200°C) oven for 25 minutes, stirring twice during cooking. Roast until vegetables are tender and meatballs are cooked. (To test, cut one in half.) Place meatballs and salsa in a large serving bowl and toss lightly.

Crispy Chicken Thighs

Shelley Tanaka, my editor, told me that this is one of her family's favorites, so I made it for my family, and it is now a favorite here, too. It is best made with chicken thighs that have the skin on, but if you can't find them, just use bone-in, skinless thighs.

Make Ahead

Chicken can be tossed in flour and refrigerated up to 30 minutes ahead, but no longer, otherwise flour will become gummy.

½ cup	all-purpose flour	125 mL
½ tsp	curry powder (approx.)	2 mL
½ tsp	paprika, or ¼ tsp (1 mL) smoked paprika (page 279)	2 mL
½ tsp	dried thyme leaves	2 mL
½ tsp	salt	2 mL
¼ tsp	black pepper	1 mL
8	large chicken thighs, with skin and bone, trimmed	8

1. In a large plastic bag, combine flour, curry powder, paprika, thyme, salt and pepper.

2. Add chicken and shake to coat all pieces. Place chicken skin side down on a lightly greased foil-lined baking sheet.

3. Convection roast in a preheated 375°F (190°C) oven for 35 to 40 minutes, or until golden and crispy, turning once during roasting.

EASY OVEN MEAL

Weeknight Dinner for 4

Crispy Chicken Thighs
Grated Potato and Onion Bake (page 151)
Steamed Green Peas
Pears with Ginger Cookies (page 263)

- Shake chicken in seasoned flour, place on baking sheet and refrigerate.
- Assemble potato and onion dish.
- Preheat oven.
- Place chicken and potatoes in oven and cook for 20 minutes while you assemble dessert.
- Add dessert to oven. Turn chicken and cook all three dishes for 15 to 20 minutes. Meanwhile, cook peas.
- Let dessert cool slightly while you are serving the main course.

Glazed Roast Duck

1	5-lb (2.5 kg) duck	1
½ tsp	dried rosemary leaves	2 mL
½ tsp	salt	2 mL
¼ tsp	black pepper	1 mL
1	onion, coarsely chopped	1
1	stalk celery, coarsely chopped	1
2 tbsp	orange juice	25 mL
2 tbsp	soy sauce	25 mL
2 tbsp	liquid honey	25 mL
1 tbsp	cider vinegar or balsamic vinegar	15 mL

Makes 4 servings

Some people think duck is fatty and difficult to cook, but it is easy to roast in the convection oven.

1. Trim excess fat from duck. Sprinkle inside and out with rosemary, salt and pepper.

2. Place onion and celery in cavity. Loosely tie legs together. Place breast side up on a lightly greased rack set over foil-lined broiler pan. Pierce skin all over with a fork. Add ¾ cup (175 mL) water to pan.

3. Convection roast in a preheated 400°F (200°C) for 30 minutes.

4. Meanwhile, in a measuring cup or small bowl, combine orange juice, soy sauce, honey and vinegar.

5. Remove duck from oven. Carefully pour off any accumulated fat. Reduce temperature to 325°F (160°C). Brush duck with some sauce and continue to roast for 50 to 60 minutes, brushing two more times, until juices run clear, skin is crisp and a meat thermometer inserted in thigh registers 180°F (82°C). Remove from oven, tent loosely with foil and let stand for 10 minutes before carving. Discard celery and onion.

Cornish Hens on Bread Stuffing

Makes 4 servings

For a fall dinner or small Thanksgiving meal, if a roast turkey is more than you need, try Cornish hens baked on top of a stuffing.

Bread Stuffing

2 tbsp	olive oil	25 mL
1	onion, chopped	1
2	cloves garlic, finely chopped	2
¼ cup	diced prosciutto	50 mL
1	red bell pepper, seeded and chopped	1
1 cup	corn kernels	250 mL
½ cup	chopped celery	125 mL
6 cups	bread cubes	1.5 L
1 tbsp	chopped fresh sage, or 1 tsp (5 mL) dried	15 mL
¾ cup	chicken stock	175 mL
½ tsp	salt	2 mL
¼ tsp	black pepper	1 mL

Cornish Hens

2	1¼ -lb (625 g) Cornish hens	2
½ cup	cranberry, grape or apple jelly	125 mL
¼ cup	apple juice or orange juice	50 mL
2 tbsp	Dijon mustard	25 mL
1 tbsp	Worcestershire sauce	15 mL

1. To prepare stuffing, in a large skillet, heat oil over medium heat. Add onion, garlic and prosciutto. Cook for 2 minutes, or until softened. Add red pepper, corn and celery and cook for 4 minutes. Remove from heat and stir in bread, sage, stock, salt and pepper.

2. Spread stuffing in a greased 13- by 9-inch (3 L) baking dish.

3. Remove wing tips from hens. Cut down either side of backbones with kitchen shears and remove backbones, then flatten and cut alongside breastbones to cut each hen in half. Place hens cut side down on stuffing.

4. Convection roast hens and stuffing in a preheated 375°F (190°C) oven for 20 minutes.

5. Meanwhile, in a small saucepan, combine jelly, juice, mustard and Worcestershire. Cook over medium heat just until jelly melts.

6. Spoon half of glaze over hens and continue to roast for 30 to 35 minutes, or until skin is golden and juices run clear and a meat thermometer registers 180°F (82°C) when inserted into inner thigh. Spoon remaining glaze over hens 10 minutes before end of cooking time.

Crusty Honey Dijon Chicken Breasts

1 cup	fresh bread crumbs	250 mL
¼ cup	sesame seeds	50 mL
2 tbsp	Dijon mustard	25 mL
2 tbsp	liquid honey	25 mL
1 tbsp	olive oil	15 mL
½ tsp	salt	2 mL
¼ tsp	black pepper	1 mL
4	6-oz (175 g) boneless, skinless chicken breasts	4

Makes 4 servings

The mustard-honey mixture adds flavor as well as providing a base for the bread crumbs to cling to. Garnish with lemon wedges.

1. In a shallow dish, combine bread crumbs and sesame seeds. In a separate shallow dish, combine mustard, honey, oil, salt and pepper.

2. Roll chicken breasts in mustard mixture, then in bread crumbs, pressing crumbs onto chicken. Place breasts, not touching, on a parchment-lined baking sheet.

3. Convection roast in a preheated 375°F (190°C) oven for 20 to 25 minutes, or until chicken is cooked through and juices run clear.

Roast Turkey with Dried Cranberry Dressing

Makes 10 servings

Turkey with all the trimmings is one of my favorite meals. Often reserved for Thanksgiving or Christmas dinners, I make this off season, even in the summer, and use leftovers in sandwiches and salads.

Many manufacturers recommend not stuffing poultry that is cooked in the convection oven. Whole turkeys and chickens roast more quickly in the convection oven than in a standard oven, sealing in juices and browning the surface. However, in the convection oven the poultry reaches its optimum temperature before the stuffing does, so for safety, the dressing is cooked separately as a side dish.

If your bread crumbs are very fresh, use less stock; use more if the bread is very dry. Day-old French or Italian bread works well.

Start with a fully defrosted bird. If your turkey is frozen, defrost it in the refrigerator.

1	10- to 12-lb (4.5 to 5 kg) turkey	1
8	large sprigs fresh rosemary, divided	8
½ tsp	salt, divided	2 mL
½ tsp	black pepper, divided	2 mL
2	onions, peeled and cut in quarters	2
2 tbsp	olive oil	25 mL

Dried Cranberry and Apricot Dressing

2 tbsp	butter	25 mL
2	onions, chopped	2
3	stalks celery, diced	3
3	cloves garlic, finely chopped	3
8 cups	coarse fresh bread crumbs	2 L
¾ cup	dried cranberries	175 mL
½ cup	diced dried apricots	125 mL
½ cup	chopped fresh parsley	125 mL
2 tbsp	chopped fresh rosemary, or 1½ tsp (7 mL) dried	25 mL
1 tsp	salt	5 mL
½ tsp	black pepper	2 mL
½ cup	toasted chopped pecans (optional)	125 mL
2¾ cups	turkey or vegetable stock	675 mL

Gravy

3 cups	turkey stock (approx.)	750 mL
3 tbsp	butter or turkey drippings	45 mL
¼ cup	all-purpose flour	50 mL
	Salt and black pepper to taste	

1. Remove giblets and neck from turkey. Pat turkey dry inside and out. Loosen breast skin of turkey and tuck in 4 sprigs of rosemary. Season cavity with ¼ tsp (1 mL) salt and ¼ tsp (1 mL) pepper. Place onions and remaining rosemary sprigs in turkey cavity.

2. Place turkey breast side up on a rack over broiler pan. Tuck wing tips under bird. Tie drumsticks together with

kitchen string. Brush turkey with olive oil. Sprinkle with remaining ¼ tsp (1 mL) salt and ¼ tsp (1 mL) pepper.

3. Convection roast in a preheated 325°F (160°C) oven for 1¾ to 2¼ hours, or until a meat thermometer inserted into inner thigh registers 180°F (82°C). Remove turkey to a platter. Cover loosely with foil and let stand for 20 minutes before carving.

4. While turkey is cooking, make dressing. In a large skillet, melt butter over medium heat. Add onions, celery and garlic. Cook for 5 minutes, stirring occasionally. Transfer to a large bowl. Add bread crumbs, cranberries, apricots, parsley, rosemary, salt, pepper and pecans, if using. Add stock and combine thoroughly. Turn into a greased 8-cup (2 L) casserole.

5. Bake stuffing, uncovered, with turkey for 1 to 1¼ hours, or until golden brown and hot throughout.

6. To prepare gravy, pour 1 cup (250 mL) stock into the roasting pan. Place on stove over high heat. Scrape bottom to loosen particles and deglaze pan. Strain into a large measuring cup. Add enough stock to make 3 cups (750 mL). Skim fat from surface.

7. In a saucepan, melt butter over medium heat. Add flour and cook, stirring, for 3 minutes, or until golden. Whisk in stock. Bring to a boil. Cook for 6 to 8 minutes, or until slightly thickened. Taste and season with salt and pepper. Serve gravy with carved turkey and dressing.

Turkey Stock

In a large saucepan, combine turkey giblets and neck with 2 peeled onions, 2 carrots and 2 stalks celery (all cut in chunks), 1 bay leaf, ½ tsp (2 mL) dried thyme leaves, ½ tsp (2 mL) whole black peppercorns and 8 cups (2 L) water. Bring to a boil. Reduce heat to low and simmer, uncovered, for 2 hours. Strain and refrigerate. (Stock can be covered and refrigerated for 2 days or frozen for up to 6 weeks.) Makes about 6 cups (1.5 L).

Turkey Meatloaf with Nacho Topping

Makes 6 servings

This meatloaf is one of the most comfy foods to make for family and friends. Ground chicken or lean ground beef can be substituted for the turkey. Leftovers make good sandwiches.

1 tbsp	vegetable oil	15 mL
1	onion, chopped	1
2	cloves garlic, finely chopped	2
1½ lbs	ground turkey	750 g
2	eggs	2
1 tbsp	Worcestershire sauce	15 mL
½ tsp	smoked paprika (page 279) or chili powder	2 mL
¾ tsp	salt	4 mL
¼ tsp	black pepper	1 mL
1 cup	fresh bread crumbs	250 mL
⅓ cup	tomato salsa or ketchup	75 mL
2 tbsp	chopped fresh cilantro or parsley	25 mL

Topping

½ cup	tomato salsa or ketchup	125 mL
½ cup	crumbled tortilla chips	125 mL
½ cup	grated Monterey Jack or Cheddar cheese	125 mL

1. In a small skillet, heat oil over medium heat. Add onion and garlic and cook for 2 minutes, or until softened.

2. In a large bowl, combine ground turkey, eggs, Worcestershire, paprika, salt, pepper, bread crumbs, salsa, cilantro and onion mixture. Mix together thoroughly.

3. Pat mixture into a lightly greased 8- by 4-inch (1.5 L) loaf pan. Convection bake in a preheated 325°F (160°F) oven for 1 hour.

4. Top meatloaf with salsa, chips and cheese. Cook for 20 minutes longer, or until internal temperature reaches 175°F (80°C). Let stand for 5 minutes. Drain off any juices.

EASY OVEN MEAL

Casual Weekend Dinner for 6

Turkey Meatloaf with Nacho Topping
Baked Potatoes
Sliced Tomatoes
Washday Pudding (page 258)

- Assemble meatloaf.
- Preheat oven. Scrub potatoes.
- Place potatoes and meatloaf in oven. If potatoes are cooked before meatloaf is done, place in a dish and cover with foil while meatloaf continues to cook and stand.
- Assemble pudding. Place in oven with meatloaf and potatoes when you add topping to meatloaf (pudding can continue to cook while you are serving main course).
- Slice tomatoes.

Baked Potatoes

Place 6 scrubbed baking potatoes (about 8 oz/250 g each) on a rack or baking sheet. Prick potatoes and convection bake in a preheated 325°F (160°C) oven for 70 minutes, or until potatoes are tender when tested with a sharp knife. (Placing potatoes directly on oven rack will give a crispy exterior all round.) Makes 6 servings.

Cider-glazed Turkey Breast

Makes 6 to 8 servings

For people who like white meat only. For a smaller family this will also provide extra for lunches. Garnish with orange sections and sage leaves.

¼ cup	cider vinegar	50 mL
2 tbsp	coarse-grain mustard	25 mL
2 tbsp	soy sauce	25 mL
2	cloves garlic, finely chopped	2
½ tsp	dried sage or savory leaves	2 mL
½ tsp	salt	2 mL
¼ tsp	black pepper	1 mL
1	3-lb (1.5 kg) turkey breast, bone in	1

1. In a small bowl, whisk together vinegar, mustard, soy sauce, garlic, sage, salt and pepper.

2. Place turkey breast skin side up on a rack over broiler pan. Spread half of vinegar mixture over turkey.

3. Convection roast in a preheated 325°F (160°C) oven for 50 minutes. Baste with vinegar mixture. Continue to roast for 30 to 40 minutes, basting every 15 minutes, until a meat thermometer registers 170°F (75°C) when inserted into thickest part. Remove turkey to a platter. Cover loosely with foil and let stand for 10 minutes before carving.

> **Variation**
> *Mediterranean Glazed Turkey Breast:* For the basting mixture, in a small bowl, whisk together 3 tbsp (45 mL) orange juice, 3 tbsp (45 mL) balsamic vinegar, 2 tbsp (25 mL) pesto, 1½ tsp (7 mL) dried thyme leaves, 1 tsp (5 mL) grated orange zest and ½ tsp (2 mL) salt.

Meat

Roast Prime Rib of Beef

Makes 6 servings

For a special and truly delicious meal, few can resist a prime roast beef dinner. Serve with pan juices, potatoes, horseradish and your favorite mustard.

¼ cup	Dijon mustard	50 mL
3	cloves garlic, finely chopped	3
1 tbsp	chopped fresh thyme, or 1 tsp (5 mL) dried	15 mL
1 tbsp	Worcestershire sauce	15 mL
¾ tsp	salt	4 mL
½ tsp	black pepper	2 mL
1	4 lb (2 kg) prime rib roast of beef	1

Sauce

2 tbsp	all-purpose flour	25 mL
1¼ cups	water	300 mL
½ cup	dry red wine	125 mL
½ tsp	salt	2 mL
¼ tsp	black pepper	1 mL

1. In a small bowl, combine mustard, garlic, thyme, Worcestershire, salt and pepper.

2. Place roast, fat side up, on a rack set over broiler pan. Rub paste mixture over top and sides of meat.

3. Convection roast in a preheated 325°F (160°C) oven for 1¾ hours, or until meat is cooked to desired doneness: 140°F (60°C) for medium-rare or 160°F (70°C) for medium. Remove roast to a carving board and cover loosely with foil. Let stand for 10 to 15 minutes before carving.

4. Meanwhile, to prepare sauce, skim fat from roasting pan and place pan of remaining meat juices on stovetop over medium-high heat. Sprinkle flour over meat juices and cook, stirring, for 2 minutes. Add water and wine. Bring to a boil, stirring and scraping any caramelized bits from bottom of pan. Reduce heat to medium and cook for 5 minutes. Add any accumulated juices from carving board to sauce. Strain sauce if desired and season with salt and pepper. Serve with sliced roast beef.

Roast Beef Tenderloin with Peppercorn Sauce

1 tbsp	Dijon mustard	15 mL
2 tsp	olive oil	10 mL
2 tsp	dried thyme leaves	10 mL
1½ tsp	salt	7 mL
1	3-lb (1.5 kg) beef tenderloin, trimmed	1

Peppercorn Sauce

3 tbsp	butter	45 mL
⅓ cup	chopped shallots	75 mL
2	cloves garlic, finely chopped	2
½ cup	Cognac, Marsala or Madeira	125 mL
2 cups	chicken or beef stock	500 mL
½ cup	whipping (35%) cream	125 mL
2 tbsp	green peppercorns	25 mL
2 tsp	Worcestershire sauce	10 mL

1. In a small bowl, combine mustard, oil, thyme and salt. Rub marinade over beef and let stand for 30 minutes.

2. Place tenderloin on a lightly greased rack set over broiler pan. Convection roast in a preheated 400°F (200°C) oven for 25 to 30 minutes, or until a meat thermometer registers 140°F (60°C) for medium-rare. Remove tenderloin to a carving board, tent loosely with foil and let stand for 10 minutes before carving.

3. While tenderloin is roasting, in a medium saucepan, melt butter over medium-high heat. Add shallots and garlic and cook, stirring, for 2 minutes, or until shallots are tender and light golden.

4. Remove pan from heat and add Cognac. Return to high heat and cook for 2 minutes. Add stock and cook for 10 minutes. Stir in cream, peppercorns and Worcestershire. Boil for 4 minutes.

5. Remove sauce from heat and add any accumulated juices from roast. Taste and adjust seasonings if necessary. Serve carved tenderloin with sauce.

Makes 8 servings

Save this — the ultimate in roast beef — for a special occasion. The circulating hot air seals the surface of the tenderloin while keeping the inside moist.

Since beef tenderloin contains little fat yet is very tender, it is best to serve it rare to medium-rare to retain the juices. Try to convince the "well-done" folks that they will be in for a treat.

Company Eye of Round Oven Roast

Makes 12 servings

Cooking for a crowd can seem overwhelming, but a roast cooked in the convection oven is easy and results in moist, perfectly cooked meat. Since eye of round is very lean, be sure not to overcook it. It will continue to cook as it stands.

Serve this with the mushroom gravy, or plain with chili sauce. Oven-cooked carrots, a cabbage salad (make a double batch if you are serving a crowd) and mashed potatoes are good accompaniments. Use any leftover beef in sandwiches (hot or cold) or salad plates.

2 tbsp	brown sugar	25 mL
1 tbsp	paprika	15 mL
2 tsp	dried savory leaves	10 mL
2 tsp	chili powder	10 mL
1 tsp	dry mustard	5 mL
2 tsp	salt	10 mL
1	6-lb (3 kg) eye of round roast	1
1 tbsp	olive oil	15 mL

Onion Mushroom Gravy

3 tbsp	butter	45 mL
2	onions, chopped	2
2 cups	sliced mushrooms	500 mL
1/3 cup	all-purpose flour	75 mL
4 cups	beef stock	1 L
1 tbsp	horseradish	15 mL
1/2 tsp	salt	2 mL
1/4 tsp	black pepper	1 mL

1. In a small bowl, combine sugar, paprika, savory, chili powder, mustard and salt. Brush roast with oil, then rub dry mixture all over roast. Place roast, fat side up, on a lightly greased rack set over a foil-lined roasting pan.

2. Preheat oven on convection roast to 500°F (260°C). Place roast in oven and reduce heat to 250°F (150°C). Roast for 2 1/4 hours, or until a meat thermometer registers 140°F (60°C) for medium-rare.

3. To prepare gravy, heat butter in a large saucepan over medium-high heat. Add onions and mushrooms and cook for 5 minutes, or until softened, stirring often. Stir in flour and cook for 4 minutes. Add beef stock and bring to a boil, stirring. Reduce heat to medium and cook for 10 minutes, stirring often. Stir in horseradish, salt and pepper. Taste and adjust seasonings if necessary.

4. Remove roast to a carving board, tent loosely with foil and let stand for 15 minutes. Pour any accumulated juices into gravy. Slice roast thinly and serve with gravy.

Slow-cooked Carrots in Orange Juice

In a baking dish, combine 3 lbs (1.5 kg) thinly sliced carrots, 1 cup (250 mL) orange juice and 2 tbsp (25 mL) maple syrup or liquid honey. Dot with 2 tbsp (25 mL) butter. Cover with foil and cook in a 250°F (150°C) oven for $1\frac{1}{4}$ to $1\frac{1}{2}$ hours, or until tender. Makes 10 to 12 servings.

Cabbage and Apple Salad

In a large bowl, combine 4 cups (1 L) shredded cabbage, 3 chopped green onions, 1 grated carrot, 2 diced red apples and $\frac{1}{4}$ cup (50 mL) chopped fresh parsley.

In a small bowl, stir together $\frac{1}{3}$ cup (75 mL) mayonnaise, $\frac{1}{3}$ cup (75 mL) sour cream or unflavored yogurt, 1 tbsp (15 mL) lemon juice, 1 tbsp (15 mL) mango chutney, $\frac{1}{2}$ tsp (2 mL) salt and $\frac{1}{4}$ tsp (1 mL) curry powder.

Toss cabbage mixture with dressing and combine well. Makes 6 servings.

Rib Eye Roast with Beer Mushroom Gravy

Makes 8 to 10 servings

Easy-cook roasts and no-fuss sauces make a roast beef dinner a breeze to prepare. Rib eye is lean, easy to carve and juicy if not overcooked.

1 tsp	dry mustard	5 mL
1 tsp	coarsely ground black pepper	5 mL
1 tsp	Worcestershire sauce	5 mL
1	3½-lb (1.75 kg) rib eye roast	1

Beer Mushroom Gravy

2 tbsp	butter or olive oil	25 mL
1 lb	mushrooms, sliced	500 g
2 tbsp	all-purpose flour	25 mL
1	12-oz (341 mL) bottle beer or apple juice	1
1 cup	water	250 mL
½ cup	tomato juice or tomato sauce	125 mL
1	1½-oz (45 g) package dry onion soup mix	1
	Salt and black pepper to taste	

1. In a small bowl, combine mustard, pepper and Worcestershire. Rub over roast. Place roast on a lightly greased rack set over broiler pan.

2. Convection roast in a preheated 350°F (180°C) oven for 1 to 1½ hours, or until internal temperature reaches 140°F (60°C) for medium-rare. Remove roast to a carving board, cover with foil and let stand for 15 minutes before carving.

3. While meat is roasting, prepare gravy. Heat butter in a large skillet over medium-high heat. Add mushrooms and cook, stirring occasionally, for 8 minutes. Add flour and cook, stirring, for 3 minutes.

4. Add beer, water, tomato juice and onion soup mix. Stir to prevent flour from sticking. Bring to a boil. Reduce heat and simmer for 15 to 20 minutes, or until onions have softened. (Add water or tomato juice if sauce reduces too much.) Season to taste with salt and pepper.

Filet Mignon Steaks with Roquefort Butter

4	6-oz (175 g) filet mignon steaks (about 1½ inches/4 cm thick)	4
1 tbsp	olive oil	15 mL
1 tsp	coarse salt	5 mL
½ tsp	coarsely ground black pepper	2 mL

Roquefort Butter

⅓ cup	butter, softened	75 mL
¼ cup	crumbled Roquefort or blue cheese	50 mL
1 tbsp	chopped fresh tarragon, or 1 tsp (5 mL) dried	15 mL

1. Brush steaks with oil. Sprinkle with salt and pepper.

2. Heat a large, heavy ovenproof skillet over high heat. (If you have a seasoned cast-iron skillet or a heavy ridged skillet that will make grill marks, use it here. In either case, make sure handles are ovenproof. If not, wrap handles well in foil and remember that they are hot when you remove steaks from oven.) When skillet is hot, place steaks in pan. Cook for 1 to 2 minutes per side, until browned.

3. Transfer skillet to a preheated 425°F (220°C) oven and convection roast for 10 to 12 minutes, or until a meat thermometer registers 140°F (60°C) for medium-rare. Turn steaks once during roasting. Let stand for 5 minutes before serving.

4. Meanwhile, to prepare seasoned butter, in a bowl, cream together butter, cheese and tarragon. Serve steaks with butter.

> **Variation**
> *Lemon Horseradish Butter:* In a bowl, cream ⅓ cup (125 mL) softened butter, 1 tbsp (15 mL) horseradish, 1 tbsp (15 mL) lemon juice, 2 tbsp (25 mL) chopped fresh parsley and ½ tsp (2 mL) salt. Makes about ½ cup (125 mL).

Makes 4 servings

This recipe is dedicated to Susan Richardson, a fabulous cook who has taken nearly every cooking class I have taught over the past twenty-five years. She prepares special dinners for friends and is always on the lookout for new ideas. Susan lives in an apartment where barbecuing is not allowed, so she relies on her convection oven and uses the chef's technique of starting the steaks on the stovetop and finishing them in the oven.

The butter is also good on baked potatoes.

Make Ahead
Butter can be prepared, covered and refrigerated up to three days ahead.

Bistro Rib Eye Steak with Shallot Sauce

Makes 4 servings

This reminds me of a steak and potato dinner I had at a small bistro in Provence — just simple, good food prepared with a minimum of fuss.

2 tsp	olive oil	10 mL
2	boneless rib steaks (about 1½ inches/ 4 cm thick)	2
½ tsp	salt	2 mL
¼ tsp	pepper	1 mL
Shallot Sauce		
2 tbsp	butter	25 mL
2	shallots, chopped	2
1 cup	beef or chicken stock	250 mL
¼ cup	whipping (35%) cream	50 mL
¼ cup	Port, Madeira or red wine	50 mL
2 tbsp	barbecue sauce	25 mL
1 tsp	coarse-grain or Dijon mustard	5 mL

1. In a large, heavy ovenproof skillet, heat oil over high heat. Season both sides of steaks with salt and pepper. When pan is hot, brown steaks for 2 minutes per side.

2. Transfer skillet to oven and convection roast in a preheated 425°F (220°C) oven for 14 to 16 minutes, turning steaks once, until a meat thermometer registers 140°F (60°C) for medium-rare. Remove to a serving platter and let rest for 5 minutes before carving.

3. While steaks are cooking, in a saucepan, combine butter, shallots, stock, whipping cream, Port, barbecue sauce and mustard. Bring to a boil. Reduce heat to medium and cook for 8 minutes. Serve steaks with sauce.

Bistro Mushrooms
In a bowl, combine 1 lb (500 g) large mushrooms, 2 tbsp (25 mL) chopped fresh parsley, 2 chopped garlic cloves, 2 tbsp (25 mL) olive oil, 2 tbsp (25 mL) lemon juice, ½ tsp (2 mL) salt and ¼ tsp (1 mL) black pepper. Spread on a parchment-lined baking sheet. Convection roast in a preheated 425°F (220°C) oven for 12 to 15 minutes, or until just cooked. Makes 4 servings.

EASY OVEN MEAL

Steak Dinner for 4

Bistro Rib Eye Steak with Shallot Sauce
Bistro Potatoes
Bistro Mushrooms
Lettuce Wedges with Blue Cheese Dressing (page 159)
Summer Berry Gratin (page 251)

- Assemble dessert, potatoes and mushrooms.
- Preheat oven.
- Sear steaks.
- Place steaks and potatoes in oven and roast for 5 minutes while starting shallot sauce.
- Place mushrooms in oven and turn steaks and potatoes. Roast all three dishes for 10 minutes while finishing sauce. Prepare salad.
- Remove steaks from oven and let rest while mushrooms and potatoes finish cooking.
- Broil dessert just before serving.

Bistro Potatoes

Cut 2 lbs (1 kg) potatoes into $\frac{1}{4}$-inch (5 mm) dice. Place in a bowl and toss with 2 tbsp (25 mL) chopped fresh parsley, 2 chopped garlic cloves, 2 tbsp (25 mL) olive oil, 2 tbsp (25 mL) lemon juice, $\frac{3}{4}$ tsp (4 mL) salt and $\frac{1}{4}$ tsp (1 mL) black pepper. Spread potatoes on a parchment-lined baking sheet. Convection roast in a preheated 425°F (220°C) oven for 20 minutes, or until cooked and golden, stirring once. Makes 4 servings.

Sirloin Steak Provençal

**Makes 4 to
5 servings**

Sirloin steak is lean
and flavorful, but for
the best results, do not
overcook it. Slice the
steak thinly like a small
roast and pour the
juices over top. Leftovers
can be cut into smaller
pieces and added to
a salad.

¼ cup	olive oil, divided	50 mL
1	2-lb (1 kg) sirloin steak (about 1½ inches/4 cm thick)	1
1 tsp	salt	5 mL
½ tsp	black pepper	2 mL
1 cup	pitted black olives	250 mL
1	head roasted garlic (page 214)	1
2	anchovy fillets, chopped, or 1 tsp (5 mL) anchovy paste	2
2 tbsp	lemon juice	25 mL
1 tbsp	chopped fresh rosemary, or ¾ tsp (4 mL) dried	15 mL

1. In a large, heavy ovenproof skillet, heat 2 tsp (10 mL) oil over high heat. Season both sides of steak with salt and pepper. Add steak to hot skillet and brown for 2 minutes per side.

2. Transfer skillet to oven and convection roast in a preheated 425°F (220°C) oven for 14 to 16 minutes, turning steak once, until a meat thermometer registers 140°F (60°C) for medium-rare. Remove to a carving board and let rest for 5 minutes.

3. While steak is roasting, chop olives coarsely in a food processor. Squeeze roasted garlic into olives. Add anchovies, remaining oil, lemon juice and rosemary and pulse until just combined but still coarse. Taste and adjust seasonings if necessary.

4. Carve steak and serve with olive mixture.

Variation
Sirloin Steak with Peanut Drizzle: Brown and roast steak as described above. Omit olive topping. While steak is roasting, in a food processor, combine ⅓ cup (75 mL) peanut butter, ⅓ cup (75 mL) coconut milk, ¼ cup (50 mL) lime juice, 2 tbsp (25 mL) hoisin sauce, 2 tbsp (25 mL) water, 1 tbsp (15 mL) fish sauce or soy sauce and ¼ tsp (1 mL) hot pepper sauce. Process until smooth. Taste and adjust seasonings if necessary. Drizzle over carved steak and sprinkle with 2 tbsp (25 mL) chopped fresh cilantro.

Danish Meat Patties

8 oz	ground beef	250 g
8 oz	ground veal or pork	250 g
1	onion, finely chopped	1
1 cup	fresh bread crumbs	250 mL
2 tbsp	all-purpose flour	25 mL
1	egg	1
1 tsp	salt	5 mL
1/2 tsp	black pepper	2 mL
1/2 tsp	allspice	2 mL
1 cup	soda water	250 mL
2 tbsp	butter, melted	25 mL
1 tbsp	olive oil	15 mL

Makes 6 servings (12 patties)

Also known as frikadeller, these patties resemble mini meatloaves. Adding soda water makes a lighter patty. The convection oven cooks these to a crispy brown without pan-frying. Serve hot or cold with pickled beets, mashed potatoes and sautéed red cabbage.

1. In a large bowl, combine ground meats, onion, bread crumbs, flour, egg, salt, pepper and allspice. Mix together well.

2. Beat in soda water until thoroughly incorporated. Cover and refrigerate for 1 hour.

3. Using a 1/3 cup (75 mL) measuring cup as a scant measure, shape mixture into 12 oval patties. Place on a parchment-lined baking sheet.

4. In a small bowl, combine melted butter and oil. Spoon over patties. Convection bake or roast in a preheated 350°F (180°C) oven for 30 to 35 minutes, or until patties are brown and starting to crisp.

Cheeseburger Pie

**Makes 6 to
8 servings**

Cheeseburgers without
the bun make an easy
weeknight dinner. Most
of the condiments are
included in the pie,
but feel free to serve
pickles, tomato slices
and lettuce alongside.
Any leftover pie makes
great sandwiches.

Make Ahead
Pie can be assembled
and refrigerated up to
four hours before baking.

1½ lbs	lean ground beef	750 g
1 cup	fresh bread crumbs	250 mL
2	eggs	2
½ cup	milk	125 mL
¼ cup	chili sauce	50 mL
¼ cup	chopped sweet pickle	50 mL
2	green onions, chopped	2
1 tsp	Dijon mustard	5 mL
½ tsp	dried oregano leaves	2 mL
¾ tsp	salt	4 mL
¼ tsp	black pepper	1 mL
1½ cups	grated Cheddar or Swiss cheese	375 mL

1. In a large bowl, combine ground beef, bread crumbs, eggs, milk, chili sauce, pickle, green onions, mustard, oregano, salt and pepper. Mix thoroughly.

2. Spoon filling into a lightly greased 10-inch (25 cm) pie plate. Convection bake in a preheated 350°F (180°C) oven for 30 minutes.

3. Sprinkle cheese over surface. Continue to bake for 10 minutes. Let stand for 5 minutes. Pour off any fat. Cut into wedges.

Deep-Dish Tamale Pie

2 tbsp	olive oil	25 mL
1	onion, chopped	1
2	cloves garlic, finely chopped	2
¼ tsp	hot pepper flakes	1 mL
1 lb	lean ground beef	500 g
2 tsp	chili powder	10 mL
½ tsp	dried oregano leaves	2 mL
¼ tsp	ground cumin	1 mL
¾ tsp	salt	4 mL
¼ tsp	black pepper	1 mL
1 cup	corn kernels	250 mL
1 cup	tomato sauce	250 mL
½ cup	chopped stuffed green olives	125 mL

Topping

1 cup	all-purpose flour	250 mL
½ cup	cornmeal	125 mL
1 tbsp	baking powder	15 mL
½ tsp	salt	2 mL
¾ cup	grated Cheddar cheese	175 mL
1 cup	buttermilk	250 mL
2 tbsp	vegetable oil	25 mL

Makes 4 to 5 servings

Tamales are Mexican snacks of mesa dough wrapped in corn husks, with a sweet or savory filling. This easy-to-prepare dish has some of the tamale flavors, though it is a far cry from the real thing.

Make Ahead

Meat mixture can be prepared and spooned into dish, covered and refrigerated for up to eight hours. Let stand at room temperature for a half hour before adding topping and baking.

1. In a large skillet, heat olive oil over medium-high heat. Add onion, garlic and pepper flakes. Cook, stirring occasionally, for 3 minutes.

2. Add beef. Continue to cook, stirring, until pinkness disappears, about 5 minutes. Remove from heat and stir in chili powder, oregano, cumin, salt, pepper, corn, tomato sauce and olives. Spoon into a lightly greased 8-inch (2 L) square baking dish.

3. To prepare topping, in a bowl, combine flour, cornmeal, baking powder, salt and Cheddar.

4. In a small bowl, combine buttermilk and vegetable oil. Add to dry ingredients. Stir just to combine. Drop batter by spoonful onto top of meat mixture.

5. Convection bake in a preheated 350°F (180°C) oven for 25 to 30 minutes, or until meat mixture is bubbling at edges and biscuit topping is cooked through at center.

Ham Steaks with Peach Sauce

Makes 6 servings

Serve this for an easy weeknight dinner. You can replace the peach slices with cranberry sauce or canned or fresh apricots.

1 cup	fresh or canned peach slices	250 mL
2 tbsp	brown sugar	25 mL
1 tbsp	Dijon mustard	15 mL
½ tsp	curry powder or ground coriander	2 mL
6	6-oz (175 g) Black Forest ham steaks	6

1. In a food processor, combine peaches, sugar, mustard and curry powder. Puree until smooth.

2. Arrange ham slices on a foil-lined baking sheet. Spoon glaze over ham. Convection roast in a preheated 375°F (190°C) oven for 12 to 14 minutes, or until ham is hot and glaze is just bubbling. For additional color, switch oven to convection broil and broil for 30 to 60 seconds, watching closely.

EASY OVEN MEAL

Family Dinner for 6

Ham Steaks with Peach Sauce
Herbed Scalloped Potatoes (page 150)
Cabbage and Apple Salad (page 97) or
*   storebought coleslaw*
Strawberry Rhubarb Crunch (page 247)

- Assemble dessert and potatoes.
- Preheat oven.
- Place dessert and potatoes in oven and cook for 30 minutes while you assemble ham steaks and make salad.
- Remove dessert from oven and let stand. Place ham in oven and cook with potatoes for 12 to 14 minutes, or until ham is hot and potatoes are tender.
- Broil ham and keep warm while potatoes stand before serving.

Jumbo Meatballs with Tuscan Tomato Sauce

1 lb	lean ground beef	500 g
8 oz	ground pork or veal	250 g
¾ cup	fresh bread crumbs	175 mL
½ cup	ketchup	125 mL
2	eggs	2
¼ cup	chopped fresh basil or parsley	50 mL
1 tsp	salt	5 mL
½ tsp	black pepper	2 mL

Tuscan Tomato Sauce

1	28-oz (796 mL) can plum tomatoes, pureed with juices	1
2 cups	fresh spinach, coarsely chopped	500 mL
¼ cup	chopped sun-dried tomatoes (oil-packed)	50 mL
2	cloves garlic, minced	2
2 tbsp	olive oil	25 mL
1 tbsp	chopped fresh rosemary, or 1 tsp (5 mL) dried	15 mL
½ tsp	salt	2 mL
¼ tsp	black pepper	1 mL

1. In a large bowl, combine beef, pork, bread crumbs, ketchup, eggs, basil, salt and pepper. Mix together well. With dampened hands, shape into 6 large meatballs. Place in a lightly greased 13- by 9-inch (3 L) baking dish.

2. In a separate large bowl, combine pureed tomatoes, spinach, sun-dried tomatoes, garlic, oil, rosemary, salt and pepper. Pour sauce over and around meatballs.

3. Convection roast in a preheated 375°F (190°C) oven for 45 to 50 minutes, or until a meat thermometer registers 170°F (75°C). Baste meatballs with sauce a couple of times during cooking.

Makes 6 servings

Large meatballs (a cross between serving meatballs and meatloaf) look more important than small ones. These can simply be served with crusty bread and a salad, or with creamy mashed potatoes or pasta tossed with Parmesan.

Make Ahead
Complete dish can be cooked, covered and refrigerated a day ahead. Reheat, covered, in a preheated 300°F (150°C) convection oven for 30 minutes, or until hot. Cooked dish can also be wrapped well and frozen. Defrost overnight in refrigerator.

Asian-flavored Meatballs

Makes 4 to 5 servings

Oyster sauce, hoisin sauce and plum sauce can be found in most supermarkets. Asian grocery stores will sell several brands of each. Add a spoonful of oyster sauce or hoisin sauce to meatloaf, burgers or stir-fries. (Mushroom vegetarian oyster sauce is also available.)

Serve these meatballs with rice. Garnish with slivered green onions.

Make Ahead

Meatballs can be cooked, covered and refrigerated up to a day ahead or packaged tightly and frozen for up to three weeks.

Meatballs

8 oz	ground beef	250 g
8 oz	ground veal or pork	250 g
½ cup	fresh bread crumbs	125 mL
1	egg	1
2 tbsp	oyster sauce	25 mL
2	green onions, finely chopped	2
1 tsp	Dijon mustard	5 mL

Sauce

¾ cup	pineapple juice	175 mL
⅓ cup	hoisin sauce	75 mL
¼ cup	plum sauce	50 mL
¼ cup	rice vinegar	50 mL
1 tbsp	sesame oil	15 mL
2	cloves garlic, minced	2
2 tsp	finely chopped gingerroot	10 mL
½ tsp	hot Asian chili sauce (optional)	2 mL

1. In a large bowl, combine beef, veal, bread crumbs, egg, oyster sauce, green onions and mustard. With dampened hands, shape into 1-inch (2.5 cm) meatballs. Place on a parchment- or foil-lined baking sheet.

2. Convection bake in a preheated 375°F (190°C) oven for 25 minutes.

3. Meanwhile, to prepare sauce, in a small saucepan, combine pineapple juice, hoisin sauce, plum sauce, vinegar, sesame oil, garlic, ginger and chili sauce, if using. Bring to a boil over medium-high heat. Reduce heat to medium and simmer, stirring occasionally, for 10 minutes, or until slightly thickened.

4. Arrange meatballs in serving dish. Pour sauce over top.

Roast Pork Loin
with Dried Fruit and Capers

¾ cup	apple juice or cider	175 mL
¼ cup	red wine vinegar	50 mL
¼ cup	maple syrup	50 mL
¼ cup	ketchup or barbecue sauce	50 mL
5	cloves garlic, peeled and smashed	5
2 tsp	dried oregano or marjoram leaves	10 mL
2	bay leaves	2
1	4-lb (2 kg) boneless pork loin	1
½ tsp	salt	2 mL
¼ tsp	black pepper	1 mL
1 cup	pitted prunes, halved	250 mL
½ cup	chopped dried apricots	125 mL
1	onion, chopped	1
½ cup	pitted black or green olives, halved	125 mL
¼ cup	capers	50 mL

1. In a bowl, combine apple juice, vinegar, maple syrup, ketchup, garlic, oregano and bay leaves.

2. Place marinade in heavy-duty resealable plastic bag. Add pork, squeezing out as much air as possible. Seal and place in a dish. Refrigerate for 2 hours or up to overnight.

3. Remove roast from bag and reserve marinade. Pat roast dry. Season with salt and pepper. Place roast in a shallow baking dish.

4. Convection roast pork in a preheated 400°F (200°C) oven for 20 minutes. Reduce temperature to 325°F (160°C) and continue to roast for 30 minutes.

5. Arrange prunes, apricots, onion, olives and capers around roast. Drizzle marinade over and around roast. Continue to roast for 35 to 40 minutes, or until a meat thermometer registers 160°F (70°C). (If fruit becomes too dry, add up to ½ cup/125 mL apple juice.) Baste twice during roasting. Remove roast to a carving board and let stand for 10 minutes. Cover fruit to keep warm. Slice roast and serve with fruit and juices.

Makes 6 to 8 servings

Don't let the long list of ingredients discourage you from making this succulent roast — it actually requires little preparation. As with other roasts cooked in the convection oven, the pork becomes golden brown but stays juicy. Since pork roasts are now very lean, they dry out easily, so take care not to overcook them. Use an instant-read thermometer or the meat probe that comes with your oven (page 13).

This fruit mixture also goes well with roast chicken.

Roast Pork Loin with Apples

**Makes 6 to
8 servings**

A succulent roast for
family and guests. The
apples and onions can
cook while the pork is
roasting. Serve with
baked beets, creamy
mashed potatoes
and a steamed green
vegetable.

  Shop for a pork loin
roast with the bones
Frenched (trimmed to
expose the bones) and
the backbone removed
for easy carving.

Pork Loin

1 tsp	dry mustard	5 mL
½ tsp	curry powder	2 mL
½ tsp	salt	2 mL
¼ tsp	black pepper	1 mL
¼ tsp	ground ginger	1 mL
1	4-lb (2 kg) pork loin rib roast	1
15	sprigs rosemary, 1 inch (2.5 cm) long	15
⅓ cup	marmalade	75 mL
¼ cup	orange juice	50 mL
2 tbsp	Dijon mustard	25 mL

Apples and Onions

5	apples, peeled, cored and quartered	5
2	onions, cut in wedges	2
2 tbsp	olive oil	25 mL
1 tbsp	fresh rosemary leaves	15 mL
¼ tsp	salt	1 mL
¼ tsp	black pepper	1 mL

1. In a small bowl, combine dry mustard, curry powder, salt, pepper and ginger. Rub mixture into roast.

2. With tip of a sharp knife, pierce roast in several places and insert rosemary sprigs. Place roast rib side down on a rack set over broiler pan.

3. Convection roast in a preheated 325°F (160°C) oven for 1¾ to 2 hours, or until a meat thermometer registers 160°F (70°C).

4. For glaze, in a small bowl, combine marmalade, orange juice and Dijon mustard. Spoon over roast at intervals during the last 45 minutes of cooking time.

5. Meanwhile, in a large bowl, toss apples and onions with olive oil, rosemary, salt and pepper. Place in a shallow baking dish. Roast with pork for 45 to 50 minutes, or until apples are tender.

6. Transfer roast to a carving board. Cover loosely with foil and let stand for 15 minutes before carving. Spoon apples and onions around carved roast. Spoon accumulated juices over meat.

Baked Ham with Apricot Glaze

1	12 lb (5.5 kg) fully cooked, bone-in smoked ham	1
2 cups	apricot juice or apple juice	500 mL
½ cup	apricot jam	125 mL
½ cup	packed brown sugar	125 mL
2 tbsp	Dijon mustard	25 mL
2 tbsp	lemon juice or cider vinegar	25 mL
½ tsp	ground ginger	2 mL

1. Trim fat from ham, leaving a layer ¼ inch (5 mm) thick. Cut through fat diagonally to create a crisscross pattern. Place ham in a foil-lined baking pan. Pour juice over ham. Convection bake in a preheated 300°F (150°C) oven for 1½ hours. Baste occasionally, adding water if juice evaporates.

2. In a small bowl, combine jam, sugar, mustard, lemon juice and ginger. Spoon glaze over ham. Continue to bake ham for 30 to 45 minutes, or until a meat thermometer registers 140°F (60°C). Baste with glaze every 15 minutes. Transfer ham to a large carving board or serving platter. Cover loosely with foil. Let stand for 15 minutes before carving.

Makes 10 to 12 servings

A great glazed ham can share the dinner table with roast turkey at Thanksgiving and Christmas, or it can hold its own as the main meat dish. This juicy ham pairs well with sweet potatoes, turnip and other vegetables. Use leftovers in salads and sandwiches.

Make Ahead
For cold baked hams, bake, cover and refrigerate for up to two days. Any meat will slice more easily when cold, so for cold meat platters, carve after chilling.

Easy Smoked Pork Chops

| 6 | smoked pork chops (about 1 inch/ 2.5 cm thick) | 6 |
| ¾ cup | barbecue sauce | 175 mL |

1. Arrange pork chops on a foil and parchment-lined baking sheet. Spread half of sauce over chops.

2. Convection roast in a preheated 300°F (150°C) oven for 15 minutes. Turn chops and spread with remaining sauce. Roast for another 15 minutes.

Makes 6 servings

Fully smoked pork chops are available in some meat shops and supermarkets. They have so much flavor on their own that little embellishment is required.

Roasted Lemon Garlic Pork Chops and Vegetables

Makes 6 servings

Pork chops can be cooked especially quickly in the convection oven. Since they can easily become dry, it is important not to overcook them. These pork chops can also be brined before roasting (page 113).

Roasting seasoned pork chops and vegetables on the same baking sheet means your entire dinner can be cooking at once. This recipe works well with boneless, skinless chicken thighs, too.

4	cloves garlic, peeled	4
½ cup	packed fresh parsley leaves	125 mL
2 tbsp	fresh rosemary leaves	25 mL
1 tbsp	grated lemon zest	15 mL
⅓ cup	olive oil	75 mL
¼ cup	lemon juice	50 mL
1 tsp	salt	5 mL
½ tsp	black pepper	2 mL
2	onions, each cut in eight wedges	2
2 lbs	potatoes, peeled and cut in chunks	1 kg
4	plum tomatoes, quartered	4
6	pork chops (about 1 inch/2.5 cm thick)	6

1. In a food processor, coarsely chop garlic. Add parsley, rosemary and lemon zest and chop until fine. Add oil, lemon juice, salt and pepper and combine.

2. In a large bowl, toss onions, potatoes and tomatoes with half of lemon mixture. Arrange vegetables on a foil- and parchment-lined baking sheet.

3. Convection roast vegetables in a preheated 375°F (190°C) oven for 30 minutes, stirring once.

4. While vegetables are cooking, rub remaining lemon mixture on both sides of pork chops.

5. In a lightly greased large skillet, brown pork chops over high heat for 2 minutes per side. Arrange pork chops over partially cooked vegetables and continue to roast for 20 to 25 minutes, or until a meat thermometer registers 160°F (70°C).

Honey Mustard Pork Tenderloin

1/3 cup	Russian-style mustard	75 mL
2 tbsp	apricot or peach jam	25 mL
1 tbsp	red wine vinegar or cider vinegar	15 mL
2	1-lb (500 g) pork tenderloins	2

Makes 4 to 6 servings

Use your favorite flavored mustard in this recipe. Leftovers are delicious cold in sandwiches, wraps and salads.

1. In a small bowl, combine mustard, jam and vinegar. Pat pork dry and coat with mustard sauce. Place tenderloins on a lightly greased rack set over a foil-lined baking pan.

2. Convection roast in a preheated 400°F (200°C) oven for 30 to 35 minutes, or until internal temperature reaches 160°F (70°C). Let stand for 5 minutes before carving.

To Brine or Not to Brine

Brining is a traditional preservation technique that is reappearing in restaurants and in home kitchens. It involves fully immersing any low-fat meat such as pork or poultry (page 70) in a seasoned salt solution. The finished product is moist and flavorful.

Today pork is often so lean that many cuts benefit from brining, but plan to brine the day before cooking.

The following makes enough brining solution for 6 pork chops or a 4-lb (2 kg) pork loin.

In a large saucepan, combine 8 cups (1 L) water, 1/3 cup (75 mL) coarse salt or 1/4 cup (50 mL) table salt, 1/4 cup (50 mL) maple syrup, 2 sprigs fresh thyme (or 1/2 tsp/2 mL dried), 2 bay leaves, 1 tsp (5 mL) black peppercorns and 1 small piece smashed gingerroot. Bring to a boil and stir until salt dissolves. Let stand at room temperature until cool, about 2 hours.

Place meat in a deep bowl or a heavy-duty resealable plastic bag. Cover with brining solution and refrigerate for 12 to 24 hours. Remove meat from brine and discard brine. Pat meat dry and proceed with selected recipe.

Stuffed Pork Tenderloin with Cranberry Glaze

Makes 4 to 5 servings

Pork tenderloins are readily available, and they can be quickly roasted on their own with some seasonings, but in this recipe, two tenderloins are butterflied and filled with stuffing. This is excellent served hot or cold with scalloped potatoes (page 150) and extra cranberry sauce.

2 tbsp	butter or olive oil	25 mL
1	onion, chopped	1
1	stalk celery, chopped	1
1½ cups	coarse fresh bread crumbs	375 mL
⅓ cup	chicken stock or apple juice	75 mL
¼ cup	dried cranberries	50 mL
½ tsp	dried savory or marjoram leaves	2 mL
½ tsp	salt	2 mL
¼ tsp	black pepper	1 mL
2	1-lb (500 g) pork tenderloins	2
¾ cup	cranberry sauce	175 mL
¼ cup	maple syrup	50 mL

1. In a small skillet, heat butter over medium heat. Add onion and celery and cook for 3 minutes, or until softened.

2. In a bowl, combine onion mixture, bread crumbs, stock, cranberries, savory, salt and pepper. Mix thoroughly.

3. Butterfly each pork tenderloin by cutting lengthwise most of the way through. Open so they lie flat. Flatten with a meat pounder until ½ inch (1 cm) thick.

4. Top one opened tenderloin with stuffing, mounding slightly along center. Top with remaining tenderloin with narrow end over wide end to create an even package. Tie tenderloins together at intervals. Place pork on a lightly greased rack set over a foil-lined baking sheet.

5. In a small bowl, combine cranberry sauce and maple syrup. Spoon a small amount over pork. Convection roast in a preheated 375°F (190°C) oven for 50 to 55 minutes, or until a thermometer inserted into stuffing registers 160°F (70°C), brushing with sauce three times during roasting. Let stand for 5 minutes before removing string and cutting carefully into thick slices.

Fall-off-the-Bone Ribs

1/3 cup	lemon or lime juice	75 mL
4	cloves garlic, minced	4
1 tbsp	sweet paprika	15 mL
1 tbsp	smoked paprika (page 279)	15 mL
1 tbsp	grated lemon zest	15 mL
1 tbsp	dried oregano leaves	15 mL
5 lbs	back or side pork ribs (about 4 racks)	2.5 kg

Barbecue Glaze

1/2 cup	ketchup	125 mL
1/3 cup	lemon or lime juice	75 mL
1/4 cup	molasses	50 mL
2 tbsp	red wine vinegar or balsamic vinegar	25 mL
1 tbsp	Dijon mustard	15 mL
2 tsp	black pepper	10 mL
1 tsp	hot pepper sauce (optional)	5 mL

Makes 6 servings

These ribs are covered with foil part way through and cooked using a moist heat method. A final cooking on high heat in the convection oven delivers nicely glazed, finger-licking ribs. The glaze can also be used on chicken or steak.

Make Ahead
Ribs can be cooked to the end of Step 3, transferred to a non-metallic dish, covered and refrigerated overnight. Glaze can also be prepared the day before and refrigerated.

1. In a small bowl, combine lemon juice, garlic, paprikas, lemon zest and oregano.

2. Place ribs in two large shallow dishes. Rub mixture into both sides of ribs. Cover and refrigerate for 2 to 24 hours.

3. Arrange ribs in a single layer in two shallow roasting pans. Pour in water to a depth of about 1/4 inch (5 mm). Convection roast in a preheated 325°F (160°C) oven for 45 minutes. Cover pans tightly with foil and roast for another 40 to 50 minutes, or until ribs test tender with tip of a sharp knife.

4. Meanwhile, in a saucepan, combine ketchup, lemon juice, molasses, vinegar, mustard, pepper and hot pepper sauce, if using. Bring to a boil over medium heat.

5. Arrange ribs bone side up on foil- and parchment-lined baking sheets. Brush with glaze. Convection roast in a preheated 425°F (220°C) oven for 6 minutes. Turn, brush with remaining glaze and cook for 6 to 9 minutes, or until sizzling.

Glazed Spareribs

**Makes 3 to
4 servings**

Serve these with
a cabbage salad
(page 97).

2 tbsp	brown sugar	25 mL
1 tsp	dried oregano leaves	5 mL
1 tsp	chili powder	5 mL
1 tsp	dry mustard	5 mL
½ tsp	ground cumin	2 mL
½ tsp	ground cinnamon	2 mL
4 lbs	pork spareribs (back or side)	2 kg
1 cup	barbecue sauce	250 mL

1. In a small bowl, combine sugar, oregano, chili powder, mustard, cumin and cinnamon.

2. Place ribs in a large flat dish. Rub seasoning mixture into both sides of ribs. Cover and refrigerate for 2 to 24 hours.

3. Arrange ribs on a lightly greased rack set over a foil-lined broiler pan or roasting pan. Convection roast in a preheated 300°F (150°C) oven for $1\frac{1}{2}$ to $1\frac{3}{4}$ hours, or until meat is tender when pierced with tip of a sharp knife. Brush with sauce during last 45 minutes. Cut ribs into serving-sized pieces.

Roasted Rack of Lamb

⅓ cup	packed fresh mint leaves	75 mL
½	jalapeño pepper, seeded	½
1 tbsp	coarsely chopped gingerroot	15 mL
2	cloves garlic, peeled	2
2 tbsp	apricot jam	25 mL
1 tbsp	soy sauce	15 mL
2	Frenched racks of lamb, about 8 bones each (1 ¼ lbs/625 g total)	2

1. In a food processor, combine mint, jalapeño, ginger, garlic, jam and soy sauce. Puree until smooth to make a paste.

2. Pat lamb dry. Spread paste over lamb. Cover and refrigerate for 3 hours.

3. Place roasting rack over broiler pan. Preheat pan and rack in a 400°F (200°C) oven on convection roast setting. When oven is hot, place lamb on rack, bone side down. Return to oven and roast for 10 minutes.

4. Reduce temperature to 350°F (180°C). Continue to roast for 15 minutes, or until internal temperature reaches 140°F (60°C) for medium-rare. Remove lamb to a carving board. Tent loosely with foil and let stand for 10 minutes before carving.

Roasted Asparagus
Toss 1 lb (500 g) trimmed asparagus (fat stalks work best) with 1 tbsp (15 mL) olive oil, ¼ tsp (1 mL) salt and ¼ tsp (1 mL) black pepper. Place on a parchment-lined baking sheet. Convection roast or bake in a preheated 350°F (180°C) oven for 12 minutes, or until just tender. Turn once during cooking. Makes 4 servings.

Makes 4 servings

For several years, I assisted Jacques Pépin when he taught at Bonnie Stern's School of Cooking. Always inspired, I would cook intensely for weeks after his classes. This is an adaptation of a quick recipe that he assembled after a class trip to the market. Although he made it with lamb loins, rack of lamb also works well. Use the marinade for chicken, turkey or pork tenderloin. Serve with roasted asparagus.

Thyme-scented Leg of Lamb with Beans

Makes 8 servings

Roasted leg of lamb is a special company meal. Slightly perfumed with fresh thyme and garlic slivers, this is excellent served as a plain roast or with the bean stew (which also works as a main course for vegetarian guests) and baked beets.

Make Ahead

Beans can be assembled, covered and refrigerated up to six hours ahead. Let stand at room temperature for 30 minutes before baking.

1	4- to 5-lb (2 to 2.5 kg) bone-in leg of lamb, trimmed	1
2 tsp	olive oil	10 mL
3	cloves garlic, slivered	3
8	sprigs fresh thyme	8
½ tsp	salt	2 mL
¼ tsp	black pepper	1 mL

Bean Stew

2 tbsp	olive oil	25 mL
2	onions, thinly sliced	2
4	cloves garlic, slivered	4
2	medium zucchini (about 8 oz/250 g each), halved and cut in ¼-inch (5 mm) slices	2
1	28-oz (796 mL) can plum tomatoes, drained (reserving ¼ cup/50 mL juices) and chopped	1
1	19-oz (540 mL) can Romano beans, rinsed and drained	1
½ tsp	dried marjoram or savory leaves	2 mL
½ tsp	salt	2 mL
¼ tsp	black pepper	1 mL

1. With tip of a sharp knife, pierce lamb in several places. Rub with olive oil. Insert garlic slivers and thyme sprigs. Sprinkle with salt and pepper. Place on a rack set over a broiler pan.

2. Convection roast in a preheated 325°F (160°C) oven for 1¼ to 1½ hours, or until a meat thermometer registers 140°F (60°C) for medium-rare. Remove to a carving board and cover loosely with foil. Let stand for 15 minutes before carving.

3. While lamb is roasting, prepare beans. Heat oil in a large skillet over medium-high heat. Add onions and garlic. Cook, stirring occasionally, for 5 minutes, until onions start to turn golden.

4. Add zucchini and cook, stirring occasionally, for 6 minutes.

5. Stir in tomatoes and reserved juices, beans, marjoram, salt and pepper. Bring to a boil. Transfer to a lightly greased 8-cup (2 L) baking dish.

6. Convection roast beans with lamb for 30 minutes, or until bubbling. (Beans will keep warm for 20 minutes if covered with foil after removing from oven.) Serve beans with carved lamb.

Baked Beets

Place 2 lbs (1 kg) trimmed, unpeeled beets (about 7 medium) on a large sheet of heavy foil. Drizzle beets with 1 tbsp (15 mL) olive oil. Wrap beets tightly in foil, place on a baking sheet and convection bake or roast at 325°F (160°C) for $1\frac{1}{2}$ hours, or until tender. When cool enough to handle, peel beets, cut into slices and place in a large bowl.

In a small bowl, combine 1 tbsp (15 mL) olive oil, 2 tbsp (25 mL) orange juice, 2 tbsp (25 mL) chopped fresh dillweed, $\frac{1}{2}$ tsp (2 mL) salt and $\frac{1}{4}$ tsp (1 mL) black pepper. Toss beets with dressing. Serve warm or at room temperature. Makes 8 servings.

Herbed Butterflied Leg of Lamb with Sweet Potatoes

Makes 6 to 8 servings

A boned and butterflied leg of lamb is easy to roast and carve. When butterflied, there are thick and not-so-thick sections. Push the meat together on the roasting rack to make a compact shape so the lamb will cook more evenly.

Sweet potatoes are my favorite vegetable to roast with the lamb. They will probably require slightly longer cooking time than the lamb, but they can finish roasting while the lamb rests and is being carved.

Boneless legs of lamb usually come in 3- to 5-lb (1.5 to 2.5 kg) weights. If the leg is not already boned, ask the butcher to do this.

4	cloves garlic, peeled	4
½ cup	packed fresh parsley	125 mL
¼ cup	packed fresh basil	50 mL
3	green onions, cut in 1-inch (2.5 cm) pieces	3
¼ cup	olive oil	50 mL
2 tbsp	coarse-grain mustard	25 mL
2 tbsp	balsamic vinegar	25 mL
1 tsp	salt	5 mL
½ tsp	black pepper	2 mL
1	4-lb (2 kg) butterflied leg of lamb, trimmed	1
3 lbs	sweet potatoes (about 5 medium), peeled and cut in 1-inch (2.5 cm) pieces	1.5 kg
2	onions, cut in 1-inch (2.5 cm) pieces	2

1. In a food processor, combine garlic, parsley, basil, green onions, oil, mustard, vinegar, salt and pepper. Process until pureed.

2. Spoon three-quarters of mixture over lamb and rub in. Marinate for 30 minutes or refrigerate for up to 8 hours. Place on a lightly greased rack set over a foil-lined broiler pan or baking sheet.

3. Place potatoes and onions on a separate parchment-lined baking sheet. Add remaining paste and toss potatoes and onions to coat lightly.

4. Convection roast potatoes and onions in a preheated 350°F (180°C) oven for 50 minutes, stirring twice, until tender. Convection roast lamb for 35 to 40 minutes, or until a meat thermometer registers 140°F (60°C) for medium-rare.

5. Remove roast to a carving board and tent loosely with foil. Let stand for 10 minutes before carving.

Quick-roasted Lamb Chops with Charmoula Sauce

1 tbsp	olive oil	15 mL
1 tbsp	Dijon mustard	15 mL
2	cloves garlic, minced	2
½ tsp	salt	2 mL
½ tsp	black pepper	2 mL
8	loin lamb chops (about 1 inch/ 2.5 cm thick)	8

Charmoula Sauce

¾ cup	mayonnaise	175 mL
2	cloves garlic, minced	2
1 tbsp	lemon juice	15 mL
½ tsp	smoked paprika (page 279)	2 mL
½ tsp	ground cumin	2 mL
2 tbsp	chopped fresh cilantro	25 mL

1. To prepare lamb chops, in a small bowl, combine oil, mustard, garlic, salt and pepper. Rub mixture over both sides of chops.

2. Arrange chops on a lightly greased rack set over a foil-lined broiler pan or baking sheet. Convection roast chops in a preheated 500°F (260°C) oven for 8 minutes for medium-rare, turning once.

3. Meanwhile, to prepare sauce, combine mayonnaise, garlic, lemon juice, paprika, cumin and cilantro. Serve lamb chops with sauce.

> **Variation**
> *Lamb Chops with Mint Sauce:* In a bowl, combine ½ cup (125 mL) chopped fresh mint, 2 chopped green onions, 2 tbsp (25 mL) lemon juice, 1 tbsp (15 mL) liquid honey, ¼ cup (50 mL) olive oil, ½ tsp (2 mL) salt and ¼ tsp (1 mL) black pepper. Serve lamb chops with mint sauce instead of charmoula.

Makes 4 servings

Charmoula is a North African (Moroccan) sauce traditionally flavored with lemon, garlic, herbs and spices such as paprika and cumin. It can serve as a marinade, condiment or topping. This version also goes well with other meats, poultry and fish, and it makes an excellent spread for wraps or sandwiches.

Fresh garlic can be replaced with half a head of roasted garlic (page 214).

Make Ahead
The charmoula can be made a day ahead and refrigerated.

Breaded Veal in Tomato Sauce

Makes 5 to 6 servings

There are as many variations of this dish as there are cooks. Sometimes the breading mixtures contain grated Parmesan; mozzarella slices and basil leaves may also be added during the last ten minutes. Thin pork cutlets, chicken and turkey work well in this recipe, too. Serve it with a simple salad.

Make Ahead

Tomato sauce can be prepared, covered and refrigerated two days in advance.

Scallopini can be breaded, covered and refrigerated four hours before cooking.

Tomato Sauce

2 tbsp	olive oil	25 mL
2	onions, chopped	2
2	cloves garlic, finely chopped	2
Pinch	hot pepper flakes	Pinch
½ cup	dry white wine	125 mL
2	28-oz (796 mL) cans plum tomatoes, pureed with juices	2
1 tsp	dried sage leaves	5 mL
¾ tsp	salt	4 mL
¼ tsp	black pepper	1 mL

Breaded Veal

1 lb	veal scallopini	500 g
½ cup	all-purpose flour	125 mL
3	eggs, beaten	3
2½ cups	fine fresh bread crumbs	625 mL
¼ cup	vegetable oil or olive oil (approx.)	50 mL

1. To prepare sauce, heat oil in a large skillet over medium heat. Add onions, garlic and pepper flakes. Cook, stirring occasionally, for 4 minutes. Add wine and cook for 3 minutes. Add tomatoes, sage, salt and pepper. Cook for 25 minutes, or until sauce thickens. Stir frequently.

2. Meanwhile, to prepare veal, pat pieces dry. Place flour, eggs and bread crumbs in three separate shallow dishes. Dip veal into flour, then into egg and finally into bread crumbs, patting in on both sides. Place veal on wax paper-lined tray.

3. In a large skillet, heat 2 tbsp (25 mL) oil over medium-high heat. Cook veal in batches for about 30 seconds per side, or until golden. Add oil as required.

4. Spoon half of tomato sauce into a 13- by 9-inch (3 L) baking dish (or use 2 smaller dishes). Arrange scallopini on sauce, overlapping slightly. Pour remaining tomato sauce over veal.

5. Convection bake in a preheated 350°F (180°C) oven for 25 to 30 minutes, or until sauce is bubbling.

One-Dish Suppers

Cabbage Roll Bake

Makes 6 servings

Enjoy cabbage roll flavors without making individual rolls. This is also a great dish to make if you have a lot of leftover cooked rice.

Make Ahead

Assemble dish. Cover and refrigerate up to six hours ahead. Bring to room temperature before baking.

4 cups	shredded cabbage	1 L
2 tbsp	olive oil	25 mL
2	onions, chopped	2
2	cloves garlic, chopped	2
12 oz	lean ground beef	375 g
8 oz	mushrooms, sliced	250 g
2 cups	tomato sauce	500 mL
2 cups	cooked white rice	500 mL
1 tsp	salt	5 mL
½ tsp	black pepper	2 mL
½ tsp	dried savory or marjoram leaves	2 mL

1. Bring a large pot of salted water to a boil. Add cabbage and cook for 5 minutes. Drain well.

2. Meanwhile, heat oil in a large skillet over medium-high heat. Add onions and garlic and cook, stirring occasionally, for 3 minutes. Add beef and cook, stirring, until pinkness disappears, about 4 minutes. Add mushrooms and cook for 4 minutes, or until moisture evaporates.

3. Stir in cabbage, tomato sauce, rice, salt, pepper and savory. Mix thoroughly and turn into a lightly greased 13- by 9-inch (3 L) baking dish.

4. Convection bake in a preheated 350°F (180°C) oven for 30 minutes, or until hot in center and bubbling at edges.

Risotto with Sausages and Tomatoes

1 tbsp	olive oil	15 mL
1 lb	sweet Italian sausages (about 4), cut in 1-inch (2.5 cm) pieces	500 g
5	tomatoes	5
2	onions, chopped	2
3	cloves garlic, coarsely chopped	3
1 cup	uncooked arborio rice	250 mL
3 cups	chicken stock	750 mL
1/3 cup	dry sherry or white wine	75 mL
2 tsp	paprika	10 mL
1/2 tsp	ground cumin	2 mL
1/2 tsp	salt	2 mL
1/2 tsp	black pepper	2 mL
1/4 cup	chopped fresh parsley	50 mL

Makes 5 to 6 servings

Traditionally, risotto is cooked on the stovetop, and it involves almost constant stirring. This oven version eliminates all that stirring, allowing you time to prepare an accompanying salad to complete the meal.

Make this dish in a large ovenproof skillet, and serve the risotto directly from the pan.

1. In a large ovenproof skillet, heat oil over medium-high heat. Add sausages and cook for 5 to 7 minutes, stirring occasionally. Pour off all but 2 tbsp (25 mL) fat.

2. Core and dice 2 tomatoes. Add onions, garlic and diced tomatoes to skillet. Cook for 4 minutes, or until softened.

3. Add rice, stock, sherry, paprika, cumin, salt and pepper. Bring mixture to a boil.

4. Core remaining 3 tomatoes and cut into wedges. Place tomato wedges on top of rice.

5. Transfer skillet to oven and convection bake, uncovered, in a preheated 350°F (180°C) oven for 45 minutes, or until rice is tender.

6. Remove skillet from oven. Cover and let stand for 15 minutes. Sprinkle rice with parsley before serving.

Pretend Lasagna

Makes 8 servings

Make a lasagna without all the fuss of layering. Leftovers are great, but you can also simply halve the recipe and bake it in an 8-inch (2 L) square baking dish.

Make Ahead

Cool meat and tomato sauce before assembling dish. Cover and refrigerate overnight. Bake for an additional 10 to 15 minutes, or until hot. Assembled dish can also be wrapped well and frozen for up to six weeks. Defrost in refrigerator overnight.

2 tbsp	olive oil	25 mL
1	onion, chopped	1
2	cloves garlic, chopped	2
¼ tsp	hot pepper flakes	1 mL
1 lb	lean ground beef, ground turkey or sweet Italian sausage removed from casings	500 g
1	28-oz (796 mL) can plum tomatoes, with juices, broken up or pureed	1
½ tsp	salt	2 mL
½ tsp	black pepper	2 mL
1 cup	corn kernels	250 mL
8 oz	lasagna noodles, broken up	250 g
1 cup	grated mozzarella cheese	250 mL
¼ cup	shredded fresh basil, or 2 tbsp (25 mL) pesto	50 mL
¼ cup	grated Parmesan cheese	50 mL

1. In a large skillet, heat oil over medium-high heat. Add onion and garlic and cook for 3 minutes, or until softened.

2. Add hot pepper flakes and beef and cook for about 8 minutes, or until pinkness disappears.

3. Add tomatoes, salt and pepper. Bring to a boil, reduce heat to medium and cook, uncovered, for 15 to 20 minutes, or until sauce has thickened slightly (juices will be absorbed by pasta, so do not make sauce too dry). Stir in corn. Taste and adjust seasonings if necessary.

4. Meanwhile, cook noodles in a large amount of boiling salted water until just tender, about 8 to 10 minutes. Drain well. Add to meat sauce along with mozzarella and basil. Stir to mix thoroughly.

5. Spoon pasta mixture into a lightly greased 13- by 9-inch (3 L) baking dish. Sprinkle with Parmesan. Convection bake in a preheated 350°F (180°C) oven for 25 minutes, or until edges are bubbling and top is golden. Let stand for 5 minutes before serving.

Chicken and Wild Rice Bake

1	6-oz (180 g) package long-grain and wild rice mix	1
2 tbsp	butter	25 mL
1	onion, chopped	1
1	stalk celery, chopped	1
1½ cups	sliced mushrooms	375 mL
1	10-oz (284 mL) can cream of chicken or mushroom soup	1
¾ cup	dry white wine or chicken stock	175 mL
2 cups	diced cooked chicken	500 mL
2 tbsp	chopped pimento or roasted red pepper	25 mL
¼ cup	grated Parmesan cheese	50 mL

1. Cook rice according to package directions and reserve.

2. In a large skillet, melt butter over medium-high heat. Add onion, celery and mushrooms. Cook, stirring occasionally, for 5 minutes.

3. Add soup, wine, cooked rice, chicken and pimento and stir together. Transfer to a lightly greased 8-cup (2 L) baking dish. Sprinkle with cheese.

4. Convection bake in a preheated 350°F (180°C) oven for 25 to 30 minutes, or until bubbling and heated through.

Makes 6 servings

When I graduated from my Foods and Nutrition program in Toronto, our professor invited the class to her home for a casual dinner that included a chicken and wild rice dish. When she supplied the recipe, we were all surprised that the ingredients included convenience foods.

The original recipe has long since been lost, but this is close to what she made. Cooked turkey can be used instead of chicken.

Make Ahead

Cool rice mixture after adding soup and wine. Stir in chicken and pimento. Transfer to prepared dish, cover and refrigerate for up to six hours. Let stand at room temperature for 30 minutes before cooking. Bake for an extra 10 minutes, or until heated through.

Tortellini Casserole

Makes 5 servings

Pasta dishes cooked in gratins and shallow baking dishes utilize the circulating air of the convection oven, resulting in a golden, crusty surface.

Here a creamy tomato sauce is combined with cheese and tortellini for an easy supper dish. Several kinds of tortellini are available in the frozen food section, so choose your family's favorite.

3 tbsp	butter	45 mL
1	onion, chopped	1
2	cloves garlic, finely chopped	2
3 tbsp	all-purpose flour	45 mL
2 cups	hot milk	500 mL
1 cup	tomato sauce	250 mL
2 tsp	chopped fresh oregano, or ½ tsp (2 mL) dried	10 mL
¾ tsp	salt	4 mL
½ tsp	black pepper	2 mL
1 lb	frozen cheese or meat tortellini	500 g
1½ cups	grated Cheddar cheese	375 mL
¼ cup	grated Parmesan cheese	50 mL

1. In a medium saucepan, melt butter over medium heat. Add onion and garlic and cook for 3 minutes, stirring occasionally, until softened. Stir in flour. Cook for 3 minutes, stirring, but do not brown.

2. Whisk in hot milk and bring to a boil. Add tomato sauce, oregano, salt and pepper. Cook, stirring often, for 3 minutes.

3. Meanwhile, bring a large pot of salted water to a boil. Add frozen tortellini and cook for 7 to 8 minutes, or until just tender. Drain well.

4. Combine tortellini with Cheddar and sauce. Pour into a lightly greased 8-cup (2 L) shallow baking dish. Sprinkle with Parmesan cheese.

5. Convection bake in a preheated 325°F (160°C) oven for 25 minutes, or until bubbling and lightly browned.

Company Eye of Round Oven Roast (page 96)
Overleaf: Asian-flavored Meatballs (page 108)

Baked Spaghetti Carbonara

1 lb	uncooked spaghetti	500 g
6	slices bacon, diced	6
1	onion, chopped	1
4	eggs	4
1 cup	light (5%) cream	250 mL
1 cup	milk	250 mL
½ cup	grated Parmesan cheese	125 mL
¼ cup	chopped fresh parsley	50 mL
¼ tsp	salt	1 mL
¼ tsp	black pepper	1 mL

1. Break spaghetti in half. Bring a large pot of salted water to a boil. Add spaghetti and cook until just tender, about 10 minutes. Drain well.

2. Meanwhile, cook bacon in a small skillet over medium-high heat until almost crispy, about 4 minutes. Drain off all but 1 tbsp (15 mL) fat.

3. Add onion and cook for 2 minutes until softened.

4. In a large bowl, beat eggs. Add cream, milk, cheese, parsley, salt and pepper. Stir in spaghetti, bacon and onion.

5. Pour into a lightly greased 8-cup (2 L) shallow baking dish. Convection bake in a preheated 325°F (160°C) oven for 22 to 25 minutes, or until set.

Makes 5 servings

This favorite pasta dish bakes quickly in the convection oven. It is an ideal dish for a brunch buffet.

Make Ahead

Assemble dish completely. Cover and refrigerate up to four hours ahead. Bake for an additional five minutes, or until set.

Overleaf: Roast Pork Loin with Apples (page 110)
Honey Mustard Pork Tenderloin (page 113)

Tuna Noodle Casserole

**Makes 8 to
10 servings**

Tuna casserole has been
a popular last-minute
dish for many years.
There are as many
variations as there are
cooks, who usually make
it the same way their
moms did. This one is
perfect for brunch or a
casual weekend dinner.
The recipe can easily
be halved.

Make Ahead
Sauce can be made a
day ahead, covered
and refrigerated. When
ready to assemble, heat
slightly, then combine
with remaining
ingredients.

3 tbsp	butter	45 mL
2	onions, chopped	2
3 cups	sliced mushrooms	750 mL
1/3 cup	all-purpose flour	75 mL
4 cups	hot milk	1 L
1 tsp	salt	5 mL
1/2 tsp	black pepper	2 mL
10 oz	egg noodles (about 4 cups/1 L)	300 g
2	6-oz (170 g) cans tuna, drained and flaked	2
2 cups	frozen peas	500 mL
2 cups	grated Cheddar or Gruyère cheese	500 mL

Topping

1 cup	fresh bread crumbs	250 mL
1/2 cup	sunflower seeds	125 mL
1/4 cup	grated Parmesan cheese	50 mL
3 tbsp	olive oil	45 mL

1. In a large saucepan, melt butter over medium-high heat. Add onions and mushrooms and cook for 5 minutes, or until softened. Stir in flour and cook for 4 minutes. Add hot milk and bring to a boil, stirring. Reduce heat to medium and cook for 5 minutes, or until slightly thickened (sauce will be thin). Season with salt and pepper.

2. Meanwhile, cook noodles in a large amount of boiling salted water for 6 to 8 minutes, or until just tender. Drain and return to cooking pot. Add sauce, tuna, peas and cheese and combine thoroughly. Transfer to a greased 13- by 9-inch (3 L) baking dish.

3. To prepare topping, in a bowl, combine bread crumbs, sunflower seeds, Parmesan and oil. Sprinkle over casserole.

4. Convection bake in a preheated 350°F (180°C) oven for 35 to 40 minutes, or until casserole is hot and bubbly and top is golden.

Black Bean Burritos

1	19-oz (540 mL) can black beans, rinsed and drained	1
1 cup	tomato salsa	250 mL
½ tsp	ground cumin (optional)	2 mL
6	7-inch (18 cm) flour tortillas	6
1½ cups	grated Monterey Jack or Cheddar cheese	375 mL
2	green onions, chopped	2
2 tbsp	chopped fresh cilantro	25 mL

1. In a bowl, combine beans, salsa and cumin, if using.
2. Arrange tortillas on a flat surface. Divide bean mixture evenly over lower half of tortillas. Roll up jellyroll style.
3. Place burritos in a lightly greased 13- by 9-inch (3 L) baking dish, seam side down. Sprinkle with cheese.
4. Convection bake in a preheated 325°F (160°C) oven for 20 to 22 minutes, or until burritos are heated through and cheese has melted. Sprinkle with green onions and cilantro.

Makes 4 to 6 servings

Easy to make, burritos make a satisfying supper or lunch dish. In this recipe, they are assembled and baked quickly in the convection oven. You can improvise on fillings by using a combination of refried beans, corn kernels, cooked potatoes and cooked sausage or bacon. Serve with sour cream or guacamole (page 37).

EASY OVEN MEAL

Late Summer Supper for 8

Tuna Noodle Casserole (page 130)
Sliced Tomatoes with Fresh Basil
Roasted Peaches (page 261)

- Assemble casserole.
- Preheat oven.
- Bake casserole for 15 minutes while you assemble peaches.
- Add peaches to oven and cook both dishes for 20 to 25 minutes, or until casserole is bubbly and peaches are tender.
- Meanwhile, prepare tomatoes. Let peaches cool while you are serving the main course.

Chicken and Broccoli Bake

Makes 4 servings

This recipe is based on a Chicken Divan recipe that I found in my mother's recipe file. It was given to her by an Aunt Edna, and it was often made with cooked chicken left over from Sunday dinner. Since my mother was either very busy on the farm or, in later years, lawn bowling and gardening, she would assemble this quickly and put it in the oven while she went out to transplant a few more seedlings. Today this dish cooks especially quickly in the convection oven.

Make Ahead

Place pasta and broccoli in baking dish and cool for 20 to 25 minutes, or until no longer warm. Assemble dish, cover and refrigerate for up to four hours. Bake casserole for an additional 5 to 10 minutes, or until hot.

4 oz	egg noodles (about 1½ cups/375 mL)	125 g
2 cups	chopped broccoli	500 mL
1½ cups	chopped cooked chicken	375 mL
1	10-oz (284 mL) can cream of chicken soup	1
¾ cup	milk or chicken stock	175 mL
¼ cup	mayonnaise	50 mL
2 tsp	lemon juice	10 mL
½ tsp	curry powder	2 mL
1 cup	grated Cheddar cheese, divided	250 mL
½ cup	fresh bread crumbs	125 mL

1. Bring a large pot of salted water to a boil. Add noodles and cook for 3 minutes. Add broccoli and continue to cook for 3 minutes, or until noodles and broccoli are just cooked. Drain well.

2. Transfer drained noodles and broccoli to a lightly greased shallow 8-cup (2 L) baking dish. Spread cooked chicken over top.

3. In a bowl, combine soup, milk, mayonnaise, lemon juice, curry powder and ½ cup (125 mL) cheese. Pour over chicken. Sprinkle with bread crumbs and remaining cheese.

4. Convection bake in a preheated 350°F (180°C) oven for 25 to 30 minutes, or until casserole is bubbling and lightly browned.

Santa Fe Chicken Wraps

3 cups	diced cooked chicken	750 mL
1	green bell pepper, seeded and diced	1
2	green onions, chopped	2
1 tsp	dried oregano leaves	5 mL
1½ cups	grated Monterey Jack or Cheddar cheese, divided	375 mL
3½ cups	salsa, divided	875 mL
8	6-inch (15 cm) flour tortillas	8

1. In a bowl, combine chicken, green pepper, green onions, oregano, ¾ cup (175 mL) cheese and 1 cup (250 mL) salsa. Mix thoroughly.

2. Arrange tortillas on a flat surface. Spread filling evenly over tortillas. Roll up tortillas.

3. Spoon 1 cup (250 mL) salsa over bottom of a lightly greased 13- by 9-inch (3 L) baking dish. Place tortillas on salsa, seam side down. Spoon remaining 1½ cups (375 mL) salsa over tortillas. Sprinkle with remaining ¾ cup (175 mL) cheese.

4. Convection bake in a preheated 350°C (180°C) oven for 20 to 25 minutes, or until hot and bubbling.

Makes 4 to 6 servings

Use leftover turkey or chicken or cooked deli chicken or diced ham in this recipe. Choose mild, medium or hot bottled salsa according to your family's tastes. Serve with fresh homemade salsa, if desired.

Make Ahead
The wraps can be assembled, covered and refrigerated up to six hours ahead. Let stand at room temperature for a half hour before cooking.

Variation
Santa Fe Tofu Wraps: Replace chicken with 3 cups (750 mL) diced extra-firm tofu.

Fresh Tomato Salsa
In a medium bowl, combine 2 cored and diced tomatoes, 1 peeled and diced avocado, 1 chopped green onion, 1 tbsp (15 mL) chopped jalapeño pepper, 2 tbsp (25 mL) chopped fresh cilantro, 3 tbsp (45 mL) lime juice or lemon juice, ¼ tsp (1 mL) salt and ¼ tsp (1 mL) black pepper. Makes about 1¾ cups (425 mL).

Clarke's Layered Casserole

Makes 8 servings

My brother has many talents, but even he admits that cooking is not one of them. However, this is the one "cooked" recipe that he makes. He even uses the convection oven because it's so easy.

Some tomato soups now are seasoned with herbs, and they will also work fine in this recipe. Ground chicken or turkey can be substituted for the beef.

1 tbsp	olive oil	15 mL
1 lb	lean ground beef	500 g
½ tsp	dried oregano leaves	2 mL
¾ tsp	salt	4 mL
¼ tsp	black pepper	1 mL
3	large Yukon Gold or all-purpose potatoes (about 1 lb/500 g), peeled and thinly sliced	3
2	onions, chopped	2
2 cups	frozen mixed vegetables	500 mL
2	10-oz (284 mL) cans tomato soup	2
1 cup	water	250 mL

1. In a large skillet, heat oil over medium-high heat. Add ground beef and cook for 10 minutes, or until pinkness disappears. Drain to remove any juices. Stir in oregano, salt and pepper.

2. Layer sliced potatoes over bottom of a greased 13- by 9-inch (3 L) baking dish. Top with chopped onions and mixed vegetables. Spoon cooked ground beef over vegetables.

3. In a bowl, whisk together soup and water. Pour over beef.

4. Convection bake, covered, in a preheated 350°F (180°C) oven for 40 minutes. Remove cover and bake for 30 minutes longer, or until potatoes test tender with tip of a sharp knife, and casserole is hot and bubbling.

Potato Gnocchi with Mushrooms

1 lb	prepared potato gnocchi	500 g
2 tbsp	olive oil, divided	25 mL
3 cups	thinly sliced mushrooms	750 mL
3 oz	diced ham, prosciutto or kielbasa (about ¾ cup/175 mL)	90 g
1 cup	whipping (35%) cream	250 mL
2 tbsp	chopped fresh sage, or ½ tsp (2 mL) dried	25 mL
¼ tsp	salt	1 mL
Pinch	ground nutmeg	Pinch
½ cup	grated Parmesan cheese	125 mL

Makes 4 to 5 servings

Using storebought gnocchi makes this dish quick and easy to assemble, but it is quite rich, so you may want to reserve it for a special occasion. Serve it with a salad and ripe fruit as a finale.

If you are using frozen gnocchi, just follow the package directions.

1. Bring a large saucepan of salted water to a boil. Add gnocchi and cook for 3 to 4 minutes, or until gnocchi rise to surface. Reserve about ¼ cup (50 mL) cooking water, then drain gnocchi well.

2. Place gnocchi in an 8-inch (2 L) baking dish. Drizzle with ½ tbsp (7 mL) oil and toss gnocchi to coat.

3. Heat remaining oil in (same) saucepan over medium-high heat. Add mushrooms and ham. Cook for 5 minutes, stirring occasionally, until mushrooms are tender (there will still be juices).

4. Add cream, reserved cooking water, sage, salt and nutmeg to saucepan. Bring to a boil and cook for 4 minutes.

5. Pour sauce over gnocchi and sprinkle with cheese. Convection bake in a preheated 400°F (200°C) oven for 18 minutes, or until mixture is bubbling and top is golden. Let stand for 5 minutes before serving.

Pantry Bean Bake

Makes 8 servings

This dish makes the most of canned goods from the pantry. Serve it with chili sauce. For a meatless version, omit the salami or use a vegetarian replacement. Turkey or beef wieners or cooked sausage can also be used instead of salami. For a spicier dish, use a hot salsa and spicy salami.

Make Ahead
Casserole can be assembled, covered and refrigerated for several hours or overnight.

1	28-oz (796 mL) can baked beans	1
1	19-oz (540 mL) can mixed beans, drained	1
1 cup	tomato salsa	250 mL
¼ cup	barbecue sauce	50 mL
2 tbsp	molasses	25 mL
2 tbsp	maple syrup or brown sugar	25 mL
1 tbsp	Dijon or Russian-style mustard	15 mL
1 cup	diced salami or other cold meat	250 mL

1. In a large bowl, combine baked beans, mixed beans, salsa, barbecue sauce, molasses, maple syrup, mustard and salami. Transfer to a lightly greased 10-cup (2.5 L) casserole.

2. Convection bake in a preheated 375°F (190°C) oven for 35 to 40 minutes, or until hot and bubbling.

EASY OVEN MEAL

Winter Menu for 6 to 8

Pantry Bean Bake
Quick Biscuits (page 213)
Cucumber Salad (page 59)
Strawberry Rhubarb Crunch (page 247)

- Preheat oven.
- Assemble beans and dessert.
- Bake beans and dessert for 20 minutes while you assemble biscuits.
- Place biscuits in oven and bake all three dishes for 15 to 20 minutes.
- Meanwhile, prepare a double batch of cucumber salad.
- Let dessert stand while you serve main course.

Eggplant with Mozzarella and Tomato Sauce

2	large eggplants (about 1¼ lbs/625 g each)	2
3 tbsp	olive oil, divided	45 mL
¼ tsp	salt	1 mL
¼ tsp	black pepper	1 mL
2 cups	tomato sauce	500 mL
1 cup	grated mozzarella cheese	250 mL
12	fresh basil leaves	12
⅓ cup	grated Parmesan cheese	75 mL

1. Cut eggplants crosswise into ½-inch (1 cm) slices. Arrange in a single layer on lightly greased baking sheets. Brush with half the olive oil. Place about 4 inches (10 cm) from heat and convection broil under preheated broiler until golden, about 6 minutes. Sprinkle with salt and pepper. Turn slices over. Brush with remaining olive oil. Broil for 6 minutes on second side.

2. Spoon 1 cup (250 mL) tomato sauce over bottom of a lightly greased 13- by 9-inch (3 L) baking dish. Arrange eggplant slices over sauce, overlapping as necessary. Sprinkle mozzarella over eggplant. Arrange basil leaves over mozzarella. Spoon over remaining tomato sauce. Sprinkle with Parmesan.

3. Convection bake in a preheated 350°F (180°C) oven for 20 minutes, or until sauce is bubbling and eggplant is hot. Remove from oven and let stand for 5 minutes before serving.

> **Variation**
> *Eggplant Salad:* Broil eggplant slices and arrange on a serving platter. Drizzle with 2 tbsp (25 mL) lemon juice, 2 tbsp (25 mL) chopped fresh parsley and 2 tsp (10 mL) chopped fresh oregano. Makes 4 to 5 servings.

Makes 4 to 5 servings

Buy firm, shiny eggplants that feel weighty in the hand. Eggplants absorb oil like a sponge, so brush sparingly.

Make Ahead
Cook up to three hours ahead and serve at room temperature. The dish can also be assembled ahead, covered and refrigerated overnight. Let stand at room temperature for a half hour before baking. (You may need to bake for an additional five minutes to heat through completely.)

Tourtière

Makes 6 servings

Tourtière is a tradition in many households during the holiday season. Serve with cabbage salad (page 97) and chili sauce or ketchup.

Make Ahead

The filling can be prepared, covered and refrigerated up to a day ahead. To freeze the pie unbaked, wrap well and freeze for up to one month. Defrost in the refrigerator for 24 hours, then bake. To freeze baked, wrap well and freeze for up to two weeks. Defrost in the refrigerator for 24 hours. Reheat at 275°F (140°C) for up to 45 minutes, or until hot in the center.

Filling

2 tbsp	olive oil	25 mL
1	onion, chopped	1
2	cloves garlic, finely chopped	2
½ cup	chopped celery	125 mL
1½ lbs	ground pork, beef, veal or chicken	750 g
1 cup	peeled and grated potato	250 mL
½ cup	water	125 mL
2 tbsp	chopped fresh parsley	25 mL
1 tsp	salt	5 mL
½ tsp	dried savory leaves	2 mL
½ tsp	dried thyme leaves	2 mL
¼ tsp	black pepper	1 mL
Pinch	ground cloves	Pinch
Pinch	ground cinnamon	Pinch

Pastry

1	double recipe All-Purpose Pastry (page 262)	1

Glaze

1	egg	1
2 tsp	milk	10 mL

1. To prepare filling, heat oil in a large skillet over medium-high heat. Add onion, garlic and celery. Cook, stirring occasionally, for 3 minutes.

2. Add meat to skillet and cook, stirring, for about 8 minutes, or until all traces of pink disappear.

3. Add potato, water, parsley, salt, savory, thyme, pepper, cloves and cinnamon. Reduce heat to low. Cover and simmer for 30 minutes, stirring occasionally. Taste and adjust seasonings if necessary.

4. Spoon filling into a bowl. Cover and refrigerate until cold (adding hot filling to pie shell will make pastry soggy).

5. Divide pastry into two pieces, one piece slightly larger than the other. Roll out larger piece on a lightly floured surface and fit into a 10-inch (25 cm) pie plate with edges overhanging about 1 inch (2.5 cm). Spoon in filling. Roll out remaining pastry and place over filling.

Seal pastry edges, trim and flute edges. Cut steam vents in upper crust.

6. In a small bowl, combine egg and milk. Brush over top of pastry. Convection roast or bake in a preheated 375°F (190°C) oven for 40 to 45 minutes, or until pastry is golden.

Cottage Potato and Ham Bake

1	5-oz (141 g) package dried scalloped potatoes	1
1 cup	diced ham	250 mL
1 tbsp	chopped fresh dillweed, or 1 tsp (5 mL) dried	15 mL
1¾ cups	boiling water	425 mL
¾ cup	milk	175 mL
½ cup	grated Cheddar cheese	125 mL

1. In a lightly greased 8-cup (2 L) baking dish, combine potatoes, sauce mix from potatoes, ham and dill. Pour boiling water and milk over potatoes and stir.

2. Convection bake in a preheated 375°F (190°C) oven for 25 minutes. Stir mixture and top with cheese. Continue to bake for 20 to 25 minutes, or until potatoes are tender and top is golden. Let stand for 10 minutes before serving to allow potatoes to thicken.

Variation
Cottage Potato and Turkey Bake: Use cooked regular or smoked turkey or chicken instead of ham.

Makes 4 to 5 servings

When my parents and their friends retreated for a well-deserved break to the family camp, the focus was on spending happy times together. Neither my mother nor my aunt were big consumers of convenience foods, but this was one time that the "cooking from scratch" routine was relaxed. Usually a fresh garden vegetable such as tomatoes or cucumbers rounded out the main course.

Turkey Shepherd's Pie

Makes 8 servings

In this recipe, ground turkey serves as a replacement for the traditional ground beef, though lean ground beef could also be used. Use Yukon Gold or an all-purpose potato that mashes well. You could also use sweet potatoes instead of all or some of the potatoes.

Make Ahead

The dish can be assembled, covered and refrigerated overnight. Let stand at room temperature for a half hour before cooking.

2 lbs	potatoes (about 4 medium), peeled and cut in 1-inch (2.5 cm) pieces	1 kg
½ cup	milk	125 mL
4 tbsp	butter, divided	50 mL
¾ tsp	salt	4 mL
½ tsp	black pepper, divided	2 mL
1	green onion, chopped	1
2 tbsp	chopped fresh parsley	25 mL
1	onion, chopped	1
2	stalks celery, diced	2
8 oz	mushrooms, sliced	250 g
½ cup	diced red bell pepper (optional)	125 mL
1½ lbs	ground turkey	750 g
2 tbsp	all-purpose flour	25 mL
1 cup	chicken stock	250 mL
3 tbsp	soy sauce	45 mL
½ tsp	dried thyme or savory leaves	2 mL
2 cups	peas	500 mL

1. In a large saucepan, cover potatoes with salted water and bring to a boil. Boil for about 20 minutes, or until tender. Drain well. Mash potatoes with milk, 2 tbsp (25 mL) butter, salt, ¼ tsp (1 mL) pepper, green onion and parsley.

2. Meanwhile, in a large skillet, melt remaining 2 tbsp (25 mL) butter over medium-high heat. Add onion and celery. Cook, stirring occasionally, for 4 minutes. Add mushrooms and red pepper, if using. Cook, stirring occasionally, for 4 minutes. Add turkey and cook, stirring, until all pinkness disappears, about 4 minutes.

3. Stir in flour and cook, stirring, for 2 minutes. Add stock, soy sauce, thyme and remaining ¼ tsp (1 mL) pepper. Cook for 4 minutes, stirring, until mixture thickens. Stir in peas.

4. Spoon turkey mixture into a lightly greased 10-cup (2.5 L) shallow baking dish. Spread potato mixture over meat.

5. Convection bake in a preheated 350°F (180°C) oven for 35 minutes, or until sauce is bubbling around outside and top is golden brown.

Italian Lentil Bake

2 tbsp	olive oil	25 mL
2	onions, chopped	2
2	cloves garlic, finely chopped	2
¼ tsp	hot pepper flakes	1 mL
¼ cup	diced roasted red peppers	50 mL
1	6-oz (170 mL) jar marinated artichoke hearts, drained and chopped	1
1	19-oz (540 mL) can lentils, drained	1
1 cup	tomato sauce	250 mL
¼ tsp	dried oregano leaves	1 mL
1 cup	diced mozzarella cheese	250 mL

Topping

½ cup	fresh bread crumbs	125 mL
¼ cup	grated Parmesan cheese	50 mL
2 tbsp	olive oil	25 mL

1. In a medium skillet, heat oil over medium heat. Add onions, garlic and hot pepper flakes and cook for 4 minutes, or until softened.

2. In a large bowl, combine roasted peppers, artichokes, lentils, tomato sauce, oregano and mozzarella. Add onions and combine well. Transfer to a lightly greased 6-cup (1.5 L) casserole.

3. To prepare topping, in the same bowl, combine bread crumbs, Parmesan and oil. Sprinkle topping over lentils.

4. Convection bake in a preheated 350°F (180°C) oven for 25 minutes, or until hot and bubbling.

Makes 6 servings

Enjoy the flavors of pizza in this meatless dish that can be quickly assembled from a well-stocked pantry. This is great for a buffet or dinner when you are trying to include a vegetarian option. It is also a good dish to serve at Thanksgiving and holiday time.

Make Ahead

Lentil bake can be assembled, covered and refrigerated up to six hours ahead of time. Add 10 minutes to baking time.

Chickpea and Vegetable Curry

Makes 4 to 5 servings

These days many people are opting for a vegetarian diet, so it's good to have a few meatless main dishes in your repertoire.

Don't let the word curry scare you. This dish is flavorful without being overspiced. Choose a curry powder that suits your taste — they range from mild to hot.

Make Ahead

Curry can be assembled a day ahead, covered and refrigerated. Bring to room temperature before baking.

2 tbsp	olive oil	25 mL
2	onions, chopped	2
1	stalk celery, chopped	1
3	cloves garlic, finely chopped	3
1 tbsp	chopped gingerroot	15 mL
1 tbsp	curry powder	15 mL
¾ tsp	salt	4 mL
2 cups	tomato juice	500 mL
1 cup	cauliflower florets	250 mL
1 cup	diced green beans	250 mL
1	19-oz (540 mL) can chickpeas, rinsed and drained	1
2 tbsp	chopped fresh cilantro or parsley	25 mL

1. In a large skillet, heat oil over medium heat. Add onions, celery, garlic and ginger. Cook, stirring occasionally, for 8 minutes. Stir in curry powder and salt. Cook for 30 seconds.

2. Stir in tomato juice, cauliflower, beans and chickpeas. Bring to a boil. Transfer to a lightly greased 8-inch (2 L) square baking dish.

3. Convection bake in a preheated 350°F (180°C) oven for 35 to 40 minutes, or until vegetables are just tender. Stir occasionally. Sprinkle with cilantro before serving.

Roasted Cauliflower

Roast leftover cauliflower to make an easy vegetable dish. Cut cauliflower into florets and toss with olive oil, salt and pepper. Place on a parchment-lined baking sheet and convection roast in a preheated 375°F (190°C) oven for 25 to 30 minutes, or until tender. Stir once during cooking.

Vegetables and Salads

Broccoli Cheddar Gratin

**Makes 5 to
6 servings**

Simply steamed and
drizzled with olive
oil and lemon juice,
broccoli adds both
color and texture to the
dinner plate; however,
this gratin is a great
accompaniment for a
roast chicken or sliced
cold meats. (In France,
a vegetable gratin is
often served as a main
dish with a simple green
salad and crusty bread.)
   Cauliflower, Brussels
sprouts and cabbage
can be used instead
of broccoli.

Make Ahead
Cool cheese sauce for
about a half hour (to
prevent broccoli from
becoming soggy). Pour
sauce over broccoli. Add
topping. Cover loosely
and refrigerate for up
to four hours. Bake for
20 to 25 minutes.

1	large bunch broccoli (about 1½ lbs/ 750 g), cut in 2-inch (5 cm) pieces	1
2 tbsp	butter	25 mL
1	onion, chopped	1
3 tbsp	all-purpose flour	45 mL
2 cups	milk	500 mL
½ tsp	salt	2 mL
¼ tsp	black pepper	1 mL
Pinch	ground nutmeg	Pinch
1 cup	grated Cheddar cheese	250 mL
⅓ cup	fresh bread crumbs	75 mL
⅓ cup	grated Parmesan cheese	75 mL

1. In a medium saucepan, bring ½ inch (1 cm) water to a boil. Add broccoli and steam, covered, for 3 to 4 minutes, or until just tender. Drain. Rinse with cold water. Drain very well. Place in a lightly greased 8-inch (2 L) square baking dish.

2. Meanwhile, to prepare sauce, melt butter in a medium saucepan over medium heat. Add onion and cook for 2 minutes. Add flour and cook, stirring, for 2 minutes, but do not let color.

3. Remove pan from heat and whisk in milk. Return to medium-high heat and bring just to a boil. Add salt, pepper and nutmeg. Reduce heat to low and simmer for 5 minutes, stirring occasionally.

4. Remove sauce from heat and stir in Cheddar. Pour sauce over broccoli.

5. In a small bowl, combine bread crumbs and Parmesan. Sprinkle over broccoli and sauce. Convection bake in a preheated 375°F (190°C) oven for 15 to 20 minutes, or until top is golden and sauce bubbles at edges.

Roasted Broccoli

2	bunches broccoli (about 1 lb/500 g each), cut in 2-inch (5 cm) pieces	2
2 tbsp	olive oil (approx.)	25 mL
¾ tsp	salt	4 mL
¼ tsp	black pepper	1 mL

1. In a large bowl, toss broccoli with oil, salt and pepper, adding more oil if desired. Transfer to a parchment-lined baking sheet.
2. Convection roast in a preheated 375°F (190°C) oven for 20 minutes, or until just tender and light golden.

Broccoli Salad

In a large bowl, combine 1 bunch roasted broccoli, cut in bite-sized pieces, ½ cup (125 mL) grated Cheddar cheese, ½ cup (125 mL) diced cooked bacon, ½ cup (125 mL) dried cranberries and ¼ cup (50 mL) pine nuts.

In a small bowl, combine ⅓ cup (75 mL) mayonnaise, 2 tbsp (25 mL) cider vinegar and 1 tbsp (15 mL) mango chutney. Toss broccoli with dressing and serve immediately or cover and refrigerate for up to 8 hours. Makes 4 to 6 servings.

Makes 6 servings

Roasted broccoli has a much different flavor from steamed broccoli. Simply tossed with a good olive oil, salt and pepper, it tastes almost rich. I always roast more than I need so I can eat it the next day in a salad.

The salad recipe is based on a dish that my friend Carol Quirk served when I was visiting her in Sydney, Australia.

Roasted Fennel and Asparagus

Makes 4 to 6 servings

This can be served hot as a side dish or at room temperature as a salad.

1 lb	asparagus, trimmed and cut in 1½-inch (4 cm) pieces	500 g
1	bulb fennel, trimmed and cut in ½-inch (1 cm) pieces	1
1	orange, peeled and cut in pieces	1
1 tbsp	olive oil	15 mL
½ tsp	salt	2 mL
¼ tsp	black pepper	1 mL
1 tbsp	rice vinegar	15 mL
1	avocado, diced (optional)	1

1. On a parchment-lined baking sheet, combine asparagus, fennel and orange. Season with oil, salt and pepper. Toss to combine and spread out.

2. Convection roast in a preheated 375°F (190°C) oven for 20 to 25 minutes, or until just tender. Toss with vinegar and top with avocado, if using.

Oven-baked Sugar Snap Peas

Remove strings from 1½ lbs (750 g) sugar snap peas. Toss peas with 1 tbsp (15 mL) vegetable oil, 1 tbsp (15 mL) soy sauce and 1 tsp (5 mL) granulated sugar. Spread on a parchment-lined baking sheet. Convection bake in a preheated 400°F (200°C) oven for 10 minutes, or until tender-crisp, stirring once during cooking time. Makes 6 servings.

Asian Vegetable Medley

2	cloves garlic, chopped	2
2 tsp	chopped gingerroot	10 mL
3	green onions, chopped	3
2	stalks celery, sliced	2
1	red bell pepper, seeded and cut in ½-inch (1 cm) pieces	1
1½ cups	green beans, cut in ½-inch (1 cm) pieces	375 mL
1 cup	quartered mushrooms	250 mL
1	Asian eggplant, cut in ½-inch (1 cm) pieces	1
2 tbsp	oyster sauce or hoisin sauce	25 mL
1 tbsp	sesame oil	15 mL
1 tbsp	sweet Asian chili sauce (optional)	15 mL

1. In a large bowl, combine garlic, ginger, green onions, celery, red pepper, beans, mushrooms and eggplant.

2. Add oyster sauce, sesame oil and sweet chili sauce, if using. Toss well to combine. Transfer mixture to a foil- and parchment-lined baking sheet.

3. Convection roast in a preheated 425°F (220°C) oven for 15 to 18 minutes, or until vegetables are tender-crisp. Stir once during cooking.

Makes 4 to 5 servings

Practically any vegetables that can be stir-fried can be roasted in the convection oven for an easy vegetable dish. Create your own combination (try asparagus, broccoli, cauliflower, carrots, etc.), but do not overload the tray. Serve with chicken or fish and rice.

Zucchini Gratin

Makes 4 servings

I always used to plant lots of zucchini, until I realized I was spending more time giving them away than eating them myself. Now I just plant a few (yellow and green), but they still yield a lot. Here is a quick-to-assemble gratin to serve as a side dish or for brunch. The prosciutto and herbs give the sometimes bland zucchini a lift. (Bresaola is a beef version of prosciutto.)

Use green and/or yellow zucchini.

3	zucchini (about 8 oz/250 g each), thinly sliced	3
¼ cup	diced prosciutto or bresaola	50 mL
2 tbsp	pesto	25 mL
2 tbsp	olive oil, divided	25 mL
½ tsp	salt	2 mL
¼ tsp	black pepper	1 mL
¼ cup	fresh bread crumbs	50 mL
2 tbsp	grated Parmesan cheese	25 mL
1 tsp	chopped fresh thyme, or ½ tsp (2 mL) dried	5 mL

1. In a large bowl, combine zucchini, prosciutto, pesto, 1 tbsp (5 mL) oil, salt and pepper. Toss to coat zucchini. Transfer to a lightly greased 8-cup (2 L) shallow baking or gratin dish.

2. In a bowl, combine bread crumbs, cheese, thyme and remaining oil. Spoon over zucchini.

3. Convection bake in a preheated 400°F (200°C) oven for 35 to 40 minutes, or until zucchini is tender and topping is golden.

Roasting Frozen Vegetables

Most frozen vegetables (e.g., mixed vegetables, cauliflower, broccoli, corn) roast well in the convection oven. Spread them in their frozen state on a parchment-lined baking sheet and convection roast (dry or drizzled with a small amount of olive oil) in a preheated 375°F (190°C) oven for 8 to 10 minutes, or until just tender (do not overcook). Toss with butter, salt, pepper and chopped fresh herbs (dill, parsley, chives).

Roasted Rosemary Potatoes

3 lbs	small new potatoes	1.5 kg
2 tbsp	olive oil	25 mL
1 tsp	salt	5 mL
½ tsp	black pepper	2 mL
2 tbsp	coarsely chopped fresh rosemary, or 1 tsp (5 mL) dried	25 mL
4	cloves garlic, thinly sliced	4

Makes 6 servings

These roasted potatoes will become your new in-house French fries, without deep-frying. The hardest part is to stop eating them. Sometimes I cut them into sticks and serve with garlic mayonnaise as an appetizer.

1. Cut potatoes into 1-inch (2.5 cm) pieces (if potatoes are small, leave whole) and place in a large bowl. Toss with olive oil, salt and pepper. Place on two parchment-lined baking sheets in a single layer. Do not crowd potatoes.

2. Convection roast in a preheated 425°F (220°C) oven for 20 minutes. Stir in rosemary and garlic. Continue to roast for 15 to 20 minutes, or until potatoes are golden, crispy and tender. Stir occasionally.

> **Variation**
> *Roasted Sweet Potatoes:* Peel 5 medium sweet potatoes (about 2½ lbs/1.25 kg total) and cut into fingers about 3 inches (7.5 cm) long and ½ inch (1 cm) thick. Place in a large bowl and toss with 2 tbsp (25 mL) olive oil, ¾ tsp (4 mL) salt, ½ tsp (2 mL) black pepper and ½ tsp (2 mL) paprika. Arrange in a single layer on a parchment-lined baking sheet and convection roast in a preheated 425°F (220°C) oven for 25 to 30 minutes, until tender and golden. Stir gently two or three times during roasting. Makes 5 to 6 servings.

Herbed Scalloped Potatoes

These creamy and rich scalloped potatoes are the ultimate comfort food. They are similar to the French version made completely with whipping cream, but here, herb cream cheese forms part of the sauce. Adding the sliced potatoes to the warmed sauce makes the assembly quick.

Serve with a salad and plain roast chicken or turkey or cold sliced meat.

6 oz	herb cream cheese	175 g
2 cups	cream (10%)	500 mL
1 tsp	salt	5 mL
¼ tsp	black pepper	1 mL
2½ lbs	Yukon Gold or all-purpose potatoes	1.25 kg
¼ cup	grated Parmesan cheese	50 mL

1. In a large saucepan, combine cream cheese, cream, salt and pepper. Place over low heat and heat just until cheese melts. Do not boil. Remove from heat.

2. Peel potatoes and slice thinly. Add to cheese mixture and stir to combine. Transfer to a greased 13- by 9-inch (3 L) baking dish. Sprinkle with Parmesan.

3. Convection bake in a preheated 375°F (190°C) oven for 40 to 45 minutes, or until tender. Let stand for 10 minutes before serving.

Brussels Sprouts with Orange Butter and Poppy Seeds

Makes 6 servings

People either love Brussels sprouts or they do not — there usually isn't any middle of the road. These sprouts, roasted in the convection oven and tossed with orange butter, may even convert the holdouts.

1½ lbs	Brussels sprouts, trimmed and quartered	750 g
3 tbsp	butter, melted	45 mL
1 tbsp	orange juice concentrate or orange juice	15 mL
2 tsp	grated orange zest	10 mL
1½ tsp	poppy seeds	7 mL
¼ tsp	salt	1 mL

1. In a large bowl, combine Brussels sprouts, melted butter, orange juice concentrate, zest, poppy seeds and salt. Transfer to a parchment-lined baking sheet.

2. Convection roast in a preheated 400°F (200°C) oven for 15 to 18 minutes, or until just tender and slightly golden.

Grated Potato and Onion Bake

2	eggs	2
3 tbsp	olive oil	45 mL
1/3 cup	cornflake crumbs	75 mL
2 tbsp	all-purpose flour	25 mL
1 tsp	baking powder	5 mL
3/4 tsp	salt	4 mL
1/4 tsp	black pepper	1 mL
1	large onion, grated or finely chopped	1
2 lbs	Yukon Gold or baking potatoes (about 4 large), peeled and grated	1 kg
1/4 tsp	paprika	1 mL

1. In a large bowl, beat eggs. Stir in oil, cornflake crumbs, flour, baking powder, salt and pepper.

2. Add onion and potatoes and stir thoroughly to combine. Transfer to a well-greased 8-inch (2 L) square baking dish. Sprinkle with paprika.

3. Convection bake in a preheated 375°F (190°C) oven for 40 to 45 minutes, or until potatoes are tender.

Makes 4 to 6 servings

Assemble this dish just before baking so the potatoes do not discolor. You can peel the potatoes ahead of time and keep them covered with cold water until using, but dry them well before grating. For an especially quick assembly, grate the onion and potatoes in a food processor.

Turnip and Apple Mash

Makes 4 to 5 servings

In this recipe, apples lighten the sometimes strong taste of turnip (rutabaga). This dish can easily be doubled or tripled to serve a crowd, especially for Thanksgiving or Christmas get-togethers.

Make Ahead

Assemble dish completely, cover and refrigerate overnight. Bring to room temperature before baking.

1	large turnip (about 2½ lbs/1.25 kg), peeled and cut in ½-inch (1 cm) pieces	1
2	apples, peeled, cored and cut in 1-inch (2.5 cm) pieces	2
2 tbsp	brown sugar	25 mL
2 tbsp	butter	25 mL
¼ tsp	salt	1 mL
¼ tsp	black pepper	1 mL
¾ cup	fresh bread crumbs	175 mL
½ tsp	paprika	2 mL
2 tbsp	butter, melted, or olive oil	25 mL

1. Cook turnip in a large saucepan of boiling salted water until almost tender, about 25 to 30 minutes. Add apples and cook until both turnip and apples are tender, about 5 to 7 minutes. Drain very well.

2. Mash turnip and apples with brown sugar, butter, salt and pepper. Spoon into a lightly greased 8-inch (2 L) square baking dish.

3. In a small bowl, combine bread crumbs, paprika and melted butter. Sprinkle bread crumbs over turnip. Convection bake in a preheated 350°F (180°C) oven for 20 to 25 minutes, or until heated through and top is golden.

Stuffed Baked Tomatoes

6	firm medium to large tomatoes	6
½ cup	uncooked instant couscous	125 mL
2	green onions, chopped	2
2 tbsp	chopped fresh dillweed, tarragon or basil	25 mL
1	clove garlic, minced	1
¼ cup	grated Parmesan cheese	50 mL
½ tsp	salt	2 mL
¼ tsp	black pepper	1 mL
2 tbsp	olive oil	25 mL

1. Cut one-quarter off round ends of tomatoes and reserve. Carefully remove pulp (a grapefruit spoon works well). Chop pulp.

2. In a bowl, combine chopped tomato pulp, couscous, green onions, dill, garlic, Parmesan, salt and pepper.

3. Arrange tomatoes cut side up in a lightly greased baking dish just large enough to hold tomatoes in one layer. Spoon filling mixture into tomatoes. Place tops over filling. Brush tomatoes with olive oil.

4. Convection bake in a preheated 350°F (180°C) oven for 25 minutes, or until couscous is softened. Cover with foil and let stand for 15 minutes, then carefully transfer to a serving platter.

Quick Tomatoes Provençal
Slice 4 tomatoes in half crosswise and place cut side up on a baking sheet. In a small bowl, combine 2 minced cloves garlic, 2 tbsp (25 mL) fresh bread crumbs, 1 tsp (5 mL) herbes de Provence or dried thyme, ¼ tsp (1 mL) salt and ¼ tsp (1 mL) black pepper. Sprinkle over tomatoes. Drizzle with 2 tbsp (25 mL) olive oil. Place 4 inches (10 cm) from heat and convection broil for 4 to 5 minutes, or until topping is golden and tomatoes are slightly soft. Makes 3 to 4 servings.

Makes 6 servings

When tomatoes are in season, nothing could be simpler than sliced ripe tomatoes with fresh basil, but for a more substantial dish, try serving these as an appetizer or side dish. Be sure to select firm tomatoes and handle them gently. If you are making this dish during the winter months, buy large vine-ripened tomatoes.

You can replace the couscous with leftover rice in this recipe. Use 1¼ cups (300 mL) cooked rice.

Make Ahead
These tomatoes are also excellent served at room temperature.

Roasted Mixed Vegetables

Makes 6 servings

The convection oven makes roasted vegetables crisp on the outside while enhancing their natural sweetness, and cooking all the vegetables together makes easy work and clean-up for the cook. Puree any leftover vegetables with chicken stock for a quick soup, or toss with a simple balsamic vinaigrette (page 158) for a roasted vegetable salad.

1	medium butternut squash (about 1½ lbs/750 g), peeled and seeded	1
2	medium sweet potatoes (about 1 lb/500 g total), peeled	2
3	parsnips (about 1 lb/500 g total), peeled	3
1	large red onion, peeled	1
10	small new potatoes (about 1¼ lbs/ 625 g total)	10
2 tbsp	olive oil	25 mL
½ tsp	dried herbs (such as thyme, oregano or marjoram)	2 mL
¾ tsp	salt	4 mL
¼ tsp	black pepper	1 mL

1. Cut squash, sweet potatoes, parsnips and onion into 1½-inch (4 cm) pieces. Combine in a bowl with potatoes, olive oil, herbs, salt and pepper. Toss well. Spread in a single layer on a large parchment-lined baking sheet.

2. Convection roast in a preheated 400°F (200°C) oven for 35 minutes, or until vegetables are just tender. Stir 2 or 3 times during cooking, burying onions under other vegetables if they are browning too quickly.

Mediterranean Vegetables with Orzo

2	onions, cut in 1-inch (2.5 cm) chunks	2
4	cloves garlic, peeled and halved	4
1	eggplant (about 1 lb/250 g), cut in 1-inch (2.5 cm) pieces	1
1	medium zucchini (about 8 oz/250 g), sliced	1
2	red bell peppers, seeded and cut in 1-inch (2.5 cm) pieces	2
3	large tomatoes, cored and cut in 1-inch (2.5 cm) pieces	3
¼ cup	olive oil	50 mL
¾ tsp	herbes de Provence or dried thyme leaves	4 mL
½ tsp	salt	2 mL
½ tsp	black pepper	2 mL
½ cup	uncooked orzo	125 mL
1 cup	crumbled chèvre or feta cheese	250 mL
½ cup	pitted black olives	125 mL
¼ cup	shredded fresh basil	50 mL

1. Place onions, garlic, eggplant, zucchini, red peppers and tomatoes in a 13- by 9-inch (3 L) baking dish. Sprinkle with olive oil, herbes de Provence, salt and pepper and toss together.

2. Convection bake in a preheated 400°F (200°C) oven for 45 to 50 minutes, or until vegetables are tender and golden. Stir several times during roasting.

3. Meanwhile, cook orzo in plenty of boiling salted water for about 8 minutes, or until tender. Drain well.

4. Toss vegetables with orzo and sprinkle with chèvre, olives and basil.

Makes 8 servings

Orzo is a rice-shaped pasta often used in soups or pilafs. If it is difficult to find, use 1½ cups (375 mL) cooked long-grain white or brown rice. Serve this as a meatless main course or side dish at a potluck or buffet (it can be served hot or at room temperature). The combination is reminiscent of ratatouille, a robust Provençal vegetable stew.

Sicilian (round) or Asian (long slender) eggplants can be used in this dish. Eggplant absorbs oil like a sponge, but try to refrain from adding more. For a juicier dish, add one or two more tomatoes or another zucchini.

Make Ahead
Vegetables can be roasted, covered and refrigerated a day ahead. Reheat at 350°F (180°C) for 20 minutes before combining with hot pasta.

Butternut Squash with Roasted Onions

Makes 6 servings

This recipe combines the most popular member of the squash family with the sweetness of roasted onions and fresh sage. Serve it with roasted sausages and potatoes.

2	butternut squash (about 2 lbs/1 kg each), peeled and cut in ½-inch (1 cm) pieces	2
2	onions, cut in ½-inch (1 cm) pieces	2
3 tbsp	olive oil	45 mL
2 tbsp	shredded fresh sage, or 1 tsp (5 mL) dried	25 mL
¾ tsp	salt	4 mL
¼ tsp	black pepper	1 mL

1. In a large bowl, combine squash, onions, oil, sage, salt and pepper. Spread over a parchment-lined baking sheet.

2. Convection roast in a preheated 400°F (200°C) oven for 35 to 40 minutes, or until vegetables are tender and golden. Stir twice during roasting.

Acorn Squash Rounds

Makes 5 servings

Acorn squash is one of the first squashes on the market in late summer. Its mild flavor lends itself to seasoning. Easy to roast in the convection oven, this can be served plain or with a scoop of creamy mashed potatoes placed in the center.

1	acorn squash (about 2½ lbs/625 g)	1
¼ cup	olive oil	50 mL
¼ cup	chopped fresh parsley	50 mL
2	cloves garlic, minced	2
1 tbsp	lemon juice	15 mL
¾ tsp	salt	4 mL
¼ tsp	curry powder or ground cumin (optional)	1 mL

1. Trim ends from squash with a heavy sharp knife. Carefully cut squash crosswise into five 1-inch (2.5 cm) rounds. Remove any seeds. Arrange rounds in a single layer on a parchment-lined baking sheet.

2. In a bowl, combine oil, parsley, garlic, lemon juice, salt and curry powder, if using. Spoon mixture over squash rounds.

3. Convection roast in a preheated 400°F (200°C) oven for 30 to 35 minutes, or until squash is tender.

Savory Pumpkin Bread Pudding

1½ cups	pumpkin puree	375 mL
4	eggs	4
1	shallot or small piece of red onion, finely chopped	1
1	clove garlic, minced	1
1 tbsp	chopped fresh marjoram or thyme	15 mL
1 tbsp	chopped fresh rosemary	15 mL
1¼ tsp	salt	6 mL
¼ tsp	black pepper	1 mL
Pinch	ground nutmeg	Pinch
3 cups	milk, divided	750 mL
4 cups	stale bread cubes (1-inch/2.5 cm pieces)	1 L

1. In a food processor or by hand, combine pumpkin puree, eggs, shallot, garlic, marjoram, rosemary, salt, pepper and nutmeg. Add 1 cup (250 mL) milk and process. Transfer to a large bowl.

2. Stir in remaining milk and bread cubes. Transfer mixture to a greased 8-cup (2 L) baking dish.

3. Convection roast in a preheated 325°F (160°C) oven for 55 to 60 minutes, or until set and browned. Let stand for 10 minutes before serving.

Makes 8 servings

In his recent cookbook, *Kitchen Sense*, which is filled with cozy and creative recipes, Mitchell Davis included this recipe for a stuffing-like dish. It is a wonderful side dish for fall and festive dinners, but Mitchell also suggests that leftovers can be sliced, fried in butter and served with eggs for breakfast or brunch.

Make Ahead
Pudding can be assembled an hour before cooking. It can also be baked a day ahead, cooled, covered and refrigerated. Convection roast or bake in a preheated 300°F (150°C) oven for 25 to 30 minutes, or until hot.

Portobello and Fennel Salad

Makes 6 servings

Portobello mushrooms appear in soups, salads, side dishes and main courses. Although not a complete protein, they are often the mainstay of vegetarian menus, perhaps because of their meaty texture. If you wish, you can use a spoon to scrape away the dark gills on the underside of the mushrooms.

Make Ahead
Prepare dressing, cover and refrigerate for up to two days.

Mushrooms and Fennel

⅓ cup	olive oil	75 mL
4	cloves garlic, minced	4
2 tsp	chopped fresh tarragon, or ¾ tsp (4 mL) dried	10 mL
½ tsp	salt	2 mL
¼ tsp	black pepper	1 mL
6	portobello mushrooms (about 1½ lbs/ 750 g total), stems removed	6
1	large bulb fennel (about 1½ lbs/750 g), trimmed and cut in 12 wedges	1

Balsamic Vinaigrette

2 tbsp	balsamic vinegar	25 mL
1 tbsp	lemon juice	15 mL
1 tsp	Dijon mustard	5 mL
2 tbsp	olive oil	25 mL
¼ tsp	salt	1 mL
¼ tsp	black pepper	1 mL

Salad

6 cups	arugula or baby spinach	1.5 L
½ cup	toasted pine nuts	125 mL

1. In a small bowl, whisk together olive oil, garlic, tarragon, salt and pepper.

2. Arrange mushrooms, round side up, on a parchment-lined baking sheet. Brush with half the oil mixture.

3. In a large bowl, toss fennel wedges with remaining oil mixture. Place on another parchment-lined baking sheet.

4. Convection roast mushrooms and fennel in a preheated 400°F (200°C) oven — mushrooms for 12 minutes, fennel for 18 to 20 minutes, or until tender. Cool both slightly. Cut each mushroom into 4 slices.

5. To prepare vinaigrette, in a small bowl or measuring cup, whisk together vinegar, lemon juice, mustard, olive oil, salt and pepper.

6. Toss arugula with vinaigrette and arrange on serving plates. Arrange mushrooms and fennel over greens. Sprinkle with pine nuts.

Pasta Salad with Cherry Tomatoes and Arugula

4 cups	cherry or grape tomatoes, halved if large	1 L
1	red onion, chopped	1
2	cloves garlic, finely chopped	2
¼ cup	olive oil	50 mL
2 tbsp	red wine vinegar or tarragon vinegar	25 mL
½ tsp	hot pepper flakes	2 mL
¼ cup	shredded fresh basil, divided	50 mL
1 tsp	salt	5 mL
¼ tsp	black pepper	1 mL
12 oz	spaghetti, broken up slightly	375 g
4 cups	coarsely chopped arugula	1 L

Makes 6 servings

If you have a cherry tomato plant that produces more than you can use or even give away, make this salad. When roasted, the seasoned tomatoes are almost like a salad on their own. Serve at room temperature or cold.

This is great lunch box or picnic fare.

Make Ahead

Tomatoes can be roasted ahead and cooled before tossing with pasta. Tomatoes and pasta can be combined, covered and refrigerated overnight before tossing with arugula.

1. In a large bowl, combine tomatoes, onion, garlic, oil, vinegar, hot pepper flakes, 2 tbsp (25 mL) basil, salt and pepper. Spread on a foil- and parchment-lined baking sheet.

2. Convection roast in a preheated 400°F (200°C) oven for 20 minutes, or until tomatoes are softened and giving off juices.

3. Meanwhile, cook pasta in a large amount of boiling salted water until just tender. Drain and toss with roasted tomatoes. Add a bit more oil if desired. Cool to room temperature and toss with arugula and remaining basil.

Lettuce Wedges with Blue Cheese Dressing

In a small bowl, combine 1 minced clove garlic, ½ tsp (2 mL) Dijon mustard, 2 tbsp (25 mL) lemon juice and ¼ tsp (1 mL) black pepper. With a fork, gradually whisk in ⅓ cup (75 mL) olive oil. Stir in ¼ cup (50 mL) crumbled blue cheese (leave slighty lumpy or mash until smooth).

Cut ½ large head iceberg lettuce into four wedges. Drizzle dressing over lettuce. Makes 4 servings.

Potato and Bean Caesar Salad

Makes 6 servings

Caesar salad, a perennial favorite, shows up in many variations. An excellent year-round salad, this version is especially good during the summer months when baby new potatoes and beans are in season.

Make Ahead

Roast vegetables up to six hours in advance and keep at room temperature. Dressing can be prepared, covered and refrigerated for up to two days.

2 lbs	new potatoes	1 kg
6 tsp	olive oil, divided	30 mL
½ tsp	salt, divided	2 mL
½ tsp	black pepper, divided	2 mL
8 oz	green beans, trimmed and cut in half	250 g

Caesar Dressing

2	cloves garlic, minced	2
2	anchovy fillets, mashed, or 1 tsp (5 mL) anchovy paste	2
1 tsp	Dijon mustard	5 mL
3 tbsp	lemon juice	45 mL
½ tsp	Worcestershire sauce	2 mL
¼ cup	olive oil	50 mL
2 tbsp	grated Parmesan cheese	25 mL
½ tsp	salt	2 mL
½ tsp	black pepper	2 mL

Salad

½	head Romaine lettuce, shredded	½
2	tomatoes, cut in sections	2
6	slices cooked bacon, crumbled	6
2 tbsp	grated Parmesan cheese	25 mL

1. Cut potatoes into 1-inch (2.5 cm) pieces and place in a large bowl. Toss with 4 tsp (20 mL) olive oil, ¼ tsp (1 mL) salt and ¼ tsp (1 mL) pepper. Place on a parchment-lined baking sheet. Toss beans with remaining oil, salt and pepper. Place on another parchment-lined baking sheet.

2. Convection roast vegetables in a preheated 400°F (200°C) oven. Remove beans from oven after 15 minutes. Cook potatoes for an additional 20 minutes, or until tender. Cool potatoes and beans to room temperature.

3. Meanwhile, to prepare dressing, in a small bowl, whisk together garlic, anchovies, mustard, lemon juice, Worcestershire, olive oil, Parmesan, salt and pepper.

4. Toss lettuce with half the dressing. Toss potatoes and beans with remaining dressing. Spoon vegetables and tomatoes over lettuce. Sprinkle with bacon and Parmesan.

Mexican Salad

Orange Chipotle Dressing

2 tbsp	orange juice concentrate	25 mL
2 tbsp	red wine vinegar	25 mL
1/2 tsp	chipotle puree (page 54) or hot pepper sauce	2 mL
1/4 cup	olive oil	50 mL
1/2 tsp	dried oregano leaves	2 mL
1/4 tsp	ground cumin	1 mL

Salad

2 cups	corn kernels	500 mL
1	red onion, chopped	1
1	red bell pepper, seeded and chopped	1
2 tbsp	olive oil	25 mL
2	tomatoes, seeded and chopped	2
1	apple, unpeeled and chopped	1
1 cup	canned black or pinto beans, rinsed and drained	250 mL
1	avocado, diced	1
1 cup	chopped Romaine lettuce	250 mL
1/2 cup	crumbled tortilla chips	125 mL

1. To prepare dressing, in a small bowl, whisk together orange juice concentrate, vinegar, chipotle, oil, oregano and cumin.

2. To prepare salad, in a bowl, combine corn, onion, red pepper and oil. Transfer to a parchment-lined baking sheet. Convection roast in a preheated 400°F (200°C) oven for 15 minutes, or until tender and light golden. Cool to room temperature.

3. To assemble, in a large bowl, combine corn mixture, tomatoes, apple, beans, avocado and lettuce. Add dressing and toss to combine. Taste and adjust seasonings if necessary. Sprinkle with tortilla chips.

Makes 6 to 8 servings

Include this salad at your next fiesta, along with Santa Fe Chicken Wraps (page 133), Southwestern Wings (page 42) or spareribs (pages 115 and 116). The roasted vegetables also make an excellent side dish. For a spicier version, increase the chipotle puree to 1 tsp (5 mL).

Make Ahead

Everything can be chopped ahead with the exception of the apple and avocado. The corn, onion and red pepper can be roasted ahead and refrigerated. For best results, assemble salad shortly before serving.

Warm Chèvre Salad with Mexican Pesto

Makes 6 servings

Although this salad consists of several steps, most can be prepared in advance. The Mexican pesto yields more than is required for the salad, so use the extra to toss with steamed vegetables, pasta or whisk into a vinaigrette.

Pumpkin seeds are available in health food and bulk food stores.

Make Ahead

Pesto can be prepared a day ahead. Cover and refrigerate. Tomatoes can be roasted up to four hours in advance and kept at room temperature. Roll cheese in tortilla chips and refrigerate until baking.

Mexican Pesto

½ cup	pumpkin seeds, toasted	125 mL
½ cup	lightly packed fresh cilantro leaves	125 mL
2	green onions, coarsely chopped	2
2	cloves garlic, chopped	2
2 tsp	chopped jalapeño pepper (or to taste)	10 mL
½ tsp	salt	2 mL
3 tbsp	olive oil	45 mL
2 tbsp	water	25 mL

Warm Chèvre Salad

3	medium tomatoes, cored and halved	3
1 tbsp	olive oil	15 mL
¼ tsp	salt	1 mL
¼ tsp	black pepper	1 mL
10 oz	chèvre, cut in 6 pieces	300 g
½ cup	crushed tortilla chips	125 mL
6 cups	arugula or shredded Romaine lettuce	1.5 L

1. To prepare pesto, place pumpkin seeds, cilantro, green onions, garlic, jalapeño and salt in a food processor or blender and process until coarsely chopped. Add olive oil and water. Process until pureed.

2. To prepare salad, arrange tomatoes in a shallow baking dish large enough to hold tomatoes in a single layer (cut small pieces from bottoms so tomatoes sit upright).

3. Sprinkle tomatoes with oil, salt and pepper. Convection bake in a preheated 400°F (200°C) oven for 10 to 12 minutes, or until tomatoes are just softened.

4. Roll chèvre in tortilla chips, flattening cheese slightly. Place on a parchment-lined baking sheet. Convection bake with tomatoes for 6 minutes.

5. To serve, arrange arugula on serving plates. Place tomato on greens. Arrange chèvre on top of tomato. Place a generous serving of pesto on top of chèvre.

Summer Peppers

3	red or yellow bell peppers, halved lengthwise and seeded	3
3	medium tomatoes, cored and cut in wedges	3
1 tbsp	capers	15 mL
3	cloves garlic, thinly sliced	3
¼ cup	shredded fresh basil	50 mL
½ cup	dry bread crumbs	125 mL
½ tsp	salt	2 mL
¼ tsp	black pepper	1 mL
2 tbsp	olive oil	25 mL

1. Arrange peppers cut side up in a lightly greased shallow baking dish just large enough to hold peppers in one layer.
2. Place tomatoes, capers and garlic in pepper cavities. Sprinkle with basil, bread crumbs, salt and pepper. Drizzle olive oil over top.
3. Convection bake in a preheated 325°F (160°C) oven for 50 to 60 minutes, or until peppers are softened and partially collapsed.

> ### Toasting Nuts and Seeds
> Place nuts or seeds in a small baking dish. Convection bake in a preheated 300°F (150°C) oven for 5 to 10 minutes, or until golden. Toasting time depends on nut and seed size (bake pumpkin seeds for 5 to 6 minutes, or until seeds pop).

Makes 6 servings

The slow roasting in this recipe releases the sweet flavors of the peppers. This dish is perfect for luncheons, buffets and picnics, if carefully packed. Serve hot or at room temperature.

Make Ahead
Bake up to four hours in advance and serve at room temperature.

Salmon Caesar Salad

Makes 4 servings

Combine two favorites in this easy lunch or light supper dish. Almost any kind of bread can be used for the croutons — even bread that is slighty stale. Leftovers are good for munching or as toppings for soups, casseroles or other salads.

Croutons

1½ cups	bread cubes	375 mL
3 tbsp	olive oil	45 mL

Salmon

4	6-oz (175 g) salmon fillets, skin removed	4
1 tbsp	olive oil	15 mL
½ tsp	salt	2 mL
¼ tsp	black pepper	1 mL
2 tbsp	grated Parmesan cheese	25 mL

Caesar Salad

6 cups	chopped Romaine lettuce	1.5 L
1 cup	shredded radicchio or red cabbage	250 mL
½ cup	Caesar dressing, storebought or homemade (page 160)	125 mL
2 tbsp	grated Parmesan cheese	25 mL
2 tbsp	chopped sun-dried tomatoes (in oil)	25 mL

1. To prepare croutons, in a bowl, toss bread cubes with oil. Place on a parchment-lined baking sheet.

2. For salmon, arrange fillets on a separate parchment-lined baking sheet. Drizzle with oil and sprinkle with salt, pepper and Parmesan.

3. Convection bake croutons and salmon in a preheated 400°F (200°C) oven. Bake croutons for 6 minutes, or until light golden. Continue to bake salmon for 4 to 6 minutes, or until just cooked.

4. Meanwhile, to prepare salad, toss Romaine and radicchio with dressing. Arrange on individual serving plates.

5. Place salmon alongside salad. Sprinkle salmon and salad with Parmesan, sun-dried tomatoes and croutons.

Roasted Onion Salad with Melon

3	onions, cut in 1-inch (2.5 cm) pieces	3
2 tbsp	olive oil	25 mL
2 tbsp	raspberry or balsamic vinegar	25 mL
2 tsp	chopped fresh rosemary, or ½ tsp (2 mL) dried	10 mL
½ tsp	salt	2 mL
¼ tsp	black pepper	1 mL
4 cups	baby arugula or watercress leaves	1 L
4 cups	watermelon, canteloupe or honeydew chunks (cut in 1-inch/2.5 cm pieces)	1 L

Dressing

3 tbsp	raspberry or red wine vinegar	45 mL
2 tsp	liquid honey or maple syrup	10 mL
½ tsp	coarse-grain mustard	2 mL
¼ cup	olive oil	50 mL
½ tsp	salt	2 mL
¼ tsp	black pepper	1 mL

1. In a large bowl, combine onions, oil, vinegar, rosemary, salt and pepper. Transfer to a parchment-lined baking sheet and convection roast in a preheated 375°F (190°C) oven for 25 minutes, or until golden and tender, stirring twice during cooking. Cool to room temperature.

2. Arrange arugula on a serving platter and top with onions and melon pieces.

3. To prepare dressing, in a small bowl, whisk together vinegar, honey, mustard, oil, salt and pepper. Drizzle over salad.

Makes 6 servings

Colorful melons combine with roasted onions for a refreshing summer lunch dish. Sweet onions such as Spanish, Maui and Vidalia are excellent, but red or regular cooking onions can be used, too.

When roasting onions, roast extra and use as a topping for pizza or pasta, or puree and spread as a "jam" on bread or crackers.

You can also top this salad with other fresh seasonal fruit such as strawberries, raspberries or blueberries, along with or instead of the melons.

Make Ahead

The dressing can be prepared two days ahead and refrigerated. The onions can be roasted, covered and refrigerated up to three days ahead.

Roasted Pear Salad with Candied Pecans and Blue Cheese

3	pears (Bartlett or Anjou), halved, peeled and cored	3
2 tbsp	olive oil	25 mL
¼ tsp	dried thyme or oregano leaves	1 mL
¼ tsp	salt	1 mL
¼ tsp	black pepper	1 mL

Candied Pecans

1 cup	pecan halves	250 mL
2 tbsp	granulated sugar	25 mL
2 tbsp	liquid honey	25 mL
2 tbsp	boiling water	25 mL
½ tsp	dried rosemary leaves	2 mL
¼ tsp	salt	1 mL

Raspberry Vinaigrette

2 tbsp	olive oil	25 mL
2 tbsp	raspberry vinegar	25 mL
1 tsp	Dijon mustard	5 mL
¼ tsp	salt	1 mL
¼ tsp	black pepper	1 mL

Salad

8 cups	baby salad greens	2 L
½ cup	crumbled blue cheese	125 mL
1 cup	fresh raspberries	250 mL

Makes 6 servings

This is the salad to serve at a special dinner party. We prepared a version of this for a fundraising dinner for 350 guests, and could have raised even more had we sold the recipe! The pears should be ripe but firm. The roasted pears can also be served on their own with baked ham, chicken or pork.

Make Ahead

Pears and pecans can be cooked up to six hours ahead. Store pecans in a dry place (away from humidity and nibblers!).

1. Place pears cut side up in a shallow baking dish. Sprinkle with olive oil, thyme, salt and pepper.

2. Convection roast in a preheated 325°F (160°C) oven for 20 to 25 minutes, or until pears are just tender. Cool to room temperature.

3. Meanwhile, in a bowl, combine pecan halves with sugar, honey, boiling water, rosemary and salt. Stir well and spoon onto a parchment-lined baking sheet.

4. Convection roast nuts in a preheated 325°F (160°C) oven for 16 to 18 minutes, or until nuts are golden and water has evaporated. Stir twice during cooking. Cool until easy to handle. Loosen from paper.

5. To prepare vinaigrette, whisk together olive oil, vinegar, mustard, salt and pepper.

6. Toss greens with dressing and arrange on individual serving plates. Place pear in center of greens. Fill cavity with cheese. Sprinkle with pecans and raspberries.

Fresh vs. Dried Herbs

Use fresh herbs whenever possible. They make your food taste like summer. Add the amount called for in the recipe and, for even more freshness, stir in a small amount to taste at the end of the cooking time.

To store fresh herbs, wash them well and spin dry or roll in a clean towel to remove excess moisture. Wrap loosely in a paper towel and refrigerate in a storage container to prevent the herbs from being crushed. The storage time will depend on the type of herb and how fresh it is (dill, cilantro and chervil, for example, do not seem to keep as long as parsley, rosemary, sage and thyme).

If fresh herbs are not available, dried herbs can be a good stand-in. The general rule for replacing fresh herbs with dried is three to one. In other words, if a recipe calls for 3 tbsp (45 mL) fresh herbs, use 1 tbsp (15 mL) dried.

When purchasing dried herbs, buy leaves and pieces rather than ground. Crush the dried leaves between your fingertips before adding them to the dish. If the aroma is weak, add a bit more. Purchase dried herbs in small quantities and store in airtight containers, away from heat and light.

Chicken and Sausage Salad with Peaches

A substantial main course salad to serve at a brunch, as part of a buffet or even for an evening meal. The peaches should be just ripe but firm; nectarines or pineapple could be substituted. For an even richer flavor, toss the meat and pepper mixture with ¼ tsp (1 mL) smoked paprika (page 279).

Make Ahead

Salad can be made ahead, covered and refrigerated for up to eight hours.

12 oz	boneless, skinless chicken breasts, cut in ½-inch (1 cm) pieces	375 g
2	sweet or hot Italian sausages, cut in ½-inch (1 cm) pieces	2
¼ cup	olive oil, divided	50 mL
2	red or yellow bell peppers, seeded and cut in 1-inch (2.5 cm) pieces	2
1	large red or sweet onion, cut in ½-inch (1 cm) pieces	1
3	peaches, unpeeled, cut in ½-inch (1 cm) pieces	3
3 tbsp	balsamic vinegar	45 mL
2 tsp	coarse-grain mustard	10 mL
2	cloves garlic, minced	2
¼ cup	coarsely chopped black olives	50 mL
¼ cup	chopped fresh parsley	50 mL
2 tbsp	chopped sun-dried tomatoes (in oil)	25 mL

1. In a bowl, combine chicken, sausages and 2 tbsp (25 mL) oil. Transfer to a parchment-lined baking sheet.

2. In same bowl, combine peppers, onion, peaches and remaining oil. Transfer to a separate parchment-lined baking sheet.

3. Convection roast chicken and sausages in a preheated 400°F (200°C) oven for 20 minutes, or until cooked and no traces of pink remain (but do not overcook). Cook peach mixture for 15 minutes, or until just tender. Let both cool to room temperature.

4. In a large bowl, combine chicken, sausages, peppers, onion and peaches with vinegar, mustard, garlic, olives, parsley and sun-dried tomatoes. Toss well to combine.

Breakfast, Brunch and Lunch

Rise and Shine Granola

Makes 8 cups (2 L)

With so many cereal products on the market, is a homemade granola really necessary? I think so, as you can control exactly what goes into it and make substitutions according to your own taste and nutritional needs. This granola is so good, many people eat it as a snack.

For gifts, package it in plastic bags with colorful ribbons and homemade labels (a great project for young cooks).

Make Ahead

The granola can be made and stored in an airtight container for up to two weeks.

3 cups	rolled oats (not instant), divided	750 mL
1 cup	whole almonds, with skins	250 mL
1 cup	pecan halves or hazelnuts	250 mL
1 cup	unsweetened shredded coconut	250 mL
1 cup	wheat germ	250 mL
1/2 cup	sesame seeds	125 mL
1/2 cup	pumpkin seeds	125 mL
1/2 cup	unsalted sunflower seeds	125 mL
1/3 cup	vegetable oil	75 mL
1/3 cup	liquid honey	75 mL

1. Place $1\frac{1}{2}$ cups (375 mL) rolled oats, almonds and pecans in a food processor. Pulse several times until coarsely chopped.

2. In a large bowl, combine chopped oat mixture with remaining $1\frac{1}{2}$ cups (375 mL) rolled oats, coconut, wheat germ, sesame seeds, pumpkin seeds and sunflower seeds. Add oil and honey and combine thoroughly.

3. Spread granola over two parchment-lined baking sheets. Convection bake in a preheated 300°F (150°C) oven for 15 minutes, or until golden. Stir occasionally. Cool completely.

Oven French Toast with Caramelized Apples

Caramelized Apples

5	apples, peeled, cored and sliced	5
1/3 cup	packed brown sugar	75 mL
2 tbsp	butter, melted	25 mL
1 tsp	grated orange zest	5 mL
1/4 tsp	ground cinnamon	1 mL

French Toast

3	eggs	3
3/4 cup	milk	175 mL
2 tbsp	granulated sugar	25 mL
1/2 tsp	vanilla	2 mL
6	slices bread (about 3/4 inch/2 cm thick)	6

1. To prepare apples, in a large bowl, combine apples, brown sugar, melted butter, orange zest and cinnamon. Spoon into a lightly greased 8-inch (2 L) square baking dish.

2. To prepare French toast, in a large shallow dish, beat together eggs, milk, granulated sugar and vanilla. Add bread slices, turning gently to absorb liquid. Arrange on a lightly buttered parchment-lined baking sheet.

3. Convection bake apples and bread in a preheated 375°F (190°C) oven for 25 minutes, or until toast is golden and slightly crispy. Turn toast once during cooking. Stir apples gently twice during cooking (do not mash apples).

4. To serve, cut toast in half diagonally. Spoon apples on toast.

Makes 4 servings

The beauty of making French toast in the oven is the ease of cooking in one operation, rather than continuous pan-frying. Select an apple that holds its shape well, such as Northern Spy, Ida Red or Golden Delicious. Thickly sliced egg bread or cinnamon bread gives the best results. Other toppings could be seasonal fresh fruit such as sliced strawberries, blueberries, sliced peaches and even diced pineapple in winter months.

Make Ahead

Apples can be baked, covered and refrigerated up to a day ahead. Reheat at 375°F (190°C) for 12 minutes, or until hot.

B & B Maple French Toast

**Makes 6 to
8 servings**

At a local bed and
breakfast where I
taught cooking classes,
the last thing the
owners did before
retiring at night was
to assemble a version
of this dish. The next
morning, the French
toast just went into the
convection oven along
with bacon and baked
pineapple while they
made coffee, emptied
the dishwasher and
set the table.

8 to 10 slices	raisin bread or challah, cubed (about 8 cups/2 L loosely packed)	8 to 10 slices
5	eggs	5
2½ cups	milk	625 mL
½ cup	maple syrup	125 mL
3 tbsp	butter, melted	45 mL
1 tsp	vanilla	5 mL
½ tsp	ground cinnamon	2 mL
¼ cup	Irish whiskey or orange liqueur (optional)	50 mL

1. Spread bread cubes in a lightly greased 13- by 9-inch (3 L) baking dish.

2. In a bowl, whisk eggs, milk, maple syrup, melted butter, vanilla, cinnamon and whiskey, if using. Pour over bread. Press bread gently to submerge. Cover and refrigerate overnight.

3. Convection bake in a preheated 325°F (160°C) oven for 45 minutes, or until slightly puffed. Let stand for 10 minutes before serving. Cut into serving portions or spoon onto serving dishes.

Baked Pineapple and Blueberries
Combine 2 cups (500 mL) diced fresh pineapple and 2 tbsp (25 mL) orange juice in an 8-inch (2 L) square baking dish. Convection bake in a preheated 325°F (160°C) oven for 20 minutes, or until pineapple is just tender. Cool for 15 minutes. Stir in 1½ cups (375 mL) fresh blueberries. Makes 6 to 8 servings.

Baked Double Smoked Bacon
On a foil- and parchment-lined baking sheet, arrange 1 lb (500 g) thickly sliced double smoked bacon, with slices overlapping slightly. Convection bake in a preheated 325°F (160°C) oven for 35 to 40 minutes, or until cooked to your liking. Drain on paper towels. Makes 6 to 8 servings.

EASY OVEN MEAL

Brunch for 6

B & B Maple French Toast (page 172)
Baked Double Smoked Bacon (page 172)
Baked Pineapple and Blueberries (page 172)

- Assemble French toast the night before, cover and refrigerate.
- Let French toast stand at room temperature for 30 minutes before baking.
- Preheat oven.
- Place French toast in oven and bake for 20 minutes.
- Arrange bacon on baking sheet. Assemble pineapple dish.
- Add pineapple and bacon to oven and cook all three dishes for 25 minutes.
- Remove French toast and pineapple from oven and let sit while bacon continues to cook for 10 minutes. Stir blueberries into pineapple and let cool slightly.
- Drain bacon. Serve French toast with bacon and pineapple dish.

Cheese Blintzes with Berries

Makes 6 servings

Blintzes are a popular brunch item, and these can even be served as a dessert. Use homemade or storebought crêpes.

Sour cream and caramelized apples (page 171) also make great accompaniments.

Make Ahead

Blintzes can be assembled, wrapped well (even individually) and frozen. Convention bake in a preheated 375°F (190°C) oven for 20 minutes, or until hot. Assembled blintzes can also be covered and refrigerated overnight before baking.

2 cups	ricotta or small curd cottage cheese	500 mL
1	egg	1
2 tbsp	granulated sugar	25 mL
1/2 tsp	vanilla	2 mL
1/2 tsp	grated lemon or orange zest	2 mL
12	crêpes	12
2 tbsp	butter, melted	25 mL
1 cup	fresh or frozen strawberries	250 mL
1 cup	fresh or frozen raspberries	250 mL
2 tbsp	liquid honey or granulated sugar	25 mL

1. In a bowl or food processor, combine ricotta, egg, sugar, vanilla and lemon zest until smooth.

2. Arrange crêpes on a flat surface. Spoon filling (about 3 tbsp/45 mL) over center of each crêpe. Fold bottom of crêpe over filling and fold in sides. Fold down top of crêpe (like an envelope). Arrange crêpes seam side down on a parchment-lined baking sheet. Brush with melted butter.

3. Place strawberries (if you are using fresh strawberries, cut them in halves or quarters), raspberries and honey in an 8-inch (2 L) baking dish. Convection bake blintzes and berries in a preheated 325°F (160°C) oven for 25 minutes, or until blintzes are light golden and hot. Serve blintzes with berries spooned over top.

Crêpes

In a food processor or blender, combine 3 eggs, 3/4 cup (175 mL) all-purpose flour, 3/4 cup (175 mL) milk, 2 tbsp (25 mL) melted butter and 1/4 tsp (1 mL) salt. Blend until smooth.

Heat an 8-inch (20 cm) nonstick skillet over medium heat and brush lightly with butter. Pour 2 tbsp (25 mL) batter into pan and swirl over pan. Cook for 40 seconds. Turn and cook second side for 20 seconds. Slide crêpe onto a plate. Repeat with remaining batter, adding butter to pan as needed. Makes about 12 crêpes.

Asparagus, Chèvre and Smoked Salmon Frittata

1 lb	asparagus	500 g
2 tbsp	butter	25 mL
1	onion, chopped	1
6	eggs	6
¾ cup	crumbled chèvre	175 mL
¾ cup	diced smoked salmon (about 4 oz/125 g)	175 mL
⅓ cup	water	75 mL
2 tbsp	chopped fresh dillweed	25 mL
½ tsp	salt	2 mL
¼ tsp	black pepper	1 mL

1. Break off tough stem ends of asparagus. Cut asparagus into ½-inch (1 cm) pieces. Cook in boiling salted water for 3 minutes, or until tender. Drain and cool under cold running water. Drain well and pat dry with paper towels.

2. In a small skillet, melt butter over medium heat. Add onion. Cook, stirring occasionally, for 4 minutes.

3. In a bowl, beat eggs until blended. Stir in asparagus, onion, chèvre, smoked salmon, water, dill, salt and pepper. Pour mixture into a lightly greased 8-inch (2 L) square baking dish.

4. Convection bake in a preheated 350°F (180°C) oven for 25 to 30 minutes, or until frittata is set in center and top is golden. Let stand for 10 minutes before serving.

Variation
Spinach, Cheddar and Ham Frittata: Instead of asparagus, cook 10 oz (300 g) fresh spinach. Drain, squeeze dry and chop. Instead of chèvre, use 1 cup (250 mL) grated Cheddar or Gruyère cheese. Use diced ham, smoked chicken or turkey instead of the smoked salmon.

Makes 4 to 6 servings

The traditional frittata is usually started on the stove and finished in the oven, but in this recipe the frittata is baked like a crustless quiche. Most of the preparation can be done ahead; just whip up a quick salad while the frittata cooks.

This is an excellent springtime dish. For a vegetarian version, omit the salmon.

Cut leftovers into cubes or slice to serve on top of a salad or in a sandwich.

Make Ahead
Prepare all ingredients up to six hours in advance, cover and refrigerate. Assemble just before baking.

Night-Before Strata

Makes 6 to 8 servings

Every August our family reunion is held in a park in Orono, Ontario. Each family takes a turn organizing games and activities before a big potluck dinner.

One year we were asked to contribute recipes for a cookbook. This is a variation of one of the recipes. It is also suitable for lunch or supper.

12	slices slightly stale bread, preferably challah	12
2 tsp	Dijon, Russian-style or coarse-grain mustard	10 mL
1	10-oz (300 g) package frozen chopped spinach, defrosted and squeezed dry	1
3	green onions, chopped	3
1 cup	grated Gruyère or Cheddar cheese	250 mL
¼ cup	grated Parmesan cheese	50 mL
½ tsp	salt	2 mL
¼ tsp	black pepper	1 mL
¼ tsp	ground nutmeg	1 mL
5	eggs	5
3 cups	milk	750 mL

Topping

½ cup	cornflake crumbs	125 mL
½ cup	grated Gruyère or Cheddar cheese	125 mL
2 tbsp	butter, melted	25 mL

1. Spread 6 bread slices with mustard.

2. In a bowl, combine spinach, green onions, Gruyère, Parmesan, salt, pepper and nutmeg.

3. Spread spinach mixture over mustard and cover with remaining bread slices to make "sandwiches." Arrange sandwiches in a buttered 13- by 9-inch (3 L) baking dish.

4. In a large bowl, beat eggs and milk. Pour mixture over bread.

5. To prepare topping, in a separate bowl, combine cornflake crumbs, cheese and melted butter. Sprinkle over bread. Cover and refrigerate for 8 hours or overnight. Let sit at room temperature for 30 minutes before baking.

6. Convection bake in a preheated 325°F (160°C) oven for 50 to 55 minutes, or until puffed and golden. Let stand for 10 minutes before serving.

Prosciutto Onion Quiche

1	unbaked 9-inch (23 cm) pie shell	1
2 tsp	Dijon mustard	10 mL
1 cup	grated Gruyère cheese	250 mL
2 tbsp	butter	25 mL
2	onions, chopped	2
4	eggs	4
1½ cups	sour cream or milk	375 mL
½ tsp	salt	2 mL
¼ tsp	black pepper	1 mL
Pinch	ground nutmeg	Pinch
½ cup	diced prosciutto	125 mL
2 tbsp	chopped fresh basil or parsley	25 mL

1. Line pastry shell with foil or parchment paper and fill with pie weights or dry beans. Convection bake or roast in a preheated 400°F (200°C) oven for 15 to 18 minutes, or until golden around edges. Carefully remove weights and foil. Cool. Brush bottom of crust with mustard and sprinkle with cheese.

2. Meanwhile, in a large skillet, melt butter over medium heat. Add onions and cook until softened and just starting to color, about 5 minutes. Cool slightly.

3. In a large bowl, beat eggs until blended. Stir in sour cream, salt, pepper, nutmeg and onions. Pour into prepared pie shell.

4. Sprinkle prosciutto and basil over top of quiche. Convection bake or roast in a preheated 350°F (180°C) oven for 25 minutes, or until center is set and top is golden. Let sit for 10 minutes before serving.

Makes 6 servings

Although quiche comes and goes in fashion, it remains a favorite of many people. Try using different cheeses, cooked vegetables and meats such as ham or smoked salmon. For a vegetarian version, just omit the prosciutto.

Partially prebaking the pastry helps to prevent a soggy bottom crust.

Make Ahead
Pastry can be prebaked up to six hours ahead and kept at room temperature before adding filling.

Asparagus and Eggs with Curried Cheese Sauce

Makes 6 to 8 servings

My aunt Evelyn would prepare tasty luncheon dishes like this for her lady friends at their church get-togethers. She served this one with a spinach and orange salad. Roast the asparagus (page 117) or steam it until just cooked, drain well and pat dry.

Make Ahead
Prepare sauce and cool. Assemble dish completely (making sure all ingredients are cold), cover and refrigerate for up to six hours. Cook for an extra 5 to 10 minutes, or until hot.

Curried Cheese Sauce

2 tbsp	butter	25 mL
2 tbsp	all-purpose flour	25 mL
1 tsp	curry powder or paste	5 mL
½ tsp	dry mustard	2 mL
2 cups	milk	500 mL
1½ cups	grated Cheddar cheese	375 mL
¾ tsp	salt	4 mL
¼ tsp	paprika	1 mL

Asparagus and Eggs

1½ lbs	asparagus, trimmed, cooked and cut in 1-inch (2.5 cm) pieces	750 g
8	hard-cooked eggs	8
¼ cup	fresh bread crumbs	50 mL
2 tbsp	grated Parmesan cheese	25 mL

1. To prepare sauce, melt butter in a saucepan over medium heat. Add flour and curry powder and cook, stirring, for 3 minutes.

2. Whisk in mustard and milk. Bring sauce to a boil, reduce heat and simmer for 6 minutes, stirring occasionally. Remove from heat and stir in Cheddar, salt and paprika.

3. Spread asparagus in a lightly greased 12- by 8-inch (3 L) baking dish. Slice eggs and arrange over asparagus. Spoon sauce over eggs. Sprinkle top with bread crumbs and Parmesan.

4. Convection bake in a preheated 325°F (160°C) oven for 30 minutes, or until bubbling and golden.

> ### Hard-cooked Eggs
> Place eggs in a large saucepan and cover with cold water. Bring to a boil, remove from heat, cover and let stand for 12 minutes. Cool completely under cold running water or in iced water.

Potato and Sausage Pie

2 lbs	potatoes, peeled and cut in 2-inch (5 cm) pieces	1 kg
1 lb	sausage meat (Italian, pork, turkey), removed from casings	500 g
½ cup	buttermilk or milk	125 mL
2 tbsp	butter or olive oil	25 mL
2	eggs, beaten	2
¼ cup	grated Parmesan cheese	50 mL
2 tbsp	chopped fresh sage, or 1 tsp (5 mL) dried	25 mL
1 tsp	salt	5 mL
¼ tsp	black pepper	1 mL
Pinch	ground nutmeg	Pinch

1. In a large saucepan, cover potatoes with plenty of salted water. Bring to a boil and cook for 20 to 25 minutes, or until tender.

2. Meanwhile, cook sausage in a skillet over medium-high heat, breaking up meat, until lightly browned. Drain off excess fat.

3. Drain potatoes and mash. Add buttermilk, butter, eggs, cheese, sage, salt, pepper and nutmeg. Stir in cooked sausage meat.

4. Spoon mixture into a well-greased 10-inch (25 cm) pie plate or a shallow 6-cup (1.5 L) baking dish. Convection roast in a preheated 350°F (180°C) oven for 30 minutes, or until top is browned. Let stand for 5 to 10 minutes before serving in wedges or by spoonfuls.

Makes 6 servings

Ireland is famous for its potatoes, and when I traveled there I ate them served many different ways (sometimes three potato dishes at the same meal). This is a version I had at one of the many bed and breakfasts where I stayed. Leftover mashed potatoes can also be used; you will need about 3 cups (750 mL).

Make Ahead
Prepare potato and sausage mixture. Cool separately. Assemble dish, cover and refrigerate for up to six hours. Cook for an extra 10 minutes, or until hot.

Potluck Corned Beef Hash

Makes 4 to 6 servings

This is a version of a recipe from Greta Holmes, who served it at her pony club brunches. She also made a version for her daughter's wedding rehearsal party.

Frozen hash browns are a popular convenience food (use them in their frozen state), but if you happen to have leftover cooked potatoes, you can use them instead. Serve the hash with eggs and chili sauce, relish or salsa. You can also omit the meat and serve this as a side dish.

Make Ahead

Assemble, cover and refrigerate for up to four hours. Bake for an extra 10 minutes, or until hot.

3 cups	frozen hash brown potatoes	750 mL
1 cup	corn kernels	250 mL
3	green onions, chopped	3
1½ cups	diced cooked corned beef, turkey or chicken	375 mL
1	10-oz (284 mL) can cream of celery soup	1
1 cup	sour cream	250 mL
1 cup	grated Cheddar cheese	250 mL
3 tbsp	chopped fresh dillweed or parsley	45 mL
½ tsp	salt	2 mL
¼ tsp	black pepper	1 mL
⅓ cup	diced roasted red pepper (optional)	75 mL
½ cup	cornflake crumbs	125 mL
2 tbsp	olive oil or melted butter	25 mL

1. In a large bowl, combine potatoes, corn, green onions, corned beef, soup, sour cream, cheese, dill, salt, pepper and roasted red pepper, if using. Spoon into a greased 6-cup (1.5 L) baking dish.

2. In a small bowl, combine cornflake crumbs and oil. Sprinkle over hash. Convection bake in a preheated 350°F (180°C) oven for 30 to 35 minutes, or until top is crispy.

Oven Home Fries
with Peameal Bacon

2 lbs	cooked potatoes, cut in ½-inch (1 cm) pieces (about 6 cups/1.5 L)	1 kg
3	onions, cut in ½-inch (1 cm) pieces	3
3	cloves garlic, coarsely chopped	3
3 tbsp	olive oil	45 mL
¾ tsp	salt	4 mL
½ tsp	dried marjoram or oregano leaves	2 mL
¼ tsp	black pepper	1 mL
¼ tsp	paprika	1 mL
1½ lbs	peameal (Canadian) bacon, sliced	750 g

1. In a large bowl, toss together potatoes, onions, garlic, olive oil, salt, marjoram, pepper and paprika. Spread in a single layer on a parchment-lined baking sheet.

2. Convection bake in a preheated 425°F (220°C) oven for 30 to 35 minutes, or until golden and slightly crispy. Stir gently twice during cooking.

3. Meanwhile, arrange bacon slices slightly overlapping on a separate parchment-lined baking sheet. Place on another shelf in oven. Cook for 10 to 12 minutes, or until golden around edges. (Timing will depend on thickness of bacon.) Serve with potatoes.

Makes 5 to 6 servings

This dish always reminds me of the hearty specials served at diners. You can add your own touches such as mushrooms, herbs or sun-dried tomatoes. My grandmother cooked home fries in a well-seasoned cast-iron frying pan using bacon fat, stale bread cubes, green onions, sage and leftover cooked potatoes — what a memory.

With the convection oven, trays of home fries can be prepared for a hungry group, with the peameal bacon added to the oven during the last half of the cooking time. Cook extra potatoes the day before to use in this dish (I usually leave the skins on).

Tuna Melt with Brie Wraps

Makes 4 wraps

Although this is served as a wrap (use regular flour or spinach tortillas), it is equally pleasing spread on hearty bread, crusty rolls or English muffins. Serve with fresh vegetables or greens. Other cheeses such as Cheddar, Havarti or provolone can also be used.

2	6-oz (170 g) cans tuna, drained	2
1/4 cup	chopped dill pickle or sweet pickle	50 mL
1	stalk celery, finely chopped	1
1/4 cup	mayonnaise	50 mL
1 tbsp	lemon juice	15 mL
4 oz	Brie, cut in small pieces	125 g
4	9-inch (23 cm) flour tortillas	4

1. In a bowl, combine tuna, pickle, celery, mayonnaise, lemon juice and cheese.
2. Place tortillas on a flat surface. Spread tuna mixture down center of each tortilla to within 2 inches (5 cm) of edge. Fold up bottom of tortilla, tuck in sides and roll up to enclose filling.
3. Arrange wraps seam side down on a parchment-lined baking sheet. Convection bake in a preheated 350°F (180°C) oven for 12 minutes. To serve, cut each wrap in half on a slight diagonal.

Open-face Reuben Sandwiches

Makes 4 servings

This adaptation of the classic sandwich is almost a full meal. Serve with dill pickles or a small green salad. Use any rye or grainy bread.

4	slices rye bread	4
1 tbsp	mayonnaise	15 mL
2 tsp	Dijon or coarse-grain mustard	10 mL
4 oz	corned beef, thinly sliced	125 g
1 cup	sauerkraut, well drained	250 mL
4	slices Swiss cheese	4

1. Arrange bread slices on a baking sheet. Top with mayonnaise, mustard, corned beef, sauerkraut and cheese.
2. Convection bake in a preheated 350°F (180°C) oven for 5 to 6 minutes, or until cheese melts.

Mushroom and Bacon Sandwiches

3 cups	thinly sliced mushrooms	750 mL
2 tbsp	olive oil	25 mL
2 tbsp	chopped fresh parsley	25 mL
2	cloves garlic, minced	2
1 tsp	chopped fresh tarragon, or ¼ tsp (1 mL) dried	5 mL
¼ tsp	salt	1 mL
¼ tsp	black pepper	1 mL
8	lean slices bacon	8
4	thick slices multigrain, seed or whole wheat bread	4
4	slices provolone or mozzarella cheese	4

1. In a medium bowl, combine mushrooms with olive oil, parsley, garlic, tarragon, salt and pepper. Spread on a parchment-lined baking sheet.

2. Arrange bacon slices on a foil-lined baking sheet.

3. Convection bake bacon in a preheated 375°F (190°C) oven for 15 minutes. Add mushrooms to oven and continue to bake for 10 minutes, or until bacon is slightly crispy. Remove bacon and mushrooms from oven. Drain bacon on paper towels.

4. Meanwhile, place bread on a baking sheet. Toast in oven for 5 minutes. Turn bread slices.

5. Spoon mushrooms over bread and top with bacon and cheese. Return to oven until cheese melts, about 3 to 4 minutes. Serve hot.

Makes 4 servings

When I worked at a hotel in Australia, the most popular sandwich was a clubhouse, so bacon was always cooked ahead. Most restaurants "tray" bacon, cooking it slightly overlapping on trays in the oven, then draining off the fat. You can use the same technique in the home convection oven.

Easy Cheese Soufflé

Makes 4 servings

For some reason, soufflés seem to alarm the novice cook. Yet a soufflé is simply a cheese sauce with beaten egg whites folded in before baking. The only tricky part is the timing — guests should be at the table when the soufflé emerges from the oven.

If you do not have a soufflé dish, use a deep casserole with straight sides. Serve with a green salad or steamed asparagus or broccoli. Cut any leftovers into small pieces and serve on top of a salad.

¼ cup	butter	50 mL
¼ cup	all-purpose flour	50 mL
1½ cups	hot milk	375 mL
½ tsp	dry mustard	2 mL
¼ tsp	salt	1 mL
¼ tsp	black pepper	1 mL
Pinch	ground nutmeg	Pinch
6	eggs, separated	6
1 cup	grated Cheddar cheese	250 mL
¼ tsp	cream of tartar	1 mL

1. In a large, heavy saucepan, melt butter over medium-low heat. Add flour and cook, stirring, for 3 minutes without browning.

2. Whisk in hot milk, mustard, salt, pepper and nutmeg. Cook, stirring constantly, for 2 minutes, or until sauce thickens. Remove from heat.

3. In a medium bowl, beat egg yolks. Stir ½ cup (125 mL) hot sauce into yolks. Add yolks back to sauce and cook for 1 minute. Remove from heat and let sit for 10 minutes. Stir in cheese.

4. In a large, very clean bowl, beat egg whites with cream of tartar until stiff (but not dry) peaks form. Stir one quarter of egg whites into cooled cheese base. Then add cheese mixture to remaining egg whites. Gently fold into whites. Turn into a buttered 8-cup (2 L) soufflé dish. Smooth surface.

5. Convection bake in a preheated 325°F (160°C) oven for 35 to 40 minutes, or until top is firm yet soufflé is slightly jiggly. Serve immediately.

Portobello Pizzas

4	large portobello mushrooms	4
2 tsp	olive oil	10 mL
1	clove garlic, minced	1
¼ tsp	salt	1 mL
¼ tsp	black pepper	1 mL
1 cup	grated mozzarella cheese	250 mL
1	large tomato, chopped	1
¼ cup	shredded fresh basil	50 mL
¼ cup	grated Parmesan cheese	50 mL

1. Remove stems from mushrooms and scrape out gills. Place mushrooms stemmed side up on a parchment-lined baking sheet.

2. Combine oil and garlic. Spoon or brush over mushrooms. Sprinkle mushrooms with salt and pepper and top with mozzarella, tomato, basil and Parmesan.

3. Convection roast "pizzas" in a preheated 400°F (200°C) oven for 10 to 12 minutes, or until mushrooms are just tender and cheese melts.

Makes 4 servings

Portobello mushrooms make perfect "crusts" for pizza toppings, and they provide a change from the traditional bready base.

These can be served as a hearty appetizer, brunch or lunch item. Serve with an arugula salad.

Fontina and Grape Flatbread
Serve this for brunch or as a snack.

Defrost half a 14-oz (397 g) package frozen puff pastry. On a lightly floured surface, roll pastry into a 16- by 6-inch (40 by 15 cm) rectangle. Place on a parchment-lined baking sheet and crimp edges slightly.

Spread pastry with 1½ cups (375 mL) diced or grated Fontina cheese. Top with 1¼ cups (300 mL) halved red seedless grapes and 2 tsp (10 mL) chopped fresh rosemary.

Convection bake in a preheated 375°F (190°C) oven for 15 to 18 minutes, or until pastry is cooked and golden brown (underside of pastry should be golden).

Gently slide pastry onto a rack and cool for 5 minutes. Cut into serving pieces. Makes 10 to 12 slices.

Homemade Pizza

**Makes two
12-inch (30 cm)
pizzas**

Homemade pizza is
easy to make. Use the
suggested toppings
or substitute your
own favorite.

Each topping
provides enough for
two pizzas (one whole
recipe of dough). You
can halve the topping
recipes to prepare
two different pizzas.

For a nice finish,
brush the edges of
the crust with olive oil
as soon as the pizzas
come out of the oven.

1	recipe Rosemary Garlic Fougasse (page 203)	1

Tomato and Mushroom Topping

2 tbsp	olive oil	25 mL
4 cups	sliced mushrooms	1 L
¼ tsp	salt	1 mL
¼ tsp	black pepper	1 mL
1 cup	tomato sauce	250 mL
3 cups	grated mozzarella cheese	750 mL
⅓ cup	grated Parmesan cheese	75 mL

Pesto and Chèvre Topping

1½ cups	lightly packed basil leaves	375 mL
1	clove garlic, peeled	1
⅓ cup	grated Parmesan cheese	75 mL
1 tsp	lemon juice	5 mL
2 tbsp	pine nuts (optional)	25 mL
4	tomatoes, thinly sliced	4
¾ cup	crumbled chèvre	175 mL

1. For dough, prepare one recipe Rosemary Garlic Fougasse (omit rosemary and garlic if desired). After dough has risen, divide into two equal portions.

2. On a lightly floured surface, roll each half into a 12-inch (30 cm) circle. (Rest dough occasionally if it springs back.) Place dough on a pizza pan or baking sheet dusted with cornmeal or semolina. Stretch dough gently if it shrinks.

3. To prepare tomato-mushroom topping, heat oil in a large skillet over medium-high heat. Add mushrooms and cook, stirring occasionally, for 10 minutes, or until mushrooms are golden and moisture has evaporated. Season with salt and pepper. Remove from heat and let sit for 10 minutes.

4. To assemble, spread tomato sauce over dough to within 1 inch (2.5 cm) of edge. Sprinkle sauce with mozzarella. Arrange mushrooms over cheese and top with Parmesan.

5. To prepare pesto topping, in a food processor or blender, combine basil, garlic, Parmesan, lemon juice and pine nuts, if using. Process until pureed.

6. To assemble pizza, spread pesto over dough to within 1 inch (2.5 cm) of edge. Arrange tomato slices in a single layer over pesto. Top with chèvre.

7. Convection bake pizzas in a preheated 425°F (220°C) oven for 15 to 18 minutes, or until crust is golden and puffed.

Nachos Pizzas

3	10-inch (25 cm) flour tortillas	3
1 cup	canned refried beans	250 mL
1 cup	grated Cheddar cheese	250 mL
½ cup	taco sauce or tomato salsa	125 mL
¼ cup	chopped red or green onion	50 mL
¼ cup	chopped jalapeño pepper	50 mL
1 cup	grated Monterey Jack cheese	250 mL
3 tbsp	chopped fresh cilantro	45 mL

1. Place each tortilla on a baking sheet (one pizza per rack). Spread tortillas with refried beans, Cheddar, taco sauce, onion, jalapeño and Monterey Jack.

2. Convection bake in a preheated 425°F (220°C) oven for 6 to 8 minutes, or until cheese is melted and bubbly. Sprinkle with cilantro.

Makes 3 individual pizzas

All the flavors of nachos show up in this quickly assembled pizza, and baking three or more is easy when you use the multiple racks of the convection oven. Use regular or flavored tortillas. Pass sour cream or guacamole (page 37) if you wish. Serve with Margaritas, sangria or lemonade.

> **Tortilla Chips**
> Cut tortillas into wedges with scissors or a sharp knife. Arrange in a single layer on parchment-lined baking sheets. Brush with olive oil. Sprinkle with coarse salt and dried herbs if desired. Convection bake in a preheated 375°F (190°C) oven for 8 to 10 minutes, or until light golden and crisp. Cool and store in a sealed container for up to three days.

Speedy Polenta Gratin

Makes 6 to 8 servings

Good-quality prepared polenta (packaged in a round tube) and tomato sauces are now readily available in most supermarkets and specialty food shops (they are often located in the pasta section). Take advantage of them to prepare this dish that can be baked quickly in the convection oven. Cook some sausages at the same time, for a complete meal.

This recipe can easily be halved.

2½ cups	tomato sauce	625 mL
2 lbs	prepared polenta, cut in ½-inch (1 cm) slices	1 kg
¼ cup	pesto	50 mL
1 cup	corn kernels	250 mL
2 cups	grated mozzarella cheese, divided	500 mL
¼ cup	grated Parmesan cheese	50 mL

1. Spoon one-third of tomato sauce over bottom of a lightly oiled 13- by 9-inch (3 L) baking dish. Arrange half of polenta slices over sauce. Spread with pesto, corn, half the mozzarella and one-third of tomato sauce. Arrange remaining polenta over sauce. Spread with remaining tomato sauce. Sprinkle with remaining mozzarella and Parmesan.

2. Convection bake in a preheated 350°F (180°C) oven for 30 to 35 minutes, or until sauce is bubbling and top is golden. Let stand for 10 minutes before serving.

Baked Italian Sausages
Arrange 6 to 8 Italian sausages on a lightly greased foil-lined baking sheet or shallow baking pan. Pierce sausages with fork. Convection bake in a preheated 350°F (180°C) oven for 35 to 40 minutes, or until browned and cooked. Turn once during cooking. Drain on paper towels. Makes 6 to 8 servings.

Baked Polenta Slices
Arrange polenta slices on a parchment-lined baking sheet. Brush with olive oil and sprinkle with cheese such as Parmesan or Gorgonzola. Convection bake in a preheated 325°F (160°C) oven for 15 minutes, or until hot and cheese has melted. Serve as a side dish or with a salad.

Tofu with Sesame Hoisin Glaze

1	12-oz (350 g) package extra-firm tofu, patted dry and cut in ½-inch (1 cm) slices	1
3 tbsp	hoisin sauce	45 mL
3 tbsp	orange juice	45 mL
1 tbsp	tomato paste	15 mL
1 tbsp	sesame oil	15 mL
2 tsp	rice vinegar	10 mL
1 tsp	liquid honey or granulated sugar	5 mL
1 tbsp	sesame seeds	15 mL
¼ tsp	hot chili paste or hot pepper sauce (optional)	1 mL
2	green onions, sliced on the diagonal	2

Makes 4 servings

Tofu is high in protein and virtually cholesterol free. To encourage family and guests to enjoy tofu, marinate it in flavored sauces rather than serving it plain.

1. Arrange tofu slices in a single layer in a lightly greased 8-inch (2 L) square baking dish.

2. In a bowl, combine hoisin sauce, orange juice, tomato paste, sesame oil, vinegar, honey, sesame seeds and hot chili paste, if using. Spoon over tofu and turn slices to coat.

3. Convection bake in a preheated 325°F (160°C) oven for 20 to 25 minutes, or until sauce is bubbling. Garnish with green onions.

Make Ahead

The tofu and sauce can be prepared and assembled a day ahead. Cover and refrigerate. Let stand at room temperature for a half hour before baking.

> **Variation**
> *Chicken with Sesame Hoisin Glaze:* Place four 6-oz (175 g) boneless, skinless chicken breasts in a single layer in baking dish. Prepare sauce and pour over chicken, turning chicken to coat with sauce. Cover and marinate, refrigerated, for up to 4 hours. Arrange chicken on a parchment-lined baking sheet. Spoon sauce over chicken. Convection bake for 25 to 30 minutes, or until juices run clear.

Vegetable Strudel

Makes 6 to 8 servings

Perfect for a brunch or luncheon, this strudel can also be served as a dinner side dish or vegetarian main course. If the leeks are large, one would be adequate.

Make Ahead

The filling can be prepared, covered and refrigerated up to a day in advance. The strudel can be rolled, covered and refrigerated up to six hours before baking.

2 tbsp	olive oil	25 mL
2	leeks, white part only, thinly sliced	2
2	cloves garlic, finely chopped	2
1	red bell pepper, seeded and diced	1
1	10-oz (300 g) package frozen chopped spinach, defrosted and squeezed dry	1
1 cup	grated Gruyère or Fontina cheese	250 mL
¼ cup	chopped fresh parsley	50 mL
¼ cup	chopped fresh dillweed	50 mL
½ tsp	salt	2 mL
¼ tsp	black pepper	1 mL
Pinch	ground nutmeg	Pinch
6	sheets phyllo pastry	6
¼ cup	butter, melted	50 mL
¼ cup	dry bread crumbs	50 mL

1. In a large skillet, heat oil over medium-high heat. Add leeks, garlic and pepper and cook, stirring frequently, for 4 minutes, or until softened. Remove vegetables to a large bowl and let stand for 20 minutes.

2. Add spinach, cheese, parsley, dill, salt, pepper and nutmeg to leek mixture. Mix thoroughly.

3. To assemble, place a sheet of phyllo on a flat surface. Brush with some melted butter and sprinkle with some bread crumbs. Place second sheet of phyllo on top of first one. Brush with butter and sprinkle with crumbs. Repeat until all phyllo is used.

4. Spoon filling lengthwise along phyllo about 2 inches (5 cm) from long edge. Roll up pastry to make a long roll. Carefully lift onto a parchment-lined baking sheet, seam side down. Brush with melted butter. Cut 6 to 8 slits in top of strudel to mark serving pieces.

5. Convection bake or roast in a preheated 350°F (180°C) oven for 30 minutes, or until golden. Let stand for 10 minutes. Cut into serving pieces along slits.

Yeast Breads

Traditional White Bread

Makes two 8- by 4-inch (1.5 L) loaves

When I teach bread making, I encourage students to start with a simple white or whole wheat bread to see how yeast works and how dough feels and reacts at various stages.

Make Ahead

Cooled bread and rolls can be packaged well and frozen for up to three weeks.

¼ cup	warm water	50 mL
1 tsp	granulated sugar	5 mL
1 tbsp	active dry yeast (1 package)	15 mL
1½ cups	warm milk	375 mL
1 cup	warm water	250 mL
2 tbsp	butter, melted, or vegetable oil	25 mL
2½ tsp	salt	12 mL
2 tbsp	granulated sugar (optional)	25 mL
6 cups	all-purpose flour (approx.)	1.5 L

1. In a large bowl, combine warm water and sugar. Sprinkle yeast over top. Let stand until foamy, about 10 minutes.

2. Add milk, water, melted butter, salt and sugar, if using. Gradually add 5 cups (1.25 L) flour to yeast mixture, stirring to combine. Stir in enough additional flour to make a soft dough.

3. Turn out onto a floured surface and knead for 8 minutes, adding just enough flour to keep dough from sticking. Place in a large, lightly oiled bowl, turning dough to coat with oil. Cover bowl with plastic wrap and let dough rise until doubled, about 1 hour.

4. Deflate dough and divide in half. Shape into 2 loaves. Place in 2 lightly greased 8- by 4-inch (1.5 L) loaf pans. Let rise for 50 to 60 minutes, or until doubled.

5. Convection bake in a preheated 350°F (180°C) oven for 30 to 35 minutes, or until loaves are browned and sound hollow when tapped on bottom. Remove loaves from pans and cool on wire racks.

Variation

White Rolls: Divide dough into 18 portions. Shape each piece of dough into a round or slightly oblong roll. Arrange rolls, at least 2 inches (5 cm) apart, on parchment-lined baking sheets and let rise for 35 to 40 minutes. Convection bake rolls for 15 minutes, or until browned. Makes 18 rolls.

Fall-off-the-Bone Ribs (page 115)

Overleaf: Chicken and Broccoli Bake (page 132)

Basic Whole Wheat Bread

1 cup	warm water	250 mL
2 tsp	granulated sugar	10 mL
2 tbsp	active dry yeast (2 packages)	25 mL
1½ cups	warm milk	375 mL
¼ cup	vegetable oil or butter, melted	50 mL
2 tbsp	molasses or liquid honey	25 mL
1 tbsp	salt	15 mL
3 cups	whole wheat flour	750 mL
3 cups	all-purpose flour (approx.)	750 mL
½ cup	natural bran or wheat germ	125 mL

Makes two 8- by 4-inch (1.5 L) loaves

Using whole wheat flour and bran results in a wholesome loaf with a nutty taste, but the bread will rise more slowly and have a slightly coarser texture than a bread made with all white flour. White whole wheat flour has also started to appear on the market; it can be substituted for regular whole wheat flour.

Make Ahead

Bread can be cooled, wrapped well and frozen for two weeks.

1. In a large bowl, combine warm water and sugar. Sprinkle yeast over top. Let stand until foamy, about 10 minutes.

2. Stir in milk, oil, molasses and salt.

3. In a separate bowl, combine whole wheat flour, 2 cups (500 mL) all-purpose flour and bran. Add gradually to yeast mixture, stirring to combine. Stir in enough additional flour to make a soft dough.

4. Turn out onto a floured surface and knead for 6 to 8 minutes, adding just enough flour to keep dough from sticking. Place in a large, lightly oiled bowl, turning dough to coat with oil. Cover bowl with plastic wrap and let dough rise until doubled, about 1 to 1¼ hours.

5. Deflate dough. Divide in half and form into 2 loaves. Place in lightly greased 8- by 4-inch (1.5 L) loaf pans. Let dough rise for 50 to 60 minutes, or until not quite doubled. (Do not let bread overrise, or it may collapse on itself. If this should happen before baking, reshape and let rise again.)

6. Convection bake in a preheated 350°F (180°C) oven for 30 to 35 minutes, or until loaves are golden-brown and sound hollow when tapped on bottom. Remove loaves from pans and cool on wire rack.

Overleaf: Warm Chèvre Salad with Mexican Pesto (page 162)
Oven French Toast with Caramelized Apples (page 171)

Whole Wheat Grain Bread

Makes two 7-inch (18 cm) loaves

A rustic-looking free-form bread to serve with cheese, or to make sandwiches and toast. The recipe easily doubles. Eight-grain cereal is available in bulk food stores (it is sometimes called seven-grain or twelve-grain cereal). Store it in the refrigerator or freezer.

Make Ahead

Baked bread can be cooled, wrapped well and frozen for up to three weeks.

2 cups	warm water	500 mL
1 tbsp	active dry yeast (1 package)	15 mL
1 tbsp	liquid honey	15 mL
1 tbsp	vegetable oil	15 mL
1½ tsp	salt	7 mL
½ cup	uncooked eight-grain cereal	125 mL
2 cups	whole wheat flour	500 mL
2 cups	all-purpose flour (approx.)	500 mL

1. In a large bowl, combine water, yeast, honey, oil and salt. Stir and let rest for 5 minutes, or until yeast becomes bubbly.

2. Add cereal, whole wheat flour and 1½ cups (375 mL) all-purpose flour. Stir to combine and form a soft dough. Add more all-purpose flour until dough is too stiff to stir, then turn out onto a floured surface. Knead for 8 minutes, adding enough flour to make a pliable dough. (If you are using an electric mixer fitted with dough hook, knead for about 5 minutes.)

3. Place dough in a lightly oiled bowl, turning to coat dough with oil. Cover bowl with plastic wrap. Let rise until doubled, about 1 hour.

4. Deflate dough and knead for 4 minutes. Divide into 2 portions. Shape into round loaves about 6 inches (15 cm) in diameter. Place seam side down on a lightly floured baking sheet. Let rise for 20 minutes.

5. Convection bake in a preheated 400°F (200°C) oven for 20 minutes. Reduce heat to 325°F (160°C) and continue to bake for 15 to 18 minutes, or until loaves are golden brown and sound hollow when tapped on bottom. Remove from pan and cool on wire racks.

Anadama Bread

2¾ cups	warm water	675 mL
1 tsp	granulated sugar	5 mL
1 tbsp	active dry yeast (1 package)	15 mL
¼ cup	butter, melted, or vegetable oil	50 mL
3 tbsp	molasses	45 mL
1 tbsp	salt	15 mL
¾ cup	cornmeal	175 mL
6 cups	all-purpose flour (approx.)	1.5 L

1. In a large bowl, combine warm water and sugar. Sprinkle yeast over top. Let stand until foamy, about 10 minutes.

2. Stir in melted butter, molasses and salt. Add cornmeal and mix well. Stir in 5 cups (1.25 L) flour. Add enough additional flour to make a soft dough.

3. Turn out onto a floured surface and knead for about 8 minutes, adding enough flour to keep dough from sticking. Shape dough into a ball. Place in a large, lightly oiled bowl, turning dough to coat with oil. Cover bowl with plastic wrap and let rise until doubled, about 1 hour.

4. Deflate dough. Divide in half and shape into 2 loaves. Place seam side down in lightly greased 8- by 4-inch (1.5 L) loaf pans. Let rise for 50 to 60 minutes, or until doubled.

5. Convection bake in a preheated 350°F (180°C) oven for 35 to 40 minutes, or until tops are brown and loaves sound hollow when tapped on bottom. Remove loaves from pans and cool on a wire rack.

> ### Variation
> *Crusty Cornmeal Rolls:* Divide dough into 18 pieces and shape into round rolls. Place seam side down, at least 2 inches (5 cm) apart, on parchment-lined baking sheets. Let rise for 40 minutes. Convection bake for 20 minutes, or until browned. Makes 18 rolls.

Makes two 8- by 4-inch (1.5 L) loaves

Apparently, a woman named Anna left her husband with only cornmeal mush, so he eventually turned it into a bread, while muttering, "Anna, damn her." There are as many variations to this story as there are for this golden bread textured with cornmeal, but it is great for toast or to serve with baked beans. You can also shape it into rolls.

Baked in the convection oven, a light crust forms early, sealing in the moisture.

Make Ahead
Bread and rolls can be baked, cooled, wrapped well and frozen for up to three weeks.

Potato Hamburger Buns

**Makes
12 large buns**

For a couple of summers I baked breads, cookies and pies to sell at the local farmer's market. Potato bread was one of the most popular items (it makes great toast!), and now, ten years later, I still bake it for special orders.

When making a potato dough, it seems as if you could keep adding flour forever. However, try not to add much more than 4½ cups (1.125 L); the dough should still be slightly sticky. Use older or baking potatoes that mash well.

Make Ahead
Cool buns completely, package and freeze for up to three weeks.

12 oz	potatoes, peeled (2 medium)	375 g
1 tbsp	active dry yeast (1 package)	15 mL
6 tsp	granulated sugar, divided	30 mL
2 tbsp	olive oil	25 mL
2 tsp	salt	10 mL
4½ cups	all-purpose flour (approx.)	1.125 L

1. In a saucepan, cover potatoes with cold salted water. Bring to a boil and cook for 25 minutes, or until tender. Drain well, reserving 1¾ cups (425 mL) potato-cooking water.

2. Mash potatoes well (but don't worry if there are still lumps). Cool potatoes and potato-cooking water until warm.

3. In a large bowl, combine yeast, 1 tsp (5 mL) sugar and warm potato water. Let stand for 10 minutes, or until mixture is foamy.

4. Stir in potatoes, oil, remaining sugar, salt and 3½ cups (875 mL) flour to make a sticky dough. Stir in additional flour until dough is too stiff to stir.

5. Turn dough onto a floured surface. Knead, adding enough flour to make a pliable dough (dough may be slightly sticky), about 10 minutes. (If you are using an electric mixer fitted with dough hook, knead for about 5 minutes.)

6. Shape dough into a ball and place in a lightly oiled bowl. Turn dough to coat with oil. Cover bowl with plastic wrap. Let dough rise for 1¼ to 1½ hours, or until doubled.

7. Deflate dough and turn out onto a floured surface. Roll roughly into a rope. Divide into 12 pieces.

8. Shape each piece into a round flattened bun about 4 inches (10 cm) in diameter. Place on two flour-dusted baking sheets. Dust tops with flour. Let rise for 15 minutes, then flatten slightly. Let rise for 20 minutes longer.

9. Convection bake in a preheated 375°F (190°C) oven for 22 to 25 minutes, or until golden. Cool on wire racks.

Rye Caraway Bread

2⅓ cups	warm water	575 mL
1 tsp	granulated sugar	5 mL
1 tbsp	active dry yeast (1 package)	15 mL
2 tbsp	molasses	25 mL
2 tbsp	butter, melted, or vegetable oil	25 mL
1 tbsp	red wine vinegar or cider vinegar	15 mL
2 tsp	grated orange zest	10 mL
2 tsp	salt	10 mL
1 tbsp	caraway seeds	15 mL
2 cups	rye flour	500 mL
3 cups	all-purpose flour (approx.)	750 mL

1. In a large bowl, combine warm water and sugar. Sprinkle yeast over top. Let stand until foamy, about 10 minutes.

2. Stir in molasses, melted butter, vinegar, orange zest, salt and caraway seeds. Stir in rye flour and 1½ cups (375 mL) all-purpose flour. Gradually stir in 1 cup (250 mL) remaining all-purpose flour to make a soft, slightly sticky dough.

3. Turn out onto a lightly floured surface and knead for 8 minutes, adding enough flour to make a soft dough. Shape into a ball. Place in a large, lightly oiled bowl, turning dough to coat with oil. Cover bowl with plastic wrap and let dough rise until doubled, about 1 hour.

4. Deflate dough and divide in half. Shape into round loaves about 6 inches (15 cm) in diameter. Place seam side down on two parchment-lined baking sheets. Let rise for 45 minutes, or until almost doubled. Dust with a little rye flour.

5. Convection bake in a preheated 375°F (190°C) oven for 30 to 35 minutes, or until loaves are browned and sound hollow when tapped on bottom. Cool on wire racks.

Makes two 8-inch (20 cm) round loaves

With so many varieties of rye bread on the market, why make your own? Well, this bread is one reason. Scented with orange zest and scattered with caraway seeds, it makes a fine bread for sandwiches and even toast. For a more peasant-style bread, use stone ground dark rye flour (buy it in small amounts and store any extra in the refrigerator or freezer to keep it fresh).

Make Ahead

Bread can be made ahead, cooled, wrapped well and frozen for up to three weeks.

Challah (Egg Bread)

**Makes two
12-inch (30 cm)
loaves**

A delicate, rich bread
that should be in
every home cook's
repertoire. Not only
is it spectacular as a
braid, it is a versatile
dough that can also be
used to make smaller
rolls or hamburger buns.

Use any extra bread
in French toast or
bread pudding.

Make Ahead
All items can be cooled,
wrapped well and frozen
for up to two weeks.

½ cup	warm water	125 mL
2 tsp	granulated sugar	10 mL
1 tbsp	active dry yeast (1 package)	15 mL
1¼ cups	milk	300 mL
⅓ cup	butter	75 mL
⅓ cup	liquid honey	75 mL
2½ tsp	salt	12 mL
3	eggs	3
7 cups	all-purpose flour (approx.)	1.75 L
Glaze		
1	egg	1
1 tbsp	milk	15 mL
1 tbsp	sesame seeds	15 mL

1. In a large bowl, combine warm water and sugar. Sprinkle yeast over top. Let stand until foamy, about 10 minutes.

2. In a saucepan, combine milk, butter, honey and salt. Heat just to lukewarm — no more than 110°F (45°C). If mixture gets too hot, cool slightly, or heat will kill yeast. Beat in eggs. Add to yeast mixture and stir in.

3. Stir in 6 cups (1.5 L) flour, adding enough flour to make a soft dough. Turn out onto a floured surface and knead for 8 to 10 minutes to make a smooth dough, adding just enough flour to keep dough from sticking. Shape into a ball. Place in a large, lightly buttered or oiled bowl, turning dough to coat with butter. Cover bowl with plastic wrap and let dough rise until doubled, about 1 hour.

4. Deflate dough and divide in half. Divide each half into three even pieces (each braid will have three ropes). Roll each piece into a rope about 12 inches (30 cm) long. For each loaf, braid together 3 ropes, pinching ends together and tucking under braid.

5. Place each loaf on a parchment-lined baking sheet. Let rise for 1 hour, or until doubled.

6. For glaze, in a small bowl, beat together egg and milk. Brush over loaves. Sprinkle with sesame seeds.

7. Convection bake in a preheated 325°F (160°C) oven for 30 to 35 minutes, or until loaves are golden brown and sound hollow when tapped on bottom. Cool on wire racks.

Variations

Dinner Rolls: Divide dough into 20 to 24 pieces. Shape into rolls and place seam side down, at least 2 inches (5 cm) apart, on parchment-lined baking sheets. Let rise for 25 minutes, or until doubled. Glaze and sesame seeds can be omitted. Convection bake for 15 minutes, or until golden. Watch carefully as they brown quickly.

Hamburger Buns: Divide dough into 14 to 16 pieces (depending on size of hamburgers). Shape into flattened rounds. Place seam side down, at least 2 inches (5 cm) apart, on parchment-lined baking sheets and let rise for about 35 to 40 minutes, or until doubled. Convection bake for 20 minutes, or until golden.

Olive and Sun-dried Tomato Focaccia

Makes 1 large focaccia

With so many mediocre focaccias sold in stores, it is a treat to have a superior homemade one. It is a bit fussy to knead in the olives and tomatoes, but well worth the effort.

For smaller focaccias, divide the dough into two to four pieces, shape, place on baking sheets and bake for 12 minutes, or until golden.

Make Ahead

After cooling, focaccia can be cut into smaller pieces, wrapped well and frozen for up to two weeks. For maximum flavor, defrost and convection bake in a preheated 350°F (180°C) oven for 8 minutes, or until warm. Or convection bake from frozen state at 300°F (150°C) for about 12 minutes.

2 cups	warm water	500 mL
2 tsp	granulated sugar	10 mL
1 tbsp	active dry yeast (1 package)	15 mL
1/3 cup	olive oil, divided	75 mL
1 tbsp	finely chopped garlic	15 mL
2 tsp	salt	10 mL
1 tsp	dried oregano leaves	5 mL
1/2 tsp	coarsely ground black pepper	2 mL
4 cups	all-purpose flour (approx.)	1 L
1/2 cup	coarsely chopped black olives	125 mL
1/2 cup	coarsely chopped sun-dried tomatoes (oil-packed)	125 mL
2 tsp	coarse salt	10 mL

1. In a large bowl, combine warm water and sugar. Sprinkle yeast over top. Let stand until foamy, about 10 minutes.

2. Stir in 3 tbsp (45 mL) oil, garlic, salt, oregano and pepper. Add 3 1/2 cups (875 mL) flour, stirring to combine. Stir in enough additional flour to make a soft dough.

3. Turn out onto a floured surface. Knead for 8 to 10 minutes, adding enough flour to keep dough from sticking. Place in large, lightly oiled bowl, turning to coat with oil. Cover bowl with plastic wrap and let dough rise until doubled, about 1 hour.

4. Deflate dough and turn out onto a lightly floured surface. Knead in olives and sun-dried tomatoes until evenly distributed. Let dough rest for 10 minutes.

5. Brush a baking sheet with half of remaining oil. With a rolling pin or oiled hands, shape dough into a rectangle roughly the size of baking sheet. Transfer to baking sheet. (Dough may be springy, so it may be necessary to rest it at intervals until it reaches edges of pan; it does not have to be perfectly shaped.) Brush with remaining oil and sprinkle with coarse salt. Let rise for 45 to 60 minutes, or until doubled.

6. Convection bake in a preheated 400°F (200°C) oven for 18 to 20 minutes, or until golden. For a darker crust, bake for another 5 minutes. Remove from pan and slide onto a wire rack.

Bread-making Tips

- Since bread doughs are slightly soft, there is a tendency for novice bakers to add too much flour, ending with a heavy result. Only knead in extra flour if your dough is very sticky.
- Once dough has been kneaded, place in an oiled bowl and cover the bowl with plastic wrap. This allows the gluten to become smooth and elastic as the dough expands (sometimes a few bubbles will show on the surface). Let the dough rise until doubled in volume. Timing will range from one to two hours depending on the type of bread, temperature of the dough, humidity and surrounding temperature.
- Let dough rise in a "warm" place — about 80°F (27°C). This could be in the oven with just the light turned on, on top of the refrigerator, or in a sun-warmed room. The warmer the air and dough temperature, the faster the dough will rise; however, the slower the rising, the better the finished product. If dough rises too quickly, the bread may have a strong flavor and coarse texture.
- If dough rises too much, it may collapse. If this happens, reshape and let rise again.
- Some convection ovens have a bread proofing (rising) setting. Consult your oven manual for directions. Using this setting creates slightly more humidity than covering the bowl with plastic and proofing at room temperature.
- To see whether the dough has risen enough, press two fingers into the dough. If the indentation remains, the dough is ready for shaping.
- To shape dough into a loaf, roughly shape into a large rectangle and fold into thirds. Starting at shorter end, tightly roll up dough. Pinch dough together on the bottom to make a seam and tuck the ends under. Place dough in prepared loaf pan, seam side down (shaped loaf should touch edges of pan).

Cranberry Cinnamon Focaccia

Makes two 9-inch (23 cm) round focaccias

Most focaccias are savory, but this slightly sweet version adds another dimension to a very popular yeast bread. Because of the milk and butter, it is very tender and delicate. Serve it as an alternative dessert with cheese, nuts and fresh fruit. It is also perfect served plain or toasted for breakfast or brunch.

Make Ahead

After cooling, wrap focaccias well and freeze for up to two weeks. Defrost and convection bake in a preheated 350°F (180°C) oven for 8 minutes, or until warm. Or convection bake from frozen state at 300°F (150°C) for about 12 minutes.

¾ cup	warm water, divided	175 mL
1 tsp	granulated sugar	5 mL
1 tbsp	active dry yeast (1 package)	15 mL
⅔ cup	warm milk	150 mL
⅓ cup	butter, melted, divided	75 mL
2 tbsp	brown sugar	25 mL
2 tsp	salt	10 mL
½ tsp	ground cinnamon	2 mL
3¼ cups	all-purpose flour (approx.)	800 mL
¾ cup	dried cranberries	175 mL
2 tbsp	coarse sugar	25 mL

1. In a large bowl, combine ¼ cup (50 mL) warm water and granulated sugar. Sprinkle yeast over top. Let stand until foamy, about 10 minutes.

2. Stir in milk, remaining warm water, ¼ cup (50 mL) melted butter, brown sugar, salt and cinnamon. Add 2¾ cups (675 mL) flour, stirring to combine. Stir in enough additional flour to make a soft dough.

3. Turn out onto a floured surface and knead for 8 minutes, adding just enough flour to keep dough from sticking. Place in a large, lightly buttered or oiled bowl, turning dough to coat with butter. Cover bowl with plastic wrap and let dough rise until doubled, about 45 minutes.

4. Deflate dough and turn out onto a lightly floured surface. Knead in cranberries. Divide dough in half. With lightly floured hands or a rolling pin, shape each half into a flat round about 8 inches (20 cm) in diameter. Place each on a parchment-lined baking sheet. Poke down cranberries that are sticking out of dough. Brush lightly with remaining melted butter and sprinkle with coarse sugar. Let rise for 35 minutes.

5. Convection bake in a preheated 350°F (180°C) oven for 25 minutes, or until golden. Cool on a wire rack. Serve warm or at room temperature.

Rosemary Garlic Fougasse

1 cup	warm water, divided	250 mL
1 tsp	granulated sugar	5 mL
1 tbsp	active dry yeast (1 package)	15 mL
½ cup	warm milk	125 mL
¼ cup	olive oil, divided	50 mL
2 tbsp	chopped fresh rosemary	25 mL
1 tbsp	finely chopped garlic	15 mL
2 tsp	salt	10 mL
3¼ cups	all-purpose flour (approx.)	800 mL
1 tsp	coarse salt	5 mL

1. In a small bowl, combine ½ cup (125 mL) warm water and sugar. Sprinkle yeast over top. Let rise until foamy, about 10 minutes.

2. In a large bowl, combine remaining warm water, warm milk, 2 tbsp (25 mL) olive oil, rosemary, garlic and salt.

3. Stir down yeast and add to rosemary mixture. Add 2½ cups (625 mL) flour, stirring to combine. Stir in enough additional flour to make a soft dough.

4. Turn out onto a floured surface and knead for 8 minutes, adding just enough flour to keep dough from sticking. Place in a large, lightly oiled bowl, turning dough to coat with oil. Cover bowl with plastic wrap and let rise until doubled in volume, about 1 hour.

5. Deflate dough. Roll into an oval about 14 by 10 inches (36 by 25 cm). Place on an oiled baking sheet.

6. Using a sharp knife or kitchen shears, cut several slashes in dough. Brush with remaining olive oil and sprinkle with coarse salt. Let rise for 45 to 60 minutes, or until doubled in volume.

7. Convection bake in a preheated 400°F (200°C) oven for 15 to 18 minutes, or until golden. Remove from oven and slide onto a rack. Serve warm or at room temperature.

Makes 1 fougasse

While working with Lydie Marshall at her cooking school in Nyons, France, we made many variations of fougasse. This oval Provençal flatbread has slashes cut into it to give a leaf-like appearance. Some are simply brushed with olive oil and sprinkled with coarse salt. Others may be flavored with coarsely chopped pitted olives or herbs.

This is best served the day it is made. Serve as a light meal with Quick Tomatoes Provençal (page 153), olives and cheese.

Country French Bread

**Makes four
10-inch (25 cm)
baguettes**

Good baguettes are
not hard to find, but
it is so easy to make
your own.

Baking the baguettes
at a high temperature
in the convection oven
gives a crusty exterior
and a chewy interior. For
a more crusty baguette,
spritz the loaves with
water a couple of times
during baking.

Make Ahead

This bread is best eaten
the day it is made. But
you can also wrap any
extra tightly and freeze
it for up to two weeks.
Convection bake frozen
baguette at 350°F (180°C)
for 8 to 10 minutes, or
until hot.

2¼ cups	warm water	550 mL
1 tsp	granulated sugar	5 mL
1 tbsp	active dry yeast (1 package)	15 mL
1 tbsp	salt	15 mL
5 cups	all-purpose flour (approx.)	1.25 L

1. In a large bowl, stir together warm water and sugar.
   Sprinkle yeast over top. Let stand for 10 minutes, or
   until foamy.

2. Stir in salt and 4 cups (1 L) flour. Add flour until a
   soft dough forms. Turn out onto a floured surface and
   knead for 6 to 8 minutes, adding only enough flour to
   keep dough from sticking. Dough should be springy
   and smooth.

3. Place dough in a dry bowl. Cover bowl with plastic
   wrap and let dough rise until tripled in volume, about
   1½ to 2 hours.

4. Deflate dough and divide into 4 pieces. Flatten each
   piece into a 10- by 4-inch (25 by 10 cm) rectangle with
   rounded ends (do not square ends). Roll up tightly
   lengthwise, rolling back and forth to make a baguette
   shape that is tapered at ends. Pinch seams to seal.

5. Place baguettes, seam side down and at least 2 inches
   (5 cm) apart, on parchment-lined or cornmeal-dusted
   baking sheets. Dust with flour. Let rise for 50 to
   60 minutes, or until doubled.

6. Convection bake in a preheated 425°F (220°C) oven
   for 22 to 25 minutes, or until loaves are golden and
   sound hollow when tapped on bottom. Cool on
   wire racks.

Cheese Batter Bread

1½ cups	warm milk	375 mL
½ tsp	granulated sugar	2 mL
1 tbsp	active dry yeast (1 package)	15 mL
3 tbsp	butter, softened	45 mL
1	egg	1
1½ tsp	salt	7 mL
3½ cups	all-purpose flour	875 mL
1 cup	grated Cheddar cheese	250 mL

1. In a large bowl, stir together milk, sugar and yeast. Let stand for 10 minutes, or until foamy.

2. Add butter, egg, salt and 2 cups (500 mL) flour. Beat for 2 minutes until thoroughly combined. Add remaining flour and cheese and beat well.

3. Spoon batter into a well-greased 9- by 5-inch (2 L) loaf pan. Smooth surface with wet fingers. Let rise to top of pan, about 35 minutes.

4. Convection bake in a preheated 350°F (180°C) oven for 45 minutes. Remove from pan and cool on a wire rack.

Yeast
Dry yeast is available in both packages and cans. The yeast recipes in this book are written for packaged active dry yeast. When purchasing yeast, check the expiry date to ensure freshness.

Makes one 9- by 5-inch (2 L) loaf

Batter breads (a method rarely used today) eliminate the kneading process. Instead, ingredients are beaten together to form a sticky batter, spooned into a prepared loaf pan, left to rise and then baked. This results in a tasty bread, though one with a coarser texture than a regular yeast bread. But it is quick — a batter bread baked in the convection oven can be ready for the bread basket in an hour and a half.

Since cheese has a tendency to stick, be sure to grease the loaf pan really well or even line the bottom and sides with parchment paper.

Make Ahead
Bread can be cooled, wrapped well and frozen for up to two weeks.

Almost Hot Cross Buns

Makes 12 buns

The "cross" on these buns is simulated by snipping the dough gently just before baking. They are perfect for ham and cheese sandwiches, breakfast or brunch; make them year round and call them fruit buns. For a simple snack, cut a bun in half and toast until golden, then top with cheese and jam or apple butter.

Make Ahead
After cooling, wrap buns well (even individually) and freeze for up to two weeks.

¼ cup	warm water	50 mL
1 tbsp	granulated sugar	15 mL
1 tbsp	active dry yeast (1 package)	15 mL
1 cup	milk	250 mL
¼ cup	butter, softened	50 mL
¼ cup	granulated sugar	50 mL
2 tsp	salt	10 mL
2	eggs, beaten	2
4 cups	all-purpose flour (approx.)	1 L
2 tsp	ground cinnamon	10 mL
½ tsp	ground allspice	2 mL
½ tsp	ground nutmeg	2 mL
½ cup	currants or raisins	125 mL
½ cup	chopped mixed candied peel	125 mL
Glaze		
1	egg	1
1 tbsp	milk or cream	15 mL

1. In a large bowl, combine warm water and 1 tbsp (15 mL) sugar. Sprinkle yeast over top. Let stand until foamy, about 10 minutes.

2. In a saucepan, combine milk, butter, ¼ cup (50 mL) sugar and salt. Warm over low heat until butter melts, about 4 minutes. Cool to lukewarm — not more than 110°F (45°C). Stir into yeast mixture along with eggs.

3. In a separate bowl, combine 2 cups (500 mL) flour, cinnamon, allspice, nutmeg, currants and peel. Stir into yeast mixture to make a wet dough. Add enough flour (about 1¾ cups/425 mL) to make a fairly stiff dough.

4. Turn dough out onto a floured surface and knead for 8 minutes until smooth and elastic, adding flour as required. Place in a large, lightly buttered bowl, turning to coat. Cover bowl with plastic wrap and let dough rise until doubled, about 1 to 1¼ hours.

5. Deflate dough. Roll dough into a log. Cut into 12 pieces. Shape each piece into a roll and place, seam side down and at least 2 inches (5 cm) apart, on parchment-lined baking sheets. Let rise for about 40 minutes, or until doubled. Using scissors dipped in flour, gently snip a cross in top of each bun.

6. To prepare glaze, beat egg with milk in a small bowl. Brush each roll with glaze.

7. Convection bake in a preheated 350°F (180°C) oven for 18 to 20 minutes, or until golden brown. Cool on wire racks.

Apple Butter
Place 5 peeled, cored and chopped apples in a saucepan with $1/4$ cup (50 mL) water, 3 tbsp (45 mL) brown sugar, $1/4$ cup (50 mL) butter, 1 tsp (5 mL) cinnamon and 1 tsp (5 mL) grated lemon zest. Bring to a boil. Cover and reduce heat to low. Cook for 10 to 15 minutes, or until apples are softened. Puree or mash until smooth. Serve warm or refrigerate, covered, for up to a week. Makes about 2 cups (500 mL).

Quick Berry Jam
In a medium saucepan, combine 2 cups (500 mL) fresh or frozen raspberries or blueberries, $1/3$ cup (75 mL) liquid honey or granulated sugar and 2 tbsp (25 mL) lemon juice. Bring to a boil, stirring often. Reduce heat to medium-low and cook, uncovered, for 12 to 15 minutes, or until thickened, stirring often. Cool to room temperature before serving or cover and refrigerate for up to a week. Makes about $1^1/2$ cups (375 mL).

Pecan Sticky Buns

Makes two 9-inch (23 cm) pans

These are an indulgence that few people can resist — a rich, sweet dough rolled with cinnamon sugar and glazed with a sticky sauce and pecans. They are baked in the convection oven for the same amount of time as in a conventional oven, but at a reduced temperature so they don't become too dark. Use pans that are at least 2 inches (5 cm) deep, otherwise the glaze will bubble out.

When I was a child, my mother would make these about once a month in the woodstove, and it seemed to be a miracle that they would be ready in time to accompany my father and me when we were making our morning farm deliveries. Now I try to continue this tradition, but baking them (with great success) in the convection oven.

You can omit the pecans or use candied red and/or green cherries with or instead of the pecans.

Dough

¼ cup	warm water	50 mL
2 tsp	granulated sugar	10 mL
1 tbsp	active dry yeast (1 package)	15 mL
1¼ cups	milk	300 mL
¼ cup	butter, softened	50 mL
¼ cup	granulated sugar	50 mL
2 tsp	salt	10 mL
2	eggs	2
5 cups	all-purpose flour (approx.)	1.25 L

Topping

½ cup	butter	250 mL
1 cup	brown sugar	250 mL
⅓ cup	corn syrup	75 mL
1 cup	pecan halves	250 mL

Filling

¾ cup	butter, softened	175 mL
1 cup	brown sugar	250 mL
2 tbsp	ground cinnamon	25 mL

1. In a large bowl, combine warm water and 2 tsp (10 mL) granulated sugar. Sprinkle yeast over top. Let stand until foamy, about 10 minutes.

2. In a saucepan, combine milk, butter, ¼ cup (50 mL) granulated sugar and salt. Warm over low heat just until butter melts, about 4 minutes. Remove from heat and beat in eggs. Make sure liquid mixture is no hotter than 110°F (45°C), or heat may kill yeast.

3. Stir liquid into yeast mixture. Stir in 4 cups (1 L) flour and combine well. Add enough flour to make a soft dough.

4. Turn out onto a floured surface. Knead dough for 8 minutes, or until smooth and elastic, adding flour as required. Place in a large, buttered bowl, turning to coat. Cover bowl with plastic wrap and let dough rise until doubled, about 1 hour.

5. To prepare topping, in a saucepan, combine butter, brown sugar and corn syrup. Warm over medium-low heat, stirring, until mixture is smooth. Spoon mixture into two buttered 9- or 10-inch (23 or 25 cm) round baking pans with 2-inch (5 cm) sides. Arrange pecans over top. Reserve.

6. Deflate dough. On a floured surface, roll into a 24- by 14-inch (60 by 35 cm) rectangle. Spread evenly with butter, leaving a 1-inch (2.5 cm) border along one long edge. Sprinkle with brown sugar and cinnamon. Roll up tightly, pinching to seal seam along unbuttered edge. Cut into 16 slices.

7. Place rolls, cut side down, over topping. Let rise for 50 to 60 minutes, or until doubled.

8. Place each pan on a foil-lined baking sheet (in case of overflow). Convection bake in a preheated 325°F (160°C) oven for 35 minutes, or until top is golden and sounds hollow when tapped. Let stand for 3 minutes.

9. Carefully invert each pan of buns onto a serving plate and let sauce drizzle over. Cool until slightly warm or at room temperature.

Make ahead

Sticky buns can be cooled, wrapped well and frozen for up to three weeks. Defrost and convection bake at 300°F (150°C) for 20 minutes, or until warm.

Chocolate Surprise Rolls

Makes 16 rolls

The sweet dough in this recipe is like the dough used for hot cross buns, without the spices but filled with a piece of chocolate like a chocolate croissant. To have the chocolate ooze from the center, serve the rolls warm. If you have buttermilk on hand, use it instead of milk; the rolls will be even more tender. (Do not be alarmed if the buttermilk separates slightly when heated.)

Make Ahead

Rolls can be cooled, individually wrapped and frozen for up to two weeks. Defrost and convection bake at 300°F (150°C) for 8 to 12 minutes, or until warm; heat for about 15 minutes if you are warming directly from the frozen state.

¼ cup	warm water	50 mL
1 tbsp	granulated sugar	15 mL
1 tbsp	active dry yeast (1 package)	15 mL
1 cup	buttermilk or milk	250 mL
¼ cup	butter, softened	50 mL
¼ cup	granulated sugar	50 mL
2 tsp	salt	10 mL
2	eggs	2
4 cups	all-purpose flour (approx.)	1 L
16	pieces bittersweet or semisweet chocolate (about ½ oz/15 g each)	16

Glaze

2 tbsp	buttermilk or milk	25 mL
1 tbsp	coarse sugar	15 mL

1. In a large bowl, combine warm water and 1 tbsp (15 mL) granulated sugar. Sprinkle yeast over top. Let stand until foamy, about 10 minutes.

2. In a saucepan, combine buttermilk, butter, ¼ cup (50 mL) granulated sugar and salt. Warm over low heat until butter melts, about 4 minutes. Remove from heat and beat in eggs. Add lukewarm (no more than 110°F/45°C) milk mixture to yeast mixture. Stir in 3 cups (750 mL) flour, adding enough flour to make a soft dough.

3. Turn out onto a floured surface. Knead dough for 8 minutes until smooth and elastic, adding flour as required. Place in a large buttered bowl, turning to coat. Cover bowl with plastic wrap and let dough rise until doubled, about 1 hour.

4. Deflate dough and roll into a log. Cut into 16 pieces. Pat each piece into a 3-inch (7.5 cm) circle. Place a piece of chocolate in center. Bring dough up around chocolate, pinching to encase chocolate. Place pinched side down, about 3 inches (7.5 cm) apart, on parchment-lined baking sheets. Let rise for 25 to 30 minutes, or until almost doubled.

5. Brush rolls with buttermilk and sprinkle with coarse sugar. Convection bake in a preheated 325°F (160°C) oven for 22 to 25 minutes, or until tops are golden.

Quickbreads, Cookies and Squares

Chive Gruyère Biscuits

Makes 10 biscuits

Serve these light and flaky savory biscuits with soups, salads or chili.

Make Ahead
Bake biscuits, cool, wrap individually and freeze for up to two weeks. Defrost and reheat at 325°F (160°C) for 10 minutes.

2 cups	all-purpose flour	500 mL
¼ cup	chopped fresh chives or green onions	50 mL
1 tbsp	baking powder	15 mL
½ tsp	salt	2 mL
½ tsp	black pepper	2 mL
½ cup	cold butter, cut in cubes	125 mL
¾ cup	grated Gruyère cheese	175 mL
1 cup	milk, divided	250 mL

1. In a large bowl, combine flour, chives, baking powder, salt and pepper. Cut in butter until mixture resembles coarse crumbs. Stir in cheese. Add all but 2 tbsp (25 mL) milk. Stir just until a soft dough forms.

2. Turn dough onto a lightly floured surface. Knead gently, making 8 turns (do not overwork dough). Pat dough down until ½ inch (1 cm) thick.

3. Cut into biscuits with a floured 2½-inch (6 cm) biscuit cutter. Reshape trimmings and cut remaining dough. Place biscuits on a baking sheet. Brush with remaining 2 tbsp (25 mL) milk.

4. Convection bake in a preheated 400°F (200°C) oven for 12 to 14 minutes, or until golden. Serve warm.

> **Variation**
> *Rosemary Cheddar Biscuits:* Use 1 tbsp (15 mL) chopped fresh rosemary instead of chives. Use grated Cheddar cheese instead of Gruyère.

Quick Biscuits

1½ cups	all-purpose flour	375 mL
¾ cup	whole wheat flour	175 mL
⅓ cup	grated Parmesan cheese	75 mL
1 tbsp	baking powder	15 mL
½ tsp	dried thyme leaves	2 mL
¼ tsp	salt	1 mL
½ cup	olive oil	125 mL
¾ cup	milk (approx.)	175 mL

1. In a large bowl, combine both flours, cheese, baking powder, thyme and salt.

2. In a measuring cup, combine oil and milk. Add to dry ingredients and stir just until batter is sticky (you may need about 1 tbsp/15 mL extra milk).

3. Drop batter by large spoonfuls (about ⅓ cup/75 mL each) onto a parchment-lined baking sheet to make 12 biscuits. Convection bake in a preheated 375°F (190°C) oven for 18 to 20 minutes, or until light golden. Cool slightly on a rack. Serve warm or at room temperature.

Makes 12 biscuits

These are quick to assemble and bake. Instead of cutting in butter, olive oil is used to tenderize the batter, which is then dropped by the spoonful onto baking sheets.

Roasted Garlic Bread

Makes 8 to 10 servings

Roasted garlic, herbs and cheese highlight a simple loaf of crusty bread. This is a good accompaniment for soups, salads and luncheon dishes.

When roasting garlic, roast several heads. Cool the extras, wrap individually and freeze. Use later to top up the flavor of spreads, soups and sauces.

Make Ahead

Garlic can be roasted, wrapped and refrigerated up to three days ahead or frozen for up to six weeks. Bring garlic to room temperature so it is easier to squeeze out of the skin. The garlic mixture can be covered and refrigerated up to a day ahead or frozen for up to two weeks.

3	heads garlic	3
5 tbsp	olive oil, divided	65 mL
¼ cup	chopped fresh parsley	50 mL
2 tbsp	chopped fresh oregano, or 1 tsp (5 mL) dried	25 mL
½ tsp	salt	2 mL
¼ tsp	black pepper	1 mL
1	loaf French or Italian bread, cut in ½-inch (1 cm) slices	1
¼ cup	grated Parmesan cheese	50 mL

1. To roast garlic, cut tops off heads to expose cloves. Pour 1 tbsp (15 mL) olive oil into a small parchment-lined baking dish. Place garlic in oil, cut side down.

2. Convection bake or roast in a 350°F (180°C) oven for 35 minutes, or until garlic is soft when squeezed. When cool enough to handle, squeeze cloves into a small bowl and mash.

3. Add remaining ¼ cup (50 mL) olive oil, parsley, oregano, salt and pepper to bowl and combine well.

4. Arrange bread slices on two parchment-lined baking sheets. Convection bake in a preheated 350°F (180°C) oven for 5 minutes. Turn bread slices. Spread with garlic mixture and sprinkle with Parmesan. Bake for 8 to 10 minutes, or until hot and lightly toasted.

Blueberry Lemon Drop Biscuits

2 cups	all-purpose flour	500 mL
¼ cup	granulated sugar	50 mL
1 tbsp	grated lemon zest	15 mL
2 tsp	baking powder	10 mL
½ tsp	baking soda	2 mL
¼ tsp	salt	1 mL
⅓ cup	cold butter, cut in cubes	75 mL
1	egg	1
¾ cup	buttermilk, unflavored yogurt or sour milk (page 217)	175 mL
1 cup	fresh or frozen blueberries	250 mL

Topping

1 tbsp	granulated sugar	15 mL

Makes 12 biscuits

Drop biscuits eliminate the rolling and cutting process, without forfeiting texture and flavor. Quick to make, these are ideal for breakfast or afternoon tea. If you are using frozen blueberries, add them in the frozen state.

1. In a large bowl, combine flour, sugar, lemon zest, baking powder, baking soda and salt. Cut in butter until mixture resembles coarse crumbs.

2. In a small bowl, combine egg and buttermilk. Add to flour mixture. Stir just until a soft dough forms. Gently stir in blueberries.

3. Drop mixture by spoonfuls in 12 mounds on a parchment-lined or lightly greased baking sheet. For topping, sprinkle with sugar.

4. Convection bake in a preheated 375°F (190°C) oven for 15 to 18 minutes, or until golden. Cool for a few minutes on a wire rack. Serve warm.

Variation
Raspberry Lemon Drop Biscuits: Use fresh or frozen raspberries instead of blueberries.

Oatmeal Currant Scones

Makes 8 servings

Fill the house with fresh-baked aromas first thing in the morning with this easy quickbread. Serve with jams and cheeses.

2 cups	all-purpose flour	500 mL
¼ cup	granulated sugar	50 mL
2 tsp	baking powder	10 mL
½ tsp	baking soda	2 mL
½ tsp	salt	2 mL
½ cup	cold butter, cut in cubes	125 mL
1 cup	rolled oats (not instant)	250 mL
½ cup	currants or golden raisins	125 mL
2 tsp	grated orange zest	10 mL
1	egg	1
1 cup	buttermilk, unflavored yogurt or sour milk (page 217)	250 mL

Topping

2 tbsp	buttermilk	25 mL
1 tbsp	granulated sugar	15 mL

1. In a large bowl, combine flour, sugar, baking powder, baking soda and salt. Cut in butter until mixture resembles coarse crumbs. Stir in rolled oats, currants and orange zest.

2. In a small bowl, combine egg and buttermilk. Add to flour mixture. Stir with a fork until just combined.

3. Turn dough onto a lightly floured surface. Roll dough into a ball and knead gently 8 times. Shape into a 9-inch (23 cm) circle with slightly raised center. Place on a parchment-lined or lightly greased baking sheet.

4. With a sharp knife, score surface with cuts ½ inch (1 cm) deep, making 8 wedges. For topping, brush surface with buttermilk and sprinkle with sugar.

5. Convection bake in a preheated 350°F (180°C) oven for 30 to 35 minutes, or until a tester inserted in center comes out clean. Serve warm.

> **Variation**
> *Oatmeal Apricot Scones:* Use diced dried apricots or cranberries instead of currants.

Cheddar Sage Muffins

2 cups	all-purpose flour	500 mL
1 tsp	baking soda	5 mL
½ tsp	salt	2 mL
2	eggs	2
3 tbsp	granulated sugar	45 mL
⅓ cup	butter, melted	75 mL
1 cup	buttermilk, unflavored yogurt or sour milk	250 mL
1¾ cups	grated Cheddar cheese, divided	425 mL
1 tbsp	chopped fresh sage, or ½ tsp (2 mL) dried	15 mL

1. In a medium bowl, combine flour, baking soda and salt.

2. In a large bowl, mix together eggs, sugar, melted butter and buttermilk. Add flour mixture and stir until just combined. Fold in 1½ cups (375 mL) cheese and sage. Spoon into greased or paper-lined medium muffin cups. Sprinkle remaining ¼ cup (50 mL) cheese over muffin tops.

3. Convection bake in a preheated 350°F (180°C) oven for 15 to 18 minutes, or until tops are golden and firm to touch. Cool in pan for 5 minutes before removing to a wire rack. Serve warm or at room temperature.

> **Sour Milk**
> To sour milk, combine 1 tbsp (15 mL) white vinegar or lemon juice with 1 cup (250 mL) milk. Let stand for 10 minutes before using.

Makes 12 medium muffins

Include these in the breakfast or dinner bread basket. Use old or extra-old Cheddar for a stronger flavor.

Make Ahead
Bake muffins and cool. Wrap individually and freeze for up to three weeks.

Cranberry Banana Muffins

Makes 12 medium muffins

The tang of cranberries is softened by the subtleness of the banana and the hint of nutmeg in this recipe. I always keep a stash of cranberries in the freezer for baking and sauces.

Make Ahead

Bake muffins and cool. Wrap individually and freeze for up to three weeks.

1	ripe banana	1
½ cup	granulated sugar	125 mL
1	egg	1
¾ cup	milk	175 mL
⅓ cup	butter, melted	75 mL
1 tbsp	grated orange zest	15 mL
2 cups	all-purpose flour	500 mL
1 tbsp	baking powder	15 mL
½ tsp	ground nutmeg	2 mL
½ tsp	salt	2 mL
1½ cups	fresh or frozen cranberries	375 mL

1. In a large bowl, mash banana. Add sugar, egg, milk, melted butter and orange zest and combine well.

2. In a medium bowl, combine flour, baking powder, nutmeg and salt. Stir into liquid ingredients until just moistened. Fold in cranberries. Spoon into greased or paper-lined medium muffin cups.

3. Convection bake in a preheated 375°F (190°C) oven for 22 to 25 minutes, or until a tester inserted in center comes out clean. Cool in pan for 5 minutes before removing to a wire rack. Serve warm or at room temperature.

Orange Sunrise Muffins

1	whole orange, unpeeled, cut in pieces	1
½ cup	coarsely chopped dates	125 mL
1	egg	1
½ cup	orange juice	125 mL
½ cup	butter, melted, or vegetable oil	125 mL
½ cup	granulated sugar	125 mL
1½ cups	all-purpose flour	375 mL
2 tsp	baking powder	10 mL
1 tsp	baking soda	5 mL
½ tsp	salt	2 mL

1. In a food processor, chop orange until coarse. Add dates and process until finely chopped.

2. In a large bowl, whisk together egg, orange juice, melted butter and sugar. Stir in orange and date mixture.

3. In a separate bowl, mix together flour, baking powder, baking soda and salt. Add to orange mixture and stir until just combined. Spoon batter into greased or paper-lined medium muffin cups.

4. Convection bake in a preheated 350°F (180°C) oven for 20 to 22 minutes, or until a tester inserted in center comes out clean. Cool in pan for 5 minutes before removing to a wire rack. Serve warm or at room temperature.

Makes 12 medium muffins

Start your day with these delicious muffins, or eat them as an afternoon snack or even as a dessert with fruit. My sister-in-law Susan uses her convection oven to make several batches of these at one time and then freezes them.

The easiest way to chop the oranges and dates is in the food processor, but make sure the dates are moist. Susan also uses the food processor to mix the batter, but if you do, do not overprocess the mixture. Raisins may be substituted for the dates.

Make Ahead
Bake muffins and cool. Wrap individually and freeze for up to three weeks.

Almost Healthy Date Bran Muffins

Makes 18 medium muffins

These moist muffins have great flavor with no added sugar. Once the dates have cooked and cooled slightly, the muffins can be baked up quickly. I usually double the recipe and — *Voilà!* — three dozen muffins in no time (and you'll use the whole container of buttermilk).

It is not necessary to chop the dates finely, as they become almost a paste on cooking.

Make Ahead
Bake muffins and cool. Wrap individually and freeze for up to three weeks.

2 cups	chopped dates	500 mL
1 cup	water	250 mL
2 cups	all-purpose flour	500 mL
2 cups	natural bran	500 mL
2 tsp	baking soda	10 mL
1 tsp	salt	5 mL
2	eggs	2
½ cup	vegetable oil	125 mL
2 tbsp	molasses	25 mL
2 cups	buttermilk	500 mL

1. In a medium saucepan, combine dates and water. Bring to a boil. Reduce heat to low and cook, uncovered, for 10 to 12 minutes, stirring and mashing, until dates are very soft and pasty and liquid has evaporated. Cool.

2. In a large bowl, combine flour, bran, baking soda and salt.

3. In a separate bowl, beat eggs. Stir in oil, molasses and buttermilk. Stir in cooled dates and combine thoroughly.

4. Add wet ingredients to dry and stir until combined but not overmixed. Scoop into greased or paper-lined medium muffin cups.

5. Convection bake in a preheated 350°F (180°C) oven for 20 minutes, or until a tester inserted in center comes out clean. Cool in pan for 5 minutes before removing to a wire rack. Serve warm or at room temperature.

Pumpkin Harvest Loaf

3 cups	all-purpose flour	750 mL
2 tsp	baking powder	10 mL
½ tsp	baking soda	2 mL
½ tsp	salt	2 mL
1 tsp	ground cinnamon	5 mL
½ tsp	ground nutmeg	2 mL
½ tsp	ground cloves	2 mL
½ tsp	ground ginger	2 mL
1 cup	chopped walnuts, pecans or hazelnuts	250 mL
3	eggs	3
1½ cups	unsweetened pumpkin puree	375 mL
1¼ cups	packed brown sugar	300 mL
½ cup	butter, melted, or vegetable oil	125 mL
½ cup	milk	125 mL

Makes two 9- by 5-inch (2 L) loaves

This loaf is especially suited to Thanksgiving and Christmas. Serve it with hearty soups, baked beans or ham salad plates. Keep one for yourself; cool the other and wrap in cellophane, tie with a pretty ribbon and take as a gift for the host or hostess.

Make Ahead
Cool baked loaf, wrap well and keep at room temperature for up to two days, or freeze for up to two months.

1. In a large bowl, combine flour, baking powder, baking soda, salt, cinnamon, nutmeg, cloves, ginger and nuts.

2. In a separate bowl, beat eggs. Stir in pumpkin, brown sugar, melted butter and milk. Pour wet ingredients into dry ingredients and mix until just combined. Spoon batter into two greased and parchment-lined 9- by 5-inch (2 L) loaf pans.

3. Convection bake in a preheated 325°F (160°C) oven for 50 to 55 minutes, or until a tester inserted in center comes out clean. Let stand for 10 minutes before removing from pan. Cool on a wire rack.

Blueberry Cinnamon Loaf

**Makes one 8- by
4-inch (1.5 L) loaf**

This easy loaf, marbled
with blueberries and
cinnamon, has a slightly
crunchy topping. Take
it on picnics, contribute
it to bake sales or
present it as a hostess
gift.

Make Ahead
Loaf can be prepared
up to two days before
serving. Or bake and
cool completely, wrap
well and freeze for up
to two months. (For
convenience, cut loaf
into serving pieces, wrap
and freeze individually.)

½ cup	butter, softened	125 mL
¾ cup	granulated sugar	175 mL
2	eggs	2
1 tsp	vanilla	5 mL
1½ cups	all-purpose flour	375 mL
1 tsp	baking powder	5 mL
½ tsp	baking soda	2 mL
¾ cup	buttermilk, sour milk (page 217) or unflavored yogurt	175 mL
1 cup	fresh or frozen blueberries	250 mL
2 tbsp	brown sugar	25 mL
2 tsp	ground cinnamon	10 mL

Topping

1 tbsp	packed brown sugar	25 mL
1 tsp	ground cinnamon	5 mL

1. In a large bowl, beat together butter and granulated sugar until light and fluffy. Beat in eggs one at a time. Beat in vanilla.

2. In a separate bowl, mix together flour, baking powder and baking soda. Add to creamed mixture alternately with buttermilk, making three dry and two liquid additions.

3. In a small bowl, combine blueberries, brown sugar and cinnamon. Gently fold blueberries into batter. Spoon batter into a parchment-lined 8- by 4-inch (1.5 L) loaf pan.

4. For topping, in a small measuring cup, combine brown sugar and cinnamon. Sprinkle topping over loaf. Convection bake in preheated 325°F (160°C) oven for 75 minutes, or until a cake tester inserted in center comes out clean. Let stand for 10 minutes before removing from pan. Cool on a wire rack.

Lunch Box Banana Bread

2	eggs	2
⅓ cup	buttermilk or sour milk (page 217)	75 mL
½ cup	packed brown sugar	125 mL
⅓ cup	butter, melted	75 mL
1 cup	mashed ripe bananas (about 2)	250 mL
1¾ cups	all-purpose flour	425 mL
1 tsp	baking powder	5 mL
1 tsp	baking soda	5 mL
¼ tsp	salt	1 mL
½ cup	chocolate chips	125 mL
½ cup	sunflower seeds	125 mL

1. In a large bowl, beat eggs. Stir in buttermilk, brown sugar, melted butter and bananas.

2. In a separate bowl, combine flour, baking powder, baking soda, salt, chocolate chips and sunflower seeds. Add dry ingredients to wet ingredients and stir to mix thoroughly, but do not overmix. Spoon batter into a greased and parchment-lined 9- by 5-inch (2 L) loaf pan.

3. Convection bake in a preheated 325°F (160°C) oven for 55 to 60 minutes, or until a tester inserted in center comes out clean. Let stand for 10 minutes before removing from pan. Cool on a wire rack.

Makes one 9- by 5-inch (2 L) loaf

When bananas are a bit beyond eating, this loaf is the answer, but it is so good that you'll also want to set bananas aside to make it. If you are really overwhelmed with overripe bananas, simply mash them, wrap well and freeze in suitable quantities to use in baking at a later time.

Make Ahead
Loaf can be baked up to two days before serving, wrapped well and stored at room temperature. Or wrap well and freeze for up to two months.

Fruitcake with Amaretto

Even people who don't
like fruitcake love this
one — a good standby
in case you don't get
around to making
traditional fruitcake.
It is basically a pound
cake with fruit and
chocolate. Made in
small loaves and
wrapped in colorful
cellophane, this is one
of the most popular
recipes from my Gifts
From the Kitchen class
(if you can't find mini
loaf pans, use the foil
ones available in most
supermarkets). It is so
easy to bake several
small loaves using the
multiple racks of the
convection oven.

Make Ahead
Once cakes have been
cooled and brushed
with Amaretto, wrap
well and keep at room
temperature for up to
two days, or place
well-wrapped cakes
in an airtight container
and freeze for up to
two months.

1½ cups	mixed candied peel	375 mL
1 cup	diced dried apricots	250 mL
1 cup	chopped bittersweet chocolate or chocolate chips	250 mL
½ cup	golden raisins	125 mL
1 tbsp	grated lemon zest	15 mL
1 tbsp	grated orange zest	15 mL
½ cup	Amaretto	125 mL
½ tsp	almond extract	2 mL
2 cups	butter, softened	500 mL
2¼ cups	granulated sugar	550 mL
7	eggs	7
3½ cups	all-purpose flour	875 mL
½ tsp	salt	2 mL
⅓ cup	Amaretto for soaking (approx.)	75 mL

1. In a bowl, combine candied peel, apricots, chocolate, raisins, lemon zest, orange zest, Amaretto and almond extract. Let stand while preparing pans and rest of cake. Stir occasionally.

2. In a large bowl, beat butter until light. Gradually beat in sugar and continue to beat until very light. Beat in eggs one at a time (mixture may appear curdled, but that is okay).

3. In a separate bowl, combine flour and salt. Add to butter mixture, mixing until just combined. Stir in reserved fruit mixture. Spoon batter into seven greased and parchment-lined 6- by 3-inch (625 mL) loaf pans. For easier handling, place loaf pans on baking sheets.

4. Convection bake in a preheated 300°F (150°C) oven for 1 hour, or until a tester inserted in center comes out clean. Let stand for 10 minutes before removing from pans, then cool completely on wire racks.

5. Brush cooled cakes all over with Amaretto (use more if needed), then wrap.

Milk Chocolate Shortbread

2 cups	butter, softened	500 mL
1 cup	granulated sugar	250 mL
3 cups	all-purpose flour	750 mL
½ cup	rice flour	125 mL
½ cup	cornstarch	125 mL
1	14-oz (400 g) milk chocolate bar, coarsely chopped	1
½ cup	confectioner's (icing) sugar, sifted	125 mL

1. In a large bowl, cream together butter and granulated sugar until light and fluffy.

2. In a separate bowl, mix together flour, rice flour and cornstarch. Add to butter mixture and stir until blended, then stir in chopped chocolate.

3. Drop batter in mounds (about 4 tsp/20 mL each and about 1½ inches/4 cm apart) onto parchment-lined baking sheets.

4. Convection bake in a preheated 300°F (150°C) oven for 22 to 25 minutes, or until cookies are just firm to touch and light golden. Cool completely. Dust with confectioner's sugar.

Variation

Lavender Shortbread: Replace chopped chocolate with 4 tsp (20 mL) fresh or dried organic lavender buds and stir until blended. Refrigerate dough for 30 to 60 minutes, or until firm enough to roll.

Shape dough into 1-inch (2.5 cm) balls. Place on parchment-lined baking sheets about 1 inch (2.5 cm) apart. Dip a cookie press in granulated sugar and press dough lightly to make an imprint. Bake as for Milk Chocolate Shortbread.

Makes about 7 dozen

This is the most popular and comforting cookie you can make. Aside from trying not to eat too many, the challenge is keeping the chocolate bar away from nibblers. I like to use a milk chocolate bar with honey and almond nougat, or use your favorite milk chocolate. To make these extra special, cut up part of another chocolate bar and press a chunk of chocolate into the top of each cookie before baking.

Make Ahead

Layer cooled cookies between sheets of waxed paper in an airtight container. Store at room temperature for up to two days or freeze for up to three weeks.

Overnight Meringues with Chocolate

Makes about 50

Rhonda Caplan is a talented recipe tester, cook, baker and instructor who excels in creating simple and delicious desserts. She shared this recipe for one of my holiday buffet classes, and I have been making the meringues ever since. The beauty is that they can be put in the convection oven before bedtime and magically, in the morning, there are finished cookies. If there is no time to deal with them in the morning, leave them until you get home from work. (Just leave a note on the oven door so everyone knows it is occupied!)

Use your favorite milk chocolate or semisweet chocolate bar in these.

Make Ahead

Meringues can be stored in tightly sealed containers and kept at room temperature for a day, or they can be frozen for up to three weeks.

4	egg whites	4
1/4 tsp	cream of tartar	1 mL
1 cup	granulated sugar	250 mL
1	14-oz (400 g) milk chocolate bar, chopped	1

1. In a large clean bowl, beat egg whites and cream of tartar until soft peaks form. Slowly beat in sugar, continuing to beat until very stiff and shiny. Fold in chopped chocolate. Spoon meringues onto three parchment-lined baking sheets — about 2 tbsp (25 mL) per meringue, placed about 1½ inches (4 cm) apart.

2. Preheat oven to 375°F (190°C) on convection bake. Place meringues in oven and turn off oven. Leave meringues in oven for 8 to 10 hours or overnight.

> **Variation**
> *Overnight Meringues with Coconut:* Replace chopped chocolate with 3 cups (750 mL) sweetened flaked coconut.

Earl Grey Cookies

1 cup	butter, softened	250 mL
2/3 cup	granulated sugar	150 mL
1	egg	1
1 tsp	vanilla	5 mL
2½ cups	all-purpose flour	625 mL
1 tbsp	Earl Grey tea leaves	15 mL
¼ tsp	salt	1 mL
½ cup	apricot jam or marmalade	125 mL

1. In a large bowl, cream together butter and sugar until light. Beat in egg and vanilla.

2. In a separate bowl, combine flour, tea and salt. Add to butter mixture and stir until just combined.

3. Roll cookies into 1-inch (2.5 cm) balls (about 1 tbsp/ 15 mL each). Place about 2 inches (5 cm) apart on parchment-lined baking sheets.

4. Dip end of a wooden spoon handle in flour and make an indentation in center of each cookie. Fill indentation with a generous ¼ tsp (1 mL) jam.

5. Convection bake in a preheated 325°F (160°C) oven for 16 to 18 minutes, or until light golden. Cool on wire racks.

Makes about 4 dozen

This is a combination of shortbread and jam thumbprint cookies, made all the more interesting by the addition of tea — something different for a cookie exchange, or package them with a fancy cup and extra tea as a gift.

You can also bake these as plain cookies without the jam. If you wish, drizzle the cooled cookies with a little melted chocolate.

Make Ahead
Layer cooled cookies between sheets of waxed paper in an airtight container. Store at room temperature for up to two days or freeze for up to three weeks.

Double Chocolate Chip Cookies

Makes about 5½ dozen

These are fairly traditional chocolate chip cookies, but with two kinds of chips.

It is so easy to make cookies in the convection oven when three trays can be baked at a time. If you have insulated baking sheets, the baking time may be increased by 3 to 4 minutes.

Make Ahead
Cookies can be stored in an airtight container for up to two days at room temperature, or well wrapped and frozen for up to three weeks.

½ cup	butter, softened	125 mL
½ cup	shortening, softened	125 mL
¾ cup	granulated sugar	175 mL
½ cup	packed brown sugar	125 mL
2	eggs	2
1 tsp	vanilla	5 mL
2¼ cups	all-purpose flour	550 mL
1 tsp	baking soda	5 mL
½ tsp	salt	2 mL
1½ cups	semisweet or milk chocolate chips	375 mL
1½ cups	white chocolate chips	375 mL

1. In a large bowl, cream together butter, shortening, granulated sugar and brown sugar until light and fluffy. Add eggs one at a time, beating until well incorporated. Beat in vanilla.

2. In a separate bowl, combine flour, baking soda and salt. Add to butter mixture along with chocolate chips, and stir until thoroughly combined. Let batter stand for 15 minutes to firm slightly.

3. Drop batter by tablespoonful, about 2 inches (5 cm) apart, onto parchment-lined baking sheets. Convection bake in a preheated 350°F (180°C) oven for 10 to 12 minutes, or until golden. Cool slightly, then remove and cool completely on wire racks.

> **Variation**
> *Traditional Chocolate Chip Cookies:* Use regular chocolate chips instead of white. Add ½ cup (125 mL) chopped pecans or walnuts to batter.

Oatmeal Crisp Cookies

1 cup	butter, softened	250 mL
¾ cup	packed brown sugar	175 mL
1 cup	granulated sugar, divided	250 mL
2	eggs	2
1 tsp	vanilla	5 mL
2½ cups	rolled oats (not instant)	625 mL
1½ cups	all-purpose flour	375 mL
1 cup	unsweetened shredded coconut	250 mL
½ tsp	salt	2 mL
½ tsp	baking soda	2 mL
½ tsp	ground cinnamon	2 mL

Makes about 6 dozen

When the newspaper that I wrote for moved to a new office, I made these cookies for the editors and staff to celebrate. The convection oven is perfect for these crisp cookies, which have a great shelf life, if they last that long! Sometimes I place a small scoop of ice cream between two cookies, wrap and freeze to make ice-cream sandwiches.

1. In a large bowl, cream together butter, brown sugar and $\frac{1}{2}$ cup (125 mL) granulated sugar until light and fluffy. Add eggs one at a time, beating until well incorporated. Beat in vanilla.

2. In a separate bowl, combine rolled oats, flour, coconut, salt, baking soda and cinnamon. Add to butter mixture and mix until all ingredients are incorporated, but do not overmix. Refrigerate dough for 3 hours or until it can be easily shaped by hand.

3. Place remaining $\frac{1}{2}$ cup (125 mL) granulated sugar in a shallow dish. Form dough into 1-inch (2.5 cm) balls and place in dish. Roll dough to coat with sugar.

4. Arrange cookies on parchment-lined baking sheets, about 2 inches (5 cm) apart. With a fork dipped in granulated sugar, press cookies to flatten to $\frac{1}{4}$-inch (5 mm) thickness.

5. Convection bake in a preheated 350°F (180°C) oven, in batches, for 10 to 12 minutes, or until firm and golden. Transfer to racks to cool.

Make Ahead
Cookies can be stored in an airtight container for up to a week at room temperature, or packaged well and frozen for up to three weeks.

Hazelnut Cinnamon Biscotti

Makes about 3 dozen

Biscotti (twice-baked cookies) are traditionally served with coffee or sweet wine, as they are perfect for dunking. Almonds, walnuts or pecans can be used instead of hazelnuts.

Make Ahead

Store cookies in an airtight container for up to three days at room temperature, or package well and freeze for up to three weeks.

⅓ cup	butter, softened	75 mL
⅓ cup	granulated sugar	75 mL
⅓ cup	packed brown sugar	75 mL
2	eggs	2
2 tsp	vanilla	10 mL
1¾ cups	all-purpose flour	425 mL
1 cup	hazelnuts, lightly toasted, skinned and coarsely chopped	250 mL
1 tsp	ground cinnamon	5 mL
1 tsp	baking powder	5 mL
¼ tsp	salt	1 mL

1. In a large bowl, cream together butter, granulated sugar and brown sugar. Beat in eggs one at a time, beating well after each addition. Beat in vanilla.

2. In a separate bowl, combine flour, nuts, cinnamon, baking powder and salt. Add to butter mixture, mixing just until combined.

3. Scrape dough onto a lightly floured surface (dough may be slightly sticky). Divide in half. Shape each into a flattish log about 12 inches (30 cm) long. Transfer to a parchment-lined baking sheet.

4. Convection bake in a preheated 325°F (160°C) oven for 25 minutes, or until lightly browned. Cool on a wire rack for 5 minutes.

5. Transfer logs to a cutting board and carefully cut on diagonal into ½-inch (1 cm) slices. Arrange slices on two parchment-lined baking sheets. Bake for an additional 15 minutes, or until lightly toasted and crisp. Cool on a wire rack.

> **Preparing Hazelnuts**
> Toast hazelnuts (page 163) and cool slightly. Wrap in a dish towel and roll to remove skins. If you use lots of hazelnuts in baking, toast and skin a large quantity and store them in the freezer. (All nuts and seeds can be stored in tightly sealed containers in the freezer to prevent them from becoming rancid.)

Toffee Chocolate Squares

1½ cups	Graham wafer crumbs	375 mL
⅔ cup	butter, melted	150 mL
1	10-oz (300 mL) can sweetened condensed milk	1
¾ cup	chopped pecans or walnuts	175 mL
¾ cup	chocolate chips	175 mL
½ cup	toffee bits or butterscotch chips	125 mL
3 tbsp	shredded sweetened coconut	45 mL

1. In a bowl, combine Graham wafer crumbs and melted butter. Pat into a lightly greased and parchment-lined 9-inch (2.5 L) square baking pan (extend parchment paper slightly beyond two sides of pan so whole recipe can be lifted out and easily cut after chilling).

2. Pour condensed milk over crumbs and spread evenly. Sprinkle nuts, chocolate chips, toffee bits and coconut over milk.

3. Convection bake in a preheated 325°F (160°C) oven for 30 to 35 minutes, or until top is golden. Chill thoroughly before removing from pan and cutting into squares.

Makes 16 to 25 squares

An instant fix for your sweet craving. A longtime staple on sweet trays at church functions, squares like these are now appearing in coffee shops. Chill thoroughly before cutting into squares, as they tend to be gooey.

Make Ahead

Squares can be made ahead and refrigerated for up to two days or wrapped well and frozen for up to a month.

Date Squares

Makes 25 squares

An old-fashioned favorite of date filling tucked between layers of tasty oatmeal. Lemon juice and zest cut the sweetness of the dates. For bake sales or easier freezing, cut the whole pan into four large squares. (Some of my customers would treat the large square as one piece!)

Make Ahead

Squares can be covered and stored at room temperature for two days or frozen for up to a month.

2½ cups	pitted dates	625 mL
3 tbsp	lemon juice	45 mL
2 tsp	grated lemon zest	10 mL
Pinch	salt	Pinch
1½ cups	water	375 mL
1½ cups	all-purpose flour	375 mL
1 cup	packed brown sugar	250 mL
½ tsp	baking powder	2 mL
¾ cup	cold butter, cut in cubes	175 mL
1½ cups	rolled oats (not instant)	375 mL

1. To prepare filling, in a medium saucepan, combine dates, lemon juice, zest, salt and water. Bring to a boil. Reduce heat to medium and simmer for 12 minutes, or until mixture is thick. Stir frequently to break up dates. Cool completely.

2. In a large bowl, combine flour, sugar and baking powder. Cut in butter until mixture resembles coarse crumbs. Stir in rolled oats and cut in slightly.

3. Pat two-thirds of crumb mixture into a lightly greased and parchment-lined 9-inch (2.5 L) square baking pan. Spread date filling over top. Spread with remaining crumb mixture and pat down lightly.

4. Convection bake in a preheated 325°F (160°C) oven for 35 minutes, or until golden brown. Cool completely in pan on a wire rack. Lift out before cutting into small squares.

Florentine Squares

Base
½ cup	butter, softened	125 mL
¼ cup	granulated sugar	50 mL
1 cup	all-purpose flour	250 mL

Topping
1 cup	sliced almonds	250 mL
½ cup	granulated sugar	125 mL
½ cup	whipping (35%) cream	125 mL
¼ cup	all-purpose flour	50 mL
¼ cup	chopped candied orange peel	50 mL
2 tbsp	butter, melted	25 mL
1 tsp	grated orange zest	5 mL
1 tsp	vanilla	5 mL

Garnish
4 oz	semisweet or bittersweet chocolate, melted	125 g

1. In a bowl, cream together butter and sugar. Add flour and combine just until mixture starts to hold together. Pat mixture into a greased and parchment-lined 9-inch (2.5 L) square baking dish. Convection bake in a preheated 375°F (190°C) oven for 12 minutes.

2. To prepare topping, in a bowl, combine almonds, sugar, cream, flour, candied peel, melted butter, orange zest and vanilla. Spread over partially baked base. Continue to bake for 18 to 20 minutes, or until top is golden. Cool in pan on a wire rack and then cut into squares.

3. Dip half of each square, diagonally, into melted chocolate and lay on a waxed paper-lined baking sheet. Refrigerate until chocolate is set.

Makes 25 squares

The traditional flavors of the delicate, lacy Florentine cookies are evident in this square. The base is shortbread-like and can be easily prepared in the food processor. This is another popular recipe from my Gifts From the Kitchen class. Make them for gifts, but keep some for yourself.

Make Ahead
Keep squares refrigerated or package well and freeze for up to three weeks.

Tangy Lemon Squares

Makes 40 squares

When you want a delicate lemon treat for a sweet tray, these are the answer. Or serve a larger piece for dessert along with fresh berries.

Be sure to grease the pan well before lining the bottom and sides with a piece of parchment paper that extends beyond two sides of the pan. It will be easier to gently lift the whole recipe out of the pan before cutting into squares (use a sharp knife dipped in hot water). Trim edges after removing from the pan. If you wish, sprinkle with sifted confectioner's sugar before serving.

Make Ahead
These are soft squares so should be served chilled. Make them a day or two ahead and refrigerate before cutting into squares.

Base
1¾ cups	all-purpose flour	425 mL
1 cup	confectioner's (icing) sugar	250 mL
1 cup	cold butter, cut in ½-inch (1 cm) pieces	250 mL

Filling
6	eggs	6
2½ cups	granulated sugar	625 mL
¾ cup	lemon juice	175 mL
2 tbsp	grated lemon zest	25 mL
½ cup	all-purpose flour	125 mL

1. To prepare base, in a food processor, combine flour and confectioner's sugar. Add butter and process until dough just starts to come together. Press into bottom of a greased and parchment-lined 13- by 9-inch (3 L) baking pan. (To prepare base by hand, in a bowl, combine flour and sugar. Cut in butter with a pastry blender until mixture resembles coarse meal and is starting to clump together.)

2. Convection bake in a preheated 325°F (160°C) oven for 25 minutes, or until light golden. Cool.

3. To prepare filling, in a bowl, whisk together eggs and granulated sugar. Whisk in lemon juice, zest and flour. Pour over cooled base. Bake for 30 to 35 minutes, or until filling is set. Cool in pan on a wire rack. Cover and chill completely before cutting into squares.

Chocolate Chunk Cookie Squares

⅓ cup	butter, softened	75 mL
⅓ cup	shortening, softened	75 mL
½ cup	packed brown sugar	125 mL
½ cup	granulated sugar	125 mL
2	eggs	2
1¾ cups	all-purpose flour	425 mL
1½ tsp	baking powder	7 mL
½ tsp	salt	2 mL
2½ cups	coarsely chopped chocolate (about 12 oz/375 g), divided	625 mL
½ cup	chopped pecans (optional)	125 mL

1. In a large bowl, cream together butter, shortening and both sugars until light. Beat in eggs one at a time.

2. In a separate bowl, combine flour, baking powder and salt. Stir into creamed mixture and blend well. Gently stir in 2 cups (500 mL) chocolate and pecans, if using.

3. Spread batter evenly over a lightly greased and parchment-lined 9-inch (2.5 L) square baking dish. Sprinkle remaining ½ cup (125 mL) chocolate over surface.

4. Convection bake in a preheated 325°F (160°C) oven for 35 minutes, or until squares are golden brown and firm to touch.

5. Cool completely in pan on a rack. Lift out of pan before cutting into squares.

Makes 25 squares

Square chocolate chip cookies! I like to use Swiss milk chocolate with honey and almonds in these cookies, but semisweet or bittersweet chocolate can also be used.

When baking squares, line the pan with parchment so the paper extends ¾ inch (2 cm) beyond two sides. The paper acts as a handle to lift the squares out of the pan completely before cutting. (Be sure to loosen the other sides with a knife.)

Make Ahead

Squares can be baked, covered and refrigerated for up to two days or frozen for up to a month.

Pan of Brownies

**Makes
40 brownies**

Brownies are always a hit, so make a big batch. Cut them into large or bite-sized pieces. For an even more special treat, spread with chocolate icing (page 246) or chocolate glaze (page 254).

Make Ahead

Brownies can be made two days ahead, or wrapped well and frozen for up to six weeks. To freeze the whole pan of brownies, run a knife around edges and lift out brownies using parchment paper as "handles." Cut into pieces and freeze.

1 cup	butter, cut in pieces	250 mL
8 oz	semisweet chocolate, coarsely chopped	250 g
1 cup	all-purpose flour	250 mL
1 tsp	baking powder	5 mL
¼ tsp	salt	1 mL
1 tsp	instant coffee powder (optional)	5 mL
1 cup	chopped walnuts or pecans (optional)	250 mL
4	eggs	4
1 cup	granulated sugar	250 mL
½ cup	packed brown sugar	125 mL
1 tsp	vanilla	5 mL
1½ cups	semisweet or white chocolate chips, or peanut butter chips	375 mL

1. In a stainless-steel bowl set over hot (not boiling) water, melt butter and chocolate and stir together. Cool slightly.

2. In a bowl, combine flour, baking powder, salt, coffee and nuts, if using.

3. In a separate large bowl, beat together eggs, sugars and vanilla. Stir in cooled chocolate mixture. Stir in flour mixture.

4. Pour batter into a greased and parchment-lined 13- by 9-inch (3 L) baking pan. Sprinkle with chocolate chips. Convection bake in a preheated 325°F (160°C) oven for 25 to 30 minutes, or just until a tester comes out clean. Do not overbake. Let cool in pan on a wire rack.

Desserts

Rhubarb Coffee Cake

**Makes one
9-inch (23 cm)
square cake**

This cake is great even without the crunchy topping. Serve it for brunch, or with coffee or tea, accompanied by fresh strawberries or other seasonal fruit.

Make Ahead

Cake can be stored in an airtight container at room temperature for up to a day. To freeze, wrap in plastic wrap, then wrap in foil and freeze for up to two weeks.

Topping

¾ cup	packed brown sugar	175 mL
½ cup	chopped pecans or almonds	125 mL
2 tsp	ground cinnamon	10 mL
2 tbsp	butter, melted	25 mL

Cake

½ cup	butter, softened	125 mL
¾ cup	granulated sugar	175 mL
1	egg	1
2 tsp	grated orange zest	10 mL
1 tsp	vanilla	5 mL
2 cups	all-purpose flour	500 mL
1 tsp	baking soda	5 mL
½ tsp	salt	2 mL
1 cup	unflavored yogurt or buttermilk	250 mL
2 cups	diced fresh or frozen rhubarb	500 mL

1. To prepare topping, in a small bowl, combine brown sugar, pecans, cinnamon and melted butter.

2. To make cake, in a large bowl, cream softened butter and granulated sugar together until light. Beat in egg, orange zest and vanilla.

3. In a separate bowl, combine flour, baking soda and salt. Stir into creamed mixture alternately with yogurt, making three additions of dry ingredients and two of yogurt. Stir in rhubarb. Spread batter in a parchment-lined or greased 9-inch (2 L) square baking pan. Sprinkle topping over cake.

4. Convection bake in a preheated 325°F (160°C) oven for 45 to 50 minutes, or until a cake tester inserted in center comes out clean. Let cool in pan on a rack.

Variations

Blueberry Coffee Cake: Use fresh or frozen blueberries instead of rhubarb.

Apple Coffee Cake: Use diced apple instead of rhubarb.

Apple Cake

Base

1 cup	all-purpose flour	250 mL
¾ cup	granulated sugar	175 mL
1 tsp	baking powder	5 mL
¼ cup	butter, cold, cut in small pieces	50 mL
1 tsp	vanilla	5 mL
1	egg, beaten	1

Filling

4	large apples (Golden Delicious, Ida Red, Northern Spy), peeled and sliced	4
2 tbsp	granulated sugar	25 mL
2 tbsp	butter, melted	25 mL
1 tbsp	lemon juice	15 mL
1 tsp	ground cinnamon	5 mL
3 tbsp	apricot jam or jelly	45 mL
2 tsp	water	10 mL

1. To prepare base, in a large bowl, combine flour, sugar and baking powder. Cut in butter until it is in tiny bits. Add vanilla and egg and mix until ingredients are combined. Pat into bottom and part way up sides of a greased 9-inch (2.5 L) springform pan.

2. To prepare filling, in same bowl, combine apples, sugar, melted butter, lemon juice and cinnamon. Spoon into prepared crust and smooth down.

3. Convection bake in a preheated 325°F (160°C) oven for 50 to 60 minutes, or until apples are tender when tested with tip of a sharp knife.

4. In a small saucepan or dish, combine jam and water. Heat or microwave until melted. Brush over apples. Cool cake in pan on a wire rack.

Makes one 9-inch (23 cm) cake

Nothing is more enticing than the aroma of an apple dessert baking in the kitchen. Serve with vanilla ice cream lightly dusted with ground cinnamon.

This cake travels well to potlucks and picnics.

Make Ahead

Cake can be baked ahead, removed from pan, covered and refrigerated for up to two days. Bring to room temperature before serving.

Orange Chiffon Cake

Makes one 10-inch (25 cm) cake

This is a tall, impressive cake, perfect to serve with fresh fruit for dessert or afternoon tea. Be sure to use a tube pan that is at least 4½ inches (12 cm) deep.

For a lovely, light presentation, surround the cake with daisies — it almost looks like a hat. You can also drizzle the cooled cake with an orange glaze.

Make Ahead

Cake can be cooled completely, removed from pan, wrapped well and frozen for up to a month.

2 cups	all-purpose flour	500 mL
1½ cups	granulated sugar, divided	375 mL
2 tsp	baking powder	10 mL
½ tsp	salt	2 mL
½ cup	vegetable oil	125 mL
6	eggs, separated	6
¾ cup	orange juice	175 mL
1 tbsp	grated orange zest	15 mL
1 tsp	vanilla	5 mL
3	egg whites	3
½ tsp	cream of tartar	2 mL

1. Sift flour, ¾ cup (175 mL) sugar, baking powder and salt into a bowl.

2. In a large bowl, combine oil, egg yolks, orange juice, orange zest and vanilla. Beat until smooth. Beat in flour mixture.

3. In a separate large clean bowl, beat all 9 egg whites and cream of tartar until soft peaks form. Gradually beat in remaining ¾ cup (175 mL) sugar until stiff peaks form.

4. Gently stir one-third of egg whites into batter, then carefully fold in remaining egg whites.

5. Pour mixture into an ungreased 10-inch (4 L) tube pan. Convection bake in a preheated 325°F (160°C) oven for 50 to 55 minutes, or until a tester inserted in cake comes out clean.

6. Invert pan on a wire rack. Cool cake completely. To remove cake from pan, use a long thin knife to loosen edges, trying not to cut into cake.

> **Orange Glaze**
> In a bowl, combine 1 cup (250 mL) confectioner's (icing) sugar, ⅓ cup (75 mL) melted butter, ⅓ cup (75 mL) orange juice and 2 tsp (10 mL) grated orange zest. Makes about 1 cup (250 mL).

Ginger Gingerbread

1½ cups	all-purpose flour	375 mL
¾ tsp	baking powder	4 mL
½ tsp	baking soda	2 mL
½ tsp	salt	2 mL
1 tsp	ground ginger	5 mL
½ tsp	ground cinnamon	2 mL
¼ tsp	ground nutmeg	1 mL
3 tbsp	chopped candied ginger	45 mL
½ cup	sour cream or buttermilk	125 mL
¼ cup	molasses	50 mL
½ cup	butter, softened	125 mL
½ cup	packed brown sugar	125 mL
2	eggs	2

Makes one 8-inch (20 cm) square cake

Candied ginger adds extra flavor to this old-fashioned cake. Serve it with pear sauce or apple sauce or cut into smaller pieces for tea time.

Make Ahead
Gingerbread can be wrapped well and frozen for up to three weeks. You can also cut the cake into individual pieces and wrap separately before freezing.

1. In a medium bowl, combine flour, baking powder, baking soda, salt, ground ginger, cinnamon, nutmeg and candied ginger. Combine well.

2. In a measuring cup, mix together sour cream and molasses.

3. In a large bowl, beat together butter and sugar until light. Beat in eggs one at a time. Add dry and liquid ingredients alternately, making three dry and two liquid additions. Spread mixture in a greased 8-inch (2 L) square baking dish.

4. Convection bake in a preheated 325°F (160°C) oven for 40 to 45 minutes, or until a cake tester inserted in center comes out clean. Cool in pan for 15 minutes before turning out onto a wire rack to cool completely.

Carrot Cake

Makes one 9-inch (23 cm) cake

For several years I baked desserts and breads for an inn, and this cake flew out of the kitchen. It has also made appearances at weddings, birthdays and picnics. Since convection cooking allows cooking on several racks, make at least three cakes at a time and freeze.

Make Ahead
Cake can be prepared, covered and refrigerated for two days with or without icing. Un-iced cake can be wrapped well and frozen for up to a month.

3	eggs	3
2 cups	grated carrots	500 mL
1 cup	packed brown sugar	250 mL
½ cup	golden raisins	125 mL
½ cup	vegetable oil	125 mL
1½ cups	all-purpose flour	375 mL
1 tsp	baking powder	5 mL
¾ tsp	baking soda	4 mL
1 tsp	ground cinnamon	5 mL
½ tsp	ground allspice	2 mL
½ tsp	salt	2 mL

Cream Cheese Icing

8 oz	cream cheese, softened	250 g
¼ cup	butter, softened	50 mL
1 cup	confectioner's (icing) sugar	250 mL
1 tsp	grated orange zest	5 mL

1. In a large bowl, combine eggs, carrots, brown sugar, raisins and oil. Mix thoroughly.

2. In a separate bowl, stir together flour, baking powder, baking soda, cinnamon, allspice and salt. Add dry ingredients to carrot mixture and stir to combine. Spread in a greased 9-inch (23 cm) round cake pan with 2-inch (5 cm) sides.

3. Convection bake in a preheated 325°F (160°C) oven for 30 minutes, or until a cake tester inserted in center comes out clean. Cool in pan for 5 minutes. Turn out onto a wire rack and cool completely.

4. Meanwhile, to prepare icing, in a large bowl, blend together cream cheese and butter until smooth. Gradually sift in confectioner's sugar and combine well. Stir in orange zest.

5. Place cake on a serving plate and spread icing over top and sides. Refrigerate to firm icing.

Peach Upside-down Cake

⅓ cup	butter, melted	75 mL
¾ cup	packed brown sugar	175 mL
1½ cups	peeled, sliced peaches (about 5)	375 mL
½ cup	butter, softened	125 mL
⅔ cup	granulated sugar	150 mL
2	eggs	2
½ tsp	almond extract or vanilla	2 mL
1½ cups	all-purpose flour	375 mL
1½ tsp	baking powder	7 mL
½ tsp	baking soda	2 mL
¼ tsp	salt	1 mL
¾ cup	buttermilk or unflavored yogurt	175 mL

Makes one 9-inch (23 cm) square cake

Celebrate the start of peach season with this irresistible cake. (Other fresh fruits such as plums, raspberries, rhubarb, nectarines and cranberries could also be used.) Serve this the same day it is baked for brunch, dessert or a picnic.

1. Pour melted butter into a 9-inch (2 L) square baking pan. Swirl butter up sides. Sprinkle brown sugar over bottom of pan. Arrange peach slices over sugar.

2. In a large bowl, cream together butter and granulated sugar until light. Add eggs one at a time. Beat in almond extract.

3. In a separate bowl, combine flour, baking powder, baking soda and salt. Add flour mixture and buttermilk alternately to egg mixture, making three dry additions and two liquid. Spread batter over peaches.

4. Convection bake in a preheated 325°F (160°C) oven for 45 minutes, or until a cake tester inserted in center comes out clean. Cool cake in pan on a rack for 15 minutes. Run knife around edge of pan and invert cake onto serving plate. Serve warm or at room temperature.

Peeling Peaches
To peel peaches easily, immerse them in boiling water for 1 to 2 minutes, or until peels loosen. Place in ice water and cool before slipping off peels.

Orange Poppyseed Cake

Makes one 9-inch (23 cm) cake

A tender cake to follow a light meal or to serve on its own with fruit for coffee break.

Make Ahead
This cake freezes well. Wrap well and freeze for up to a month.

Filling

1/3 cup	packed brown sugar	75 mL
1 tsp	ground cinnamon	5 mL

Batter

2/3 cup	milk	150 mL
2 tsp	white vinegar or lemon juice	10 mL
1/4 cup	poppy seeds	50 mL
2/3 cup	butter, softened	150 mL
3/4 cup	granulated sugar	175 mL
3	eggs	3
2 tsp	grated orange zest	10 mL
1/2 tsp	vanilla	2 mL
1 3/4 cups	all-purpose flour	425 mL
1 1/2 tsp	baking powder	7 mL
1/2 tsp	baking soda	2 mL
1/4 tsp	salt	1 mL

1. For filling, in a small bowl, combine brown sugar and cinnamon.

2. For batter, in a measuring cup, combine milk, vinegar and poppy seeds. Let stand for 15 minutes.

3. In a large bowl, cream together butter and granulated sugar until light. Beat in eggs one at a time. Beat in orange zest and vanilla.

4. In a separate bowl, stir together flour, baking powder, baking soda and salt. Add to egg mixture alternately with milk mixture, beating just to combine.

5. Spread half of batter in a greased and parchment-lined 9-inch (23 cm) cake pan with 2-inch (5 cm) sides. Sprinkle with sugar filling. Spread with remaining batter.

6. Convection bake in a preheated 325°F (160°C) oven for 35 minutes, or until a tester inserted in center comes out clean. Cool in pan for 5 minutes. Turn out onto a wire rack and cool completely.

Almond Angel Cake

1½ cups	granulated sugar, divided	375 mL
1 cup	cake flour	250 mL
1¾ cups	egg whites (about 14 eggs), at room temperature	425 mL
1 tsp	cream of tartar	5 mL
½ tsp	salt	2 mL
1 tsp	almond extract	5 mL
½ tsp	vanilla	2 mL

1. In a bowl, sift together ¾ cup (175 mL) sugar and flour. Sift again.

2. In a large clean bowl, combine egg whites with cream of tartar and salt. Beat egg whites until soft peaks form. Gradually add remaining ¾ cup (175 mL) sugar, beating until egg whites are firm. Beat in almond extract and vanilla.

3. Sift one-third of flour mixture over egg whites and fold in gently. Repeat twice with remaining flour, folding in carefully after each addition. Spoon mixture into an ungreased 10-inch (4 L) tube pan. Run knife gently through batter to release any large air bubbles. Smooth surface lightly.

4. Convection bake in a preheated 325°F (160°C) oven for 40 to 45 minutes, or until cake is firm to the touch. Remove from oven. Invert pan on a wire rack and cool completely before removing from pan.

> **Variation**
> *Mocha Chocolate Chip Angel Cake:* Add 1 tbsp (15 mL) crushed instant coffee powder to flour mixture. Omit almond extract. Fold 1 cup (250 mL) chocolate chips into cake after last flour addition. Serve with Chocolate Bourbon Sauce (page 255).

Makes one 10-inch (25 cm) cake

This is the very first cake I ever made. It is my mother's recipe and I first made it when I was nine (for special occasions, we would ice it with fluffy frosting).

Angel cake has recently regained popularity as a lower-fat dessert. Serve it with fresh fruit or lemon curd (page 253).

Make Ahead

Store in an airtight container at room temperature for up to two days or wrap well and freeze for up to a month.

Chocolate Cupcakes

**Makes
24 cupcakes**

These yummy cupcakes are so easy and quick to make (they bake in the convection oven in fifteen minutes) that they may become one of your signature desserts. Whip up the icing while the cupcakes are baking.

Make Ahead
Cupcakes can be baked, placed in a tightly sealed container and frozen with or without icing for up to four weeks.

2	eggs	2
1 cup	granulated sugar	250 mL
¾ cup	vegetable oil	175 mL
½ cup	buttermilk or sour milk (page 217)	125 mL
2 cups	all-purpose flour	500 mL
½ cup	cocoa powder	125 mL
1 tsp	baking powder	5 mL
1 tsp	baking soda	5 mL
¼ tsp	salt	1 mL
1 cup	boiling water	250 mL

Chocolate Icing

½ cup	butter, softened	125 mL
1½ cups	confectioner's (icing) sugar	375 mL
½ cup	cocoa powder, sifted	125 mL
1 tsp	instant coffee powder	5 mL
⅓ cup	milk	75 mL
1 tsp	vanilla	5 mL

1. In a large bowl, beat eggs and granulated sugar. Beat in oil and then buttermilk.

2. In a separate bowl, sift together flour, cocoa, baking powder, baking soda and salt. Add flour mixture to liquid mixture and beat lightly to combine. Add boiling water and beat just until incorporated. Batter will be thin.

3. Transfer batter (in batches if necessary) to a large measuring cup. Pour batter into paper-lined medium muffin cups until slightly more than half full.

4. Convection bake in a preheated 350°F (180°C) oven for 15 minutes, or until cupcakes have risen and a tester inserted in center comes out clean. Let stand for 5 minutes before removing from pans. Cool on a wire rack.

5. Meanwhile, to prepare icing, beat butter until soft. Add confectioner's sugar, cocoa, coffee powder, milk and vanilla and beat until smooth and creamy. Refrigerate for up to 20 minutes until spreadable, then ice cooled cupcakes.

Strawberry Rhubarb Crunch

3½ cups	sliced fresh or frozen rhubarb	875 mL
3 cups	sliced fresh or frozen strawberries	750 mL
½ cup	granulated sugar	125 mL

Topping

¼ cup	butter	50 mL
¼ cup	liquid honey	50 mL
1 cup	rolled oats (not instant)	250 mL
½ cup	all-purpose flour	125 mL
½ cup	chopped hazelnuts or pecans	125 mL
¼ cup	packed brown sugar	50 mL
¼ tsp	ground nutmeg	1 mL

1. In an 8-inch (2 L) square baking dish, combine rhubarb and strawberries. Sprinkle fruit with granulated sugar and mix with a fork.

2. In a small saucepan, combine butter and honey. Heat over low heat for a few minutes, stirring until melted.

3. In a large bowl, combine rolled oats, flour, nuts, brown sugar and nutmeg. Add butter mixture and stir to moisten ingredients. Spread crumb mixture over fruit.

4. Convection bake in a preheated 375°F (190°C) oven for 30 to 35 minutes, or until rhubarb is tender. (If crunch is browning too much near end of cooking time, cover loosely with foil.) Let stand for 30 minutes before serving.

Makes 5 to 6 servings

The tangy sweet combination of strawberry and rhubarb appears in compotes, pies, jams and desserts. Flour has been omitted from the base so the filling will be juicy (the crunch topping will absorb the juices on standing). However, if you are using frozen fruit, add 2 tbsp (25 mL) flour to the fruit.

Make Ahead

Topping can be prepared up to eight hours ahead, but do not taste it or you will need to make it again!

Mincemeat Apple Crisp

Makes 8 servings

This crisp is an easy replacement for mincemeat pie or tarts. Apples and cranberries help cut the richness of mincemeat. Serve warm with ice cream.

Make Ahead

Crisp can be cooked up to a day ahead. Cover loosely and refrigerate. Convection bake at 300°F (150°C) for 25 minutes, or until warm.

2 cups	prepared mincemeat	500 mL
3	apples, peeled and chopped	3
1 cup	fresh or frozen cranberries	250 mL
¼ cup	brandy, apple juice or orange juice	50 mL

Topping

¾ cup	granola or rolled oats (not instant)	175 mL
½ cup	all-purpose flour	125 mL
⅓ cup	packed brown sugar	75 mL
½ tsp	ground allspice or cinnamon	2 mL
⅓ cup	butter, melted	75 mL

1. In a large bowl, combine mincemeat, apples, cranberries and brandy. Transfer to a greased 8-cup (2 L) baking dish.

2. To prepare topping, in a separate bowl, combine granola, flour, brown sugar and allspice. Stir in melted butter. Sprinkle topping over fruit.

3. Convection roast in a preheated 325°F (160°C) oven for 35 to 40 minutes, or until apples and cranberries are tender and top is golden. Serve warm or at room temperature.

Upside-down Plum Cobbler

Base

1¼ cups	all-purpose flour	300 mL
¼ cup	granulated sugar	50 mL
2 tsp	baking powder	10 mL
¼ tsp	ground cinnamon	1 mL
¼ tsp	ground nutmeg	1 mL
¼ tsp	salt	1 mL
1	egg	1
¾ cup	milk	175 mL
¼ cup	butter, melted	50 mL

Fruit

3 cups	pitted and sliced plums	750 mL
⅓ cup	packed brown sugar	75 mL
¼ tsp	ground cinnamon	1 mL

1. To prepare base, in a large bowl, combine flour, granulated sugar, baking powder, cinnamon, nutmeg and salt.

2. In a separate bowl, beat egg, milk and melted butter. Add to dry ingredients and stir just to combine. Spoon into a greased 8-inch (2 L) baking dish.

3. To prepare fruit, in a separate bowl, toss together plums, brown sugar and cinnamon. Spoon over base.

4. Convection bake in a preheated 350°F (180°C) oven for 35 minutes, or until cobbler has risen and a tester inserted in base comes out clean. Serve warm.

Makes 8 servings

Cobblers usually consist of a fruit mixture topped with a biscuit-like batter. This one has the fruit on top. Try a mixture of fruits such as raspberries, pitted and quartered apricots, sliced peaches or nectarines. Serve on its own or with Orange Butterscotch Sauce (page 256).

Apple Cranberry Strudel

Makes 8 servings

Phyllo pastry simplifies the strudel-making process, and it cooks beautifully in the convection oven. Use apples that hold their shape well, such as Northern Spy, Golden Delicious or Ida Red. Strudel is best served the same day it is baked. Serve with vanilla ice cream.

For easier cleanup, line the baking sheet with both foil and parchment-paper, as the apple juices tend to run and burn onto the pan.

4	large apples, peeled and sliced	4
½ cup	dried cranberries	125 mL
⅓ cup	granulated sugar	75 mL
¼ cup	chopped pecans	50 mL
1 tsp	grated lemon zest	5 mL
½ tsp	ground cinnamon	2 mL
6	sheets phyllo pastry	6
¼ cup	butter, melted (approx.)	50 mL
⅓ cup	dry bread crumbs	75 mL

1. In a large bowl, combine apples, cranberries, sugar, pecans, lemon zest and cinnamon.

2. Place a sheet of phyllo pastry on a flat surface. Brush lightly with melted butter and sprinkle with 1 tbsp (15 mL) bread crumbs. Place a second sheet of phyllo on top of first. Brush with butter and sprinkle with bread crumbs. Continue to layer phyllo, butter and crumbs.

3. Spoon apple mixture lengthwise along pastry about 2 inches (5 cm) from long edge. Roll up pastry to enclose apples. Carefully place strudel, seam side down, on a foil- and parchment-lined baking sheet. Tuck in any escaping apples. With a serrated knife, make 7 cuts through top of pastry to mark 8 servings. Brush top with melted butter.

4. Convection bake or roast in a preheated 350°F (180°C) oven for 35 minutes, or until apples are tender and pastry is golden. Cool in pan on a wire rack. Serve warm.

Summer Berry Gratin

2 cups	assorted fresh berries (raspberries, blueberries, blackberries, sliced strawberries)	500 mL
⅓ cup	lemon curd, apricot jam or marmalade	75 mL
½ cup	sour cream or whipping (35%) cream	125 mL
2 tsp	grated lemon zest	10 mL
2 tbsp	orange liqueur (optional)	25 mL
3 tbsp	brown sugar or confectioner's (icing) sugar	45 mL

1. Divide fruit evenly among four ovenproof dishes.
2. In a bowl, stir together lemon curd, sour cream, lemon zest and liqueur, if using. Spoon over fruit and smooth slightly.
3. Just before serving, sprinkle with sugar. Convection broil under a preheated broiler about 5 inches (12.5 cm) from heat, watching constantly, for 30 to 60 seconds, or until top is golden brown and sugar has just melted.

Makes 4 servings

This simple recipe was a highlight at a Simply Summer class that I taught. It is a breeze to assemble a few hours ahead. Just keep it covered and refrigerated until broiling. Other fresh fruits such as plums, orange segments, mango, papaya and pineapple can also be used.

Buy a good-quality storebought lemon curd or make your own (page 253). Use ovenproof ramekins (about 6 oz/175 g) or a shallow gratin dish.

Ruby Fruit

2 cups	fresh strawberries, hulled and quartered	500 mL
1 cup	fresh blueberries	250 mL
1 cup	fresh raspberries	250 mL
¼ cup	strawberry jam	50 mL
¼ cup	orange juice	50 mL

1. In a 6-cup (1.5 L) baking dish, combine strawberries, blueberries, raspberries, jam and orange juice.
2. Convection roast in a preheated 375°F (190°C) oven for 20 to 25 minutes, or until fruit has just softened. Serve warm or cold.

Makes 4 servings

A colorful and full-flavored dessert to serve with angel cake, ice cream or frozen yogurt.

Amaretto Jellyroll

Makes 10 to 12 servings

In this recipe the old-fashioned jellyroll is embellished with a luscious cream filling. Use your favorite liqueur (orange, coconut, coffee flavored, etc.) or 1 tsp (5 mL) really good pure vanilla extract.

Make Ahead

Freeze filled jellyroll on baking sheet, then wrap whole or cut in half and wrap and freeze for up to four days. Defrost in refrigerator. Roll can also be carefully cut when still frozen. Garnish before serving.

5	eggs, separated	5
1 cup	granulated sugar	250 mL
⅓ cup	water	75 mL
2 tsp	grated lemon zest	10 mL
1 tsp	vanilla	5 mL
1 cup	all-purpose flour	250 mL
¾ tsp	baking powder	4 mL
1 tbsp	confectioner's (icing) sugar	15 mL
Filling		
½ cup	raspberry jam	125 mL
1 cup	whipping (35%) cream	250 mL
3 tbsp	Amaretto liqueur	45 mL
Garnish		
1½ cups	fresh raspberries or sliced strawberries	375 mL
¼ cup	sliced almonds, toasted	50 mL
	Fresh mint leaves	

1. Grease a 17- by 11-inch (45 by 29 cm) baking sheet. Line with parchment paper so edges extend slightly beyond long edges (this will help you remove cake from pan). Lightly grease and flour parchment paper, shaking off excess flour.

2. In a large bowl, beat egg yolks and granulated sugar until very thick and lemon colored. Beat in water, lemon zest and vanilla.

3. In a small bowl, stir together flour and baking powder. Slowly beat into egg mixture in three additions (mixture will be thick).

4. In a separate large, clean bowl, beat egg whites until soft peaks form. Whisk one-third of beaten whites into base, then gently fold in remaining whites. Spread mixture over prepared pan, smoothing evenly.

5. Convection bake in a preheated 300°F (150°C) oven for 20 minutes, or until firm to touch and light golden. Cool in pan on a wire rack.

6. Sprinkle surface generously with confectioner's sugar. Loosen edges of cake. Place a clean tea towel over top and invert. Remove pan. Gently remove parchment paper. Spread cake with jam to within 1 inch (2.5 cm) of one long edge.

7. In a large bowl, whip cream until stiff peaks form. Beat in Amaretto. Spread whipped cream over jam.

8. Using tea towel to help, roll up jellyroll lengthwise and gently guide onto a serving platter or baking sheet. Cover and chill for 1 to 5 hours.

9. To serve, cut roll into serving pieces with a knife dipped in hot water. Garnish with berries, almonds and mint.

Lemon Curd

In a heavy saucepan, combine 4 eggs, 1 cup (250 mL) granulated sugar, $3/4$ cup (175 mL) lemon juice and 1 tbsp (15 mL) grated lemon zest. Stir well to incorporate eggs. Place over medium heat and bring to a boil, stirring constantly. Cook for 2 minutes, or until thickened. Remove from heat and stir in 2 tbsp (25 mL) butter. Place in a bowl, cover surface directly with plastic wrap and refrigerate until cold and firm (up to 5 days). Makes $2^1/2$ cups (625 mL).

Chocolate Almond Torte

Makes one 8-inch (20 cm) torte

This flourless torte is small, but it is dense and rich and will satisfy any chocolate lover. It can be served without the glaze (just dust with icing sugar or add a dollop of whipped cream), but the chocolate glaze does add a sleek finishing touch.

The chocolate can be melted in a microwave on Medium heat. Watch it carefully. Remove the chocolate from the oven just when it collapses and stir until completely melted. For the best flavor and texture, grind the almonds yourself in a food processor or with a rotary hand grater rather than buying preground almonds.

Make Ahead
Torte can be glazed, covered and refrigerated for up to two days or frozen, unglazed, for up to six weeks.

½ cup	butter, softened	125 mL
⅔ cup	granulated sugar	150 mL
3	eggs	3
4 oz	semisweet or bittersweet chocolate, melted and slightly cooled	125 g
1¼ cups	ground almonds	300 mL
1 tsp	grated orange zest	5 mL

Glaze

4 oz	semisweet or bittersweet chocolate, chopped (about 1 cup/250 mL)	125 g
¼ cup	whipping (35%) cream	50 mL
1 tbsp	orange liqueur	15 mL

1. To prepare cake, cream butter and sugar in a large bowl. Beat in eggs one at a time. Slowly beat in melted chocolate. Stir in almonds and orange zest. Turn mixture into a lightly greased and parchment-lined 8-inch (20 cm) round cake pan.

2. Convection bake in a preheated 350°F (180°C) oven for 25 to 28 minutes, or until a skewer inserted in center comes out almost clean (cake may appear a bit soft in center). Cool in pan on a rack for 30 minutes. Run knife around edge of cake. Invert and cool completely.

3. To prepare glaze, place chopped chocolate and cream in a stainless-steel bowl set over hot water. Melt and stir together. Remove from heat and add liqueur. Cool glaze until thick enough to spread (to speed up this process, place over a bowl of ice water and stir).

4. Place cake on a serving plate. Pour glaze over cake, letting it run down sides.

Chocolate Bread Pudding with Chocolate Bourbon Sauce

Chocolate Bread Pudding

1/3 cup	butter	75 mL
6 oz	semisweet chocolate, chopped (about 1 1/2 cups/375 mL)	175 g
5	eggs	5
1/2 cup	granulated sugar	125 mL
1 1/2 cups	milk	375 mL
1 1/2 cups	light (5%) cream	375 mL
1 tsp	vanilla	5 mL
6 cups	egg bread or cinnamon bread cubes	1.5 L

Chocolate Bourbon Sauce

6 oz	semisweet chocolate, chopped (about 1 1/2 cups/375 mL)	175 g
1/4 cup	butter	50 mL
1/4 cup	corn syrup	50 mL
1/2 cup	whipping (35%) cream	125 mL
3 tbsp	Bourbon	45 mL

Makes 8 servings

What a way to update an old-fashioned dessert! Orange, raspberry or coffee liqueur can be used in the sauce instead of Bourbon. You can also serve the sauce with angel cake (page 245), chocolate squares (page 235), ice cream or fresh fruit.

Make Ahead
Sauce can be covered and refrigerated for up to a week. It will thicken when refrigerated, so soften slowly in a microwave or over hot water. Pudding can be covered and refrigerated overnight. Serve cold or convection bake in a 225°F (110°C) oven for 20 minutes.

1. To prepare pudding, melt butter and chocolate in a stainless-steel bowl over simmering water. Stir together and cool slightly.

2. In a large bowl, whisk together eggs and sugar. Stir in milk, light cream, vanilla and melted chocolate. Stir in bread cubes. Let stand for 30 minutes.

3. Pour mixture into a buttered 8-inch (2 L) square baking dish. Place on a baking sheet in case of overflow. Convection bake in a preheated 325°F (160°C) oven for 35 to 40 minutes, or until a knife inserted in center comes out clean. Cool for at least 45 minutes before serving.

4. Meanwhile, to prepare sauce, combine chocolate, butter, corn syrup, whipping cream and Bourbon in a stainless-steel bowl. Place over hot water until chocolate melts. Whisk to blend ingredients together. Serve warm or at room temperature.

Cranberry Croissant Bread Pudding

Makes 8 to 10 servings

Another version of bread pudding. Serving it with butterscotch sauce will put it over the top.

Make Ahead

Although pudding is best served warm, it can be made a day ahead, covered and refrigerated. Warm slightly if desired to take off the chill before serving. You could also assemble and refrigerate overnight before baking.

6	eggs	6
2 cups	milk	500 mL
2 cups	light (5%) cream	500 mL
¾ cup	granulated sugar	175 mL
1 tsp	vanilla	5 mL
½ tsp	ground cinnamon	2 mL
6	large (5- by 3-inch/12 by 8 cm) croissants	6
1 cup	cranberry sauce	250 mL

1. In a large bowl, whisk eggs. Whisk in milk, cream, sugar, vanilla and cinnamon.

2. Cut croissants into 1-inch (2.5 cm) cubes. Place half the cubes in a well-buttered 13- by 9-inch (3 L) baking dish. Spoon cranberry sauce over bread. Top with remaining croissant cubes.

3. Gently pour liquid mixture over top. Let stand for 15 minutes, poking down cubes to make sure they are evenly distributed and immersed in liquid.

4. Convection bake in a preheated 325°F (160°C) oven for 50 to 55 minutes, or until a knife inserted in center comes out clean. Serve slightly warm or at room temperature.

> **Orange Butterscotch Sauce**
> In a medium saucepan, combine ⅓ cup (75 mL) butter, ⅔ cup (150 mL) packed brown sugar, ½ cup (125 mL) whipping cream, ⅓ cup (75 mL) orange juice and 2 tsp (10 mL) grated orange zest. Heat just to a boil. Serve warm. Sauce can be made ahead, covered and refrigerated for up to three days. Reheat before using. Makes about 1½ cups (375 mL).

Pecan Sticky Buns (page 208)
Overleaf: Earl Grey Cookies (page 227)

Bonnie Stern's Pavlova

4	egg whites	4
1 cup	granulated sugar	250 mL
2 tsp	white vinegar	10 mL
1½ cups	yogurt cheese	375 mL
2 tbsp	liquid honey or confectioner's (icing) sugar	25 mL
1 tsp	vanilla	5 mL
4 cups	fresh blueberries, raspberries or strawberries, or a combination	1 L

1. In a large, very clean bowl, beat egg whites until light.

2. Gradually add granulated sugar to egg whites and beat until firm. Beat in vinegar.

3. Outline a 10-inch (25 cm) circle on a piece of parchment paper and place on a baking sheet. Spoon egg whites inside circle and spread in loose waves.

4. Convection bake in a preheated 250°F (120°C) oven for 2 hours. Remove from oven and cool. (If kitchen is very humid, store pavlova in a dry place such as a turned-off oven; leave a note on the oven door so you don't forget it's in there!)

5. For the filling, combine yogurt cheese with honey and vanilla. Just before serving, spread yogurt mixture over meringue. Top with berries. Serve immediately.

> ### Yogurt Cheese
> Line a strainer with cheesecloth, paper towel or coffee filter. Place strainer over a bowl. (You can also use a yogurt strainer, now readily available.) Place 3 cups (750 mL) unflavored yogurt in strainer. Cover and refrigerate for 3 hours or overnight. Discard liquid. Spoon thickened yogurt cheese into another container. Cover and refrigerate. Makes about 1½ cups (375 mL).

Makes 8 servings

This is one of the great HeartSmart dessert recipes from Bonnie Stern, owner of her own cooking school in Toronto and the author of twelve delicious cookbooks. The convection oven is fabulous for cooking meringues because of its continuous circulating heat.

Overleaf: Rhubarb Coffee Cake (page 238)
Apple Pie with Cheddar Pastry (page 260)

Washday Pudding

Makes about 9 servings

I remember this pudding from my childhood. My mother called it Washday Pudding, because she would whip it up on Mondays in the midst of doing laundry. It is also known as Cottage Pudding. This version is based on a recipe from Cathy Angus, a prolific knitter and very busy woman who calls it Unemployment Cake. Whatever the name, it is so easy to bake in the convection oven along with the rest of dinner.

This is a very sweet dessert, so you may want to serve some fresh fruit with it to offset the sweetness.

Sauce

1¼ cups	water	300 mL
1¼ cups	packed brown sugar	300 mL
1 tbsp	lemon juice	15 mL

Cake

⅓ cup	butter, softened	75 mL
¾ cup	granulated sugar	175 mL
2	eggs	2
1 tsp	vanilla	5 mL
1½ cups	all-purpose flour	375 mL
2 tsp	baking powder	10 mL
¼ tsp	salt	1 mL
¾ cup	milk	175 mL

1. To prepare sauce, in a medium saucepan, combine water, brown sugar and lemon juice. Bring to a boil. Pour into a greased 9-inch (2.5 L) square baking dish (preferably glass).

2. In a bowl, cream together butter and granulated sugar until light. Beat in eggs one at a time. Beat in vanilla.

3. In a separate bowl, combine flour, baking powder and salt. Add to butter mixture alternately with milk, mixing lightly after each addition. Spoon batter over sugar mixture.

4. Convection bake in a preheated 325°F (160°C) oven for 35 to 40 minutes, or until a tester inserted in center comes out clean. Serve warm or at room temperature.

> **Variation**
> *Plain White Cake:* Mix cake batter and turn into a greased and parchment-lined 8-inch (2 L) square baking pan. Bake for 35 minutes, or until a tester comes out clean. Serve plain or as a base for fruit shortcakes.

Toffee Chocolate Crunch Cheesecake

Base

1¼ cups	chocolate cookie crumbs	300 mL
½ cup	finely chopped pecans	125 mL
⅓ cup	butter, melted	75 mL

Filling

2 lbs	cream cheese, softened	1 kg
1 cup	granulated sugar	250 mL
4	eggs	4
¼ cup	sour cream	50 mL
2 tbsp	all-purpose flour	25 mL
2 tsp	vanilla	10 mL
4	1½-oz (39 g) chocolate-covered toffee crunch bars, chopped (about 1 cup/250 mL)	4

1. To prepare base, in a bowl, combine cookie crumbs, pecans and melted butter. Press into bottom and partway up sides of a greased 9-inch (2.5 L) springform pan.

2. To prepare filling, in a large bowl, beat cream cheese and sugar until well blended and very light. Beat in eggs one at a time, scraping down sides of bowl. Stir in sour cream, flour and vanilla just until combined. Fold in half of candy bars.

3. Pour mixture into prepared pan. Sprinkle with remaining candy bar. Convection bake in a preheated 300°F (150°C) oven for 50 to 55 minutes, or until just set (center may seem slightly jiggly, but do not overbake). Turn off oven and let cool in oven with door slightly ajar for 30 minutes. Cool completely in refrigerator for 6 hours or overnight.

Makes one 9-inch (23 cm) cheesecake

Slow baking in the convection oven produces a smooth chocolate- and caramel-studded cheesecake. For a special presentation, drizzle with chocolate and caramel sauces and garnish with fresh berries and chocolate shavings.

Cheesecakes are rich, and this should make at least twelve servings. Broken toffee crunch chocolate bars are available in bulk food stores.

Make Ahead

After cooling, cheesecake can be covered and refrigerated for up to three days or wrapped well and frozen for up to a month. Defrost in refrigerator. Individual pieces can also be wrapped well and frozen.

Apple Pie with Cheddar Pastry

**Makes one
9-inch (23 cm) pie**

A variation on an old favorite. Serve with a dollop of whipped cream or yogurt cheese (page 257). The added Cheddar results in a crusty pastry. I often use this pastry for meat or chicken pies, too.

Cheddar Pastry

1½ cups	all-purpose flour	375 mL
½ cup	grated Cheddar cheese	125 mL
½ tsp	salt	2 mL
¼ cup	cold butter, cut in pieces	50 mL
¼ cup	cold lard or shortening, cut in pieces	50 mL
5 tbsp	ice-cold water (approx.)	65 mL

Filling

6	apples (Northern Spy, Ida Red, Golden Delicious), peeled and sliced	6
⅓ cup	granulated sugar	75 mL
2 tbsp	all-purpose flour	25 mL
1 tbsp	lemon juice	15 mL
1 tbsp	cold butter, cut in bits	15 mL

Topping

⅓ cup	all-purpose flour	75 mL
⅓ cup	packed brown sugar	75 mL
½ cup	grated Cheddar cheese	125 mL
1 tsp	ground cinnamon	5 mL
¼ cup	cold butter, cut in pieces	50 mL

1. To prepare pastry, combine flour, cheese and salt in a large bowl. Using a pastry blender, cut in butter and lard until mixture resembles coarse crumbs with a few larger pieces. Drizzle ice water over dry ingredients, stirring with a fork until a rough dough forms. Bring dough together and shape into a disc. Wrap in plastic and refrigerate for 20 minutes.

2. On a lightly floured surface, roll dough into an 11-inch (28 cm) circle. Ease into a 9-inch (23 cm) pie plate. Fold overhang under at rim. Flute edge.

3. For filling, in a large bowl, combine apples, granulated sugar, flour, lemon juice and butter. Combine thoroughly. Turn into prepared pie shell, mounding apples in center.

4. For topping, in a small bowl, combine flour, brown sugar, cheese and cinnamon. Cut in butter until it is in tiny bits. Sprinkle topping over apples.

5. Convection roast or bake in a preheated 400°F (200°C) oven for 15 minutes. Reduce heat to 325°F (160°C) and continue to bake for 45 to 50 minutes, or until apples are tender. Cool on a rack.

Roasted Peaches

¼ cup	chopped candied ginger	50 mL
12	peaches, peeled and quartered	12
⅓ cup	packed brown sugar	75 mL
¼ cup	butter, melted	50 mL
⅓ cup	peach liqueur or peach juice (approx.)	75 mL

1. Sprinkle ginger over bottom of a 13- by 9-inch (3 L) baking dish. Arrange peaches over ginger in as much of a single layer as possible. Sprinkle with brown sugar and drizzle with melted butter. Turn peaches slightly to coat.

2. Convection bake in a preheated 350°F (180°C) oven for 25 to 30 minutes, or until peaches are just tender. Timing depends on ripeness of peaches. Do not overcook. Cool slightly, then pour liqueur over peaches.

Makes 8 to 10 servings

Cooking peaches in the convection oven highlights their flavor. For color, select peaches with a rosy blush. Serve with ice cream, whipped cream or yogurt.

This recipe can easily be halved.

Make Ahead
Peaches can be cooked, covered and refrigerated up to two days ahead. For the best flavor, bring to room temperature before serving.

Pumpkin Praline Pie

**Makes one
9-inch (23 cm) pie**

The praline surprise is tucked under the shiny surface of this classic pumpkin pie. Serve with or without whipped cream.

Make Ahead

The pastry, praline and filling can all be prepared ahead and refrigerated overnight (this is particularly helpful if you are making several pies at once). Before baking, simply pour the filling into the prepared pie shells and bake.

All-purpose Pastry

1½ cups	all-purpose flour	375 mL
1 tsp	salt	5 mL
¼ cup	cold butter, cut in cubes	50 mL
¼ cup	cold lard, cut in cubes	50 mL
1 tsp	lemon juice or white vinegar	5 mL
⅓ cup	ice-cold water (approx.)	75 mL

Praline

3 tbsp	butter	45 mL
½ cup	packed brown sugar	125 mL
½ cup	chopped pecans or hazelnuts	125 mL

Filling

2	eggs	2
1	14-oz (398 mL) can pumpkin puree	1
¾ cup	packed brown sugar	175 mL
1¼ cups	evaporated milk	300 mL
1 tsp	ground cinnamon	5 mL
½ tsp	ground ginger	2 mL
¼ tsp	salt	1 mL
Pinch	ground cloves	Pinch
Pinch	ground nutmeg	Pinch

1. To make pastry, in a large bowl, combine flour and salt. Add butter and lard and cut in until mixture is in tiny bits. Combine lemon juice and water and sprinkle over flour. Mix together gently with a fork until mixture starts to come together. If it is too dry, add water 1 tsp (5 mL) at a time until mixture can be formed into a ball. (To make pastry in a food processor, combine flour and salt in bowl fitted with metal blade and pulse on/off. Add butter and lard and pulse until fat is in small bits. Combine lemon juice with ¼ cup/50 mL cold water and pour over flour. Pulse just until dough starts to come together. Remove dough from food processor and form into ball.)

2. On a lightly floured surface, roll pastry into a 12-inch (30 cm) circle. Line a 9-inch (23 cm) pie plate and double pastry over at rim to make a high fluted edge. Refrigerate.

3. To make praline, in a small saucepan, melt together butter and sugar over medium heat. Stir in pecans. Remove from heat and refrigerate until cool. Sprinkle praline over bottom of prepared pastry.

4. To prepare filling, in a large bowl, mix together eggs, pumpkin and sugar. Whisk in evaporated milk, cinnamon, ginger, salt, cloves and nutmeg. Pour mixture into pie shell.

5. Convection roast or bake in a preheated 400°F (200°C) oven for 10 minutes. Reduce heat to 325°F (160°C) and continue to bake for 45 to 50 minutes, or until a sharp knife inserted in center comes out clean. Cool completely on a rack.

Pears with Ginger Cookies

4	pears, halved and cored	4
¼ cup	orange juice	50 mL
1 tbsp	lemon juice	15 mL
2 tbsp	butter, cut in bits	25 mL
2 tbsp	brown sugar	25 mL
½ cup	coarsely crumbled ginger cookies	125 mL

Makes 4 servings

Pears and ginger are a favorite combination. Serve warm or at room temperature as is or with whipped cream, yogurt, ice cream or fresh berries. Any ginger cookie works well; just crumble them up by hand.

Select pears that are slightly firm but not too hard; buy them a few days ahead to let them ripen.

1. Arrange pears skin side down in a shallow baking dish (an 8-inch/2 L square baking dish works well). Drizzle orange juice and lemon juice over pears and top with butter bits, brown sugar and cookie crumbs.

2. Convection roast in a preheated 375°F (190°C) oven for 20 minutes, or until pears test tender with tip of a sharp knife.

Blueberry Lemon Crumb Pie

Makes one 9-inch (23 cm) pie

Wild blueberries are so precious that they seldom make it into a pie, but if there is an opportunity to stock up and freeze them, this pie can easily be made with frozen berries. Fresh or frozen domestic blueberries also work well. If you use storebought pastry, be sure to purchase a deep shell and place the pie on a baking sheet in case of overflow.

5 cups	blueberries	1.25 L
½ cup	granulated sugar	125 mL
¼ cup	all-purpose flour	50 mL
½ tsp	grated lemon zest	2 mL
1	unbaked 9-inch (23 cm) deep pie shell (page 266)	1

Topping

⅓ cup	all-purpose flour	75 mL
⅓ cup	packed brown sugar	75 mL
1 tbsp	grated lemon zest	15 mL
¼ cup	butter, cut in small pieces	50 mL

1. In a large bowl, combine blueberries, granulated sugar, flour and lemon zest. Spoon into prepared pie shell. Place on a baking sheet.

2. Convection roast or bake pie in a preheated 400°F (200°C) oven for 15 minutes. Reduce temperature to 325°F (160°C) and bake for 15 minutes. (At this time, some sugar and flour may be visible on top of pie. With a knife or fork, gently swirl into fruit.)

3. Meanwhile, to prepare topping, in a bowl, combine flour, brown sugar and lemon zest. Cut in butter until it is in tiny bits.

4. Sprinkle topping over pie. Continue to bake for 15 to 20 minutes, or until filling is bubbling and top is golden. Cool in pan on a wire rack.

Open-face Apricot Tart

Pastry

2 cups	all-purpose flour	500 mL
2 tbsp	granulated sugar	25 mL
¼ tsp	salt	1 mL
¾ cup	cold butter, cut in pieces	175 mL
1	egg yolk	1
⅓ cup	ice-cold water	75 mL

Filling

¼ cup	chopped pecans or almonds	50 mL
¼ cup	all-purpose flour	50 mL
⅓ cup	granulated sugar, divided	75 mL
1½ lbs	fresh apricots, pitted and quartered	750 g
1 tbsp	butter	15 mL
¼ cup	apricot jam	50 mL

> **Makes one 10-inch (25 cm) tart**
>
> This is a versatile recipe; instead of apricots you can use almost any seasonal fruit, such as plums, peaches, pears, rhubarb and apples (apricots and plums work well together).
>
> If you do not have a rimless baking sheet, turn a rimmed baking sheet upside down to allow the tart to slide off easily.

1. To prepare pastry, combine flour, sugar and salt in a large bowl. Cut in butter until mixture resembles coarse crumbs with a few larger pieces. In a measuring cup, combine egg yolk and water. Pour over flour mixture, stirring with a fork. Bring mixture together to form a ball, adding more liquid if necessary. Shape into a disc. Wrap in plastic and refrigerate for 30 minutes.

2. On a lightly floured surface, roll pastry into a 14-inch (35 cm) circle. Transfer to a rimless baking sheet.

3. For filling, in a small bowl, combine nuts, flour and ¼ cup (50 mL) sugar. Sprinkle over pastry to within 2 inches (5 cm) of edge.

4. Arrange apricots over nut mixture. Fold up border over fruit, crimping or folding pastry as necessary. Sprinkle fruit with remaining 2 tbsp (25 mL) sugar and dot with butter.

5. Convection roast or bake in a preheated 400°F (200°C) oven for 15 minutes. Reduce heat to 350°F (180°C) and continue to bake for 35 to 40 minutes, or until pastry is golden and fruit is tender. Carefully remove tart from oven. Cool for 4 minutes before gently sliding onto a rack.

6. Melt jam in a small saucepan over low heat. Spoon or brush melted jam over filling.

Quebec Sugar Tart

Makes one 9-inch (23 cm) tart

While on a ski vacation to Mont Tremblant in Quebec, I ate various versions of this tart. The pastry can also be easily prepared in a food processor (page 262).

Serve this tart warm or at room temperature. If you don't have a tart pan, just use a regular 9-inch (23 cm) pie plate.

Make Ahead

Pastry can be rolled, covered and refrigerated up to a day ahead or wrapped and frozen for up to two weeks. The prepared tart shell can be baked, cooled and kept in a dry place at room temperature for up to a day before filling.

Pastry

1½ cups	all-purpose flour	375 mL
1 tbsp	granulated sugar	15 mL
¼ tsp	salt	1 mL
¾ cup	cold butter, cut in pieces	175 mL
5 tbsp	ice-cold water (approx.)	65 mL

Filling

3	eggs	3
1 cup	packed brown sugar	250 mL
½ cup	whipping (35%) cream	125 mL
½ cup	maple syrup	125 mL
2 tbsp	butter, melted	25 mL
1 tbsp	lemon juice or cider vinegar	15 mL

1. To prepare pastry, combine flour, granulated sugar and salt in a large bowl. Using a pastry blender, cut in butter until mixture resembles coarse crumbs with a few larger pieces. Drizzle ice water over dry ingredients, stirring with a fork until a rough dough forms. Gather dough together and shape into a disc. Wrap in plastic and refrigerate for 30 minutes.

2. Roll dough out on a lightly floured surface to fit a 9-inch (23 cm) tart pan with a 1-inch (2.5 cm) pastry overhang. Ease pastry into pan and fold edge over to make a double thickness that is about ¼ inch (5 mm) higher than pan (to allow for shrinking). Place on a baking sheet (for easier handling). Line pastry with parchment paper and fill with pie weights or dried beans.

3. Convection roast in a preheated 400°F (200°C) oven for 15 minutes. Remove weights and paper and bake for 10 minutes, or until pastry is light brown. Reduce temperature to 325°F (160°C).

4. Meanwhile, to prepare filling, in a large bowl, beat eggs. Beat in brown sugar, cream, maple syrup, melted butter and lemon juice. Pour into tart shell.

5. Convection roast or bake for 30 to 35 minutes, or until filling is set but still slightly jiggly. Cool in pan on a wire rack.

Convection Toaster Oven

Mediterranean Stuffed Mushrooms

Makes 5 to 6 servings

Serve these as a starter or as a side dish to accompany fish or poultry dishes. If jumbo mushrooms are unavailable, just use more of the smaller ones. To prevent mushrooms from wobbling, cut a small slice off the bottoms so they will sit flat. Six portobello mushrooms could also be substituted.

Make Ahead

Filling can be made ahead and refrigerated for up to six hours.

10 to 12	jumbo mushrooms (2½ to 3 inches/ 6 to 8 cm) in diameter	10 to 12
¾ cup	cooked brown or white rice	175 mL
2 tbsp	chopped sun-dried tomatoes (oil packed)	25 mL
1	clove garlic, finely chopped	1
2	green onions, finely chopped	2
2 tbsp	chopped fresh dillweed	25 mL
2 tbsp	chopped fresh parsley	25 mL
½ cup	crumbled feta cheese	125 mL
½ tsp	salt	2 mL
¼ tsp	black pepper	1 mL
¼ cup	currants (optional)	50 mL
2 tbsp	olive oil	25 mL
2 tbsp	lemon juice	25 mL

1. Remove stems from mushrooms. Arrange in one layer on oven pan.

2. In a bowl, combine rice, sun-dried tomatoes, garlic, green onions, dill, parsley, feta, salt, pepper and currants, if using. Spoon into mushroom caps, mounding in center.

3. In a small measuring cup, combine olive oil and lemon juice. Drizzle over mushrooms.

4. Convection bake in a preheated 350°F (180°C) convection toaster oven for 12 to 15 minutes, or until mushrooms are cooked and filling is hot. Let stand for 2 minutes before serving.

Baked Brie

1	7-oz (200 g) round Brie cheese	1
⅓ cup	peach or apricot jam	75 mL
⅓ cup	cranberry sauce	75 mL
2 tbsp	pine nuts	25 mL

1. Place Brie on parchment-lined oven pan (make sure paper does not hang over edges).
2. In a bowl, combine peach jam, cranberry sauce and pine nuts. Spoon over Brie.
3. Convection bake in a preheated 350°F (180°C) convection toaster oven for 8 to 10 minutes, or until cheese has softened.

Makes 4 to 8 servings

A creamy, oozing spread that can be served at almost any time — for brunch, afternoon tea, as an appetizer or dessert. Serve with crackers, breads, raw vegetables or fruit.

Crab Melts

1	7-oz (200 g) package frozen crab meat, defrosted	1
½ cup	diced Cheddar, Brie or Asiago cheese	125 mL
¼ cup	finely chopped celery	50 mL
¼ cup	finely chopped red bell pepper	50 mL
¼ cup	finely chopped green onion	50 mL
⅓ cup	mayonnaise	75 mL
1 tsp	Russian-style mustard	5 mL
½ tsp	salt	2 mL
¼ tsp	black pepper	1 mL
3	English muffins	3

1. Place crab in a sieve and press gently to squeeze out moisture. In a medium bowl, combine crab, cheese, celery, red pepper, green onion, mayonnaise, mustard, salt and pepper.
2. Cut English muffins in half horizontally. Place on oven pan. Convection bake in a preheated 350°F (180°C) convection toaster oven for 5 minutes.
3. Spread crab mixture evenly over muffins. Bake for 7 to 8 minutes, or until topping is heated through and cheese has melted slightly.

Makes 6 pieces

This mixture also makes a great sandwich filling. As a substitute for crab, use diced imitation crab or even canned tuna.

Pizza Dip

Makes 4 to 6 servings

Enjoy all the flavors of pizza, without the crust, in this winning appetizer. Serve with pita crisps (page 28), crackers or raw vegetables.

Make Ahead
Dip can be assembled and refrigerated several hours ahead.

8 oz	cream cheese, softened	250 g
3 tbsp	olive oil	45 mL
½ tsp	dried Italian herbs or oregano leaves	2 mL
2 tbsp	chopped green olives	25 mL
2 tbsp	chopped sun-dried tomatoes (oil-packed)	25 mL
¼ cup	chopped red bell pepper	50 mL
¼ cup	diced pepperoni or ham	50 mL
¾ cup	grated mozzarella cheese	175 mL
2 tbsp	grated Parmesan cheese	25 mL

1. In a food processor or by hand, blend together cream cheese, oil and herbs. Spread over bottom of a lightly greased shallow 8-inch (20 cm) ovenproof serving dish. Sprinkle with olives, sun-dried tomatoes, red pepper, pepperoni, mozzarella and Parmesan.

2. Convection bake in a preheated 350°F (180°C) convection toaster oven for 10 minutes, or until cheese has melted.

Havarti and Mango Croissant

Makes 2 servings

This lovely combination of cheese and fruit makes an interesting combination. Serve warm with a green salad. Try other cheeses such Brie or Camembert, or any mild cheese that will melt slightly. Use peaches or nectarines in season instead of mango.

2	large croissants, halved lengthwise	2
2 tbsp	red pepper jelly	25 mL
6	thin slices fresh mango (approx.)	6
2	slices Havarti cheese	2

1. Place bottom halves of croissants on oven pan. Spread with jelly. Top with mango and cheese. Top with remaining croissant halves.

2. Convection bake in a preheated 350°F (180°C) convection toaster oven for 8 to 10 minutes, or until warmed through. Cool slightly, then cut each "sandwich" in half or in thirds.

Tomato and Olive Bruschetta

¼ cup	olive oil, divided	50 mL
2	cloves garlic, minced	2
6	slices French or Italian bread, about 1 inch (2.5 cm) thick	6
3	tomatoes, cored and diced	3
½ cup	chopped green or black olives	125 mL
2 tbsp	balsamic vinegar	25 mL
¼ cup	shredded fresh basil	50 mL
¼ tsp	salt	1 mL
¼ tsp	black pepper	1 mL
6	thin slices Parmesan cheese (optional)	6

Makes 3 to 6 servings

Serve this bruschetta as a hearty starter. The generous topping is piled on top and tumbles down the sides of the bread, so provide knives and forks.

1. In a small bowl, combine 2 tbsp (25 mL) olive oil and garlic. Arrange bread slices on oven pan and brush with garlic oil.

2. Convection bake in a preheated 325°F (160°C) convection toaster oven for 8 to 10 minutes, or until slightly colored and toasty.

3. Meanwhile, in a medium bowl, combine tomatoes, olives, vinegar, remaining 2 tbsp (25 mL) oil, basil, salt and pepper.

4. Arrange toasts on serving plates. Spoon tomato mixture over bread. Top with Parmesan slices, if using.

Old-fashioned Macaroni and Cheese

**Makes 4 to
6 servings**

Convection baking in a
shallow casserole gives
this old-time favorite
a golden, crispy crust.

1½ cups	uncooked macaroni (about 6 oz/175 g)	375 mL
2 tbsp	butter	25 mL
1	onion, chopped	1
2 tbsp	all-purpose flour	25 mL
2 cups	milk	500 mL
½ tsp	dry mustard	2 mL
¼ tsp	paprika	1 mL
¾ tsp	salt	4 mL
¼ tsp	black pepper	1 mL
1½ cups	grated Cheddar cheese	375 mL
1 cup	fresh bread crumbs	250 mL
2 tbsp	butter, melted	25 mL

1. In a large saucepan, cook macaroni in a large amount of boiling salted water for 8 to 10 minutes, or until just tender. Drain well.

2. Meanwhile, melt butter in a large saucepan over medium heat. Add onion and cook, stirring occasionally, for 3 to 4 minutes, or until softened. Add flour and cook, stirring, for 3 minutes.

3. Whisk in milk. Bring sauce to a boil, reduce heat and simmer, stirring occasionally, for 6 minutes. Remove from heat. Season with mustard, paprika, salt and pepper. Stir in cheese and drained macaroni. Spoon macaroni into a lightly greased 6-cup (1.5 L) shallow baking dish.

4. In a small bowl, stir together bread crumbs and melted butter. Sprinkle bread crumbs over macaroni.

5. Convection bake in a preheated 350°F (180°C) convection toaster oven for 25 minutes, or until golden and bubbling.

Stuffed Baked Potatoes

3	large baking potatoes	3
⅓ cup	sour cream or unflavored yogurt	75 mL
2 tbsp	olive oil or butter	25 mL
1½ cups	grated Gruyère or Cheddar cheese, divided	375 mL
¼ cup	chopped green onion or chives	50 mL
2 tsp	chopped fresh tarragon, or ½ tsp (2 mL) dried	10 mL
½ tsp	salt	2 mL
¼ tsp	black pepper	1 mL
½ cup	diced cooked bacon or ham	125 mL

Makes 4 to 6 servings

Potatoes bake beautifully in the convection oven, especially when embellished with fresh herbs and cheese. Serve with cold meats, poultry or fish, or just with a salad for a light meal.

1. Pierce potatoes with a fork. Convection bake in a preheated 400°F (200°C) convection toaster oven, directly on rack, for 50 minutes, or until tender when pierced with a skewer. Cool slightly.

2. Carefully cut potatoes in half lengthwise. Gently scoop out potato pulp, leaving enough shell to act as a container. Place pulp in a large bowl and mash. Add sour cream, olive oil, ¾ cup (175 mL) cheese, green onion, tarragon, salt, pepper and bacon. Mix well.

3. Spoon mixture into potato shells, mounding in center. Sprinkle with remaining ¾ cup (175 mL) cheese.

4. Arrange potatoes on oven pan. Convection bake in a preheated 400°F (200°C) convection toaster oven for 12 to 15 minutes, or until potatoes are heated through and cheese has melted.

Potato Cakes

Makes 4 servings

When you find your refrigerator full of leftover mashed potatoes, it is time to make potato cakes. After Christmas or Thanksgiving, I will add about 1 cup (250 mL) finely chopped turkey or ham (or even leftover stuffing). Serve them for brunch, lunch or supper with cold meat and a salad.

The quantity of mayonnaise or milk may vary slightly according to the wetness of the potatoes.

Make Ahead

Cakes can be assembled, covered and refrigerated for several hours. Bake for an additional 8 to 10 minutes, watching to make sure cakes do not brown too much.

3 cups	mashed potatoes	750 mL
½ cup	cooked corn kernels	125 mL
¼ cup	chopped green onion	50 mL
¼ cup	chopped celery (optional)	50 mL
¼ cup	mayonnaise or milk (approx.)	50 mL
1	egg, beaten	1
½ tsp	dried thyme or sage leaves	2 mL
½ tsp	salt	2 mL
¼ tsp	black pepper	2 mL
2 tbsp	butter, melted	25 mL

1. In a large bowl, combine potatoes, corn, green onion and celery, if using. Stir in mayonnaise, egg, thyme, salt and pepper. Shape into 4 cakes.

2. Place cakes on lightly greased or parchment-lined oven pan. Brush tops and sides with melted butter.

3. Convection bake in a preheated 400°F (200°C) convection toaster oven for 20 to 25 minutes, or until golden and hot.

Rainbow Pepper Salad

3	bell peppers (red, yellow and orange), seeded and cut in 1-inch (2.5 cm) pieces	3
2 tbsp	olive oil	25 mL
1	onion, thinly sliced	1
4	cloves garlic, peeled and cut in slivers	4
½ tsp	salt	2 mL
¼ tsp	black pepper	1 mL
2 tbsp	balsamic vinegar	25 mL
2 tsp	capers	10 mL
2 tsp	chopped fresh oregano or basil, or ½ tsp (2 mL) dried	10 mL
Pinch	granulated sugar	Pinch
2	anchovy fillets, chopped (optional)	2

Makes 4 to 5 servings

Make this versatile salad in late summer when multi-colored peppers are overflowing at the market. Serve it with egg dishes, polenta, pasta, fish and poultry. Cut the peppers into smaller pieces to use as a topping for grilled bread or as a sandwich filling.

1. In a large bowl, combine peppers, olive oil, onion, garlic, salt and pepper. Toss.
2. Turn peppers into a lightly greased baking dish that will fit in oven. Convection bake in a preheated 400°F (200°C) convection toaster oven for 30 minutes, stirring twice during baking.
3. Remove peppers from oven and let cool for 15 minutes. Stir in vinegar, capers, oregano, sugar and anchovies, if using. Taste and adjust seasonings if necessary.

Make Ahead
Salad can be served at room temperature or covered and refrigerated for up to two days.

Baked Lemon Salmon with Mango Salsa

Makes 4 servings

This is perfect for a quick weeknight meal. Papaya or pineapple could be used in place of mango. Serve hot or cold as part of a salad plate.

Make Ahead

Prepare salsa, cover and refrigerate for up to six hours before serving. Cook salmon, cover and refrigerate up to a day ahead.

2 tbsp	lemon juice	25 mL
1 tbsp	olive oil	15 mL
1 tbsp	grated lemon zest	15 mL
2 tsp	Russian-style mustard	10 mL
½ tsp	black pepper	2 mL
4	6-oz (175 g) salmon fillets, skin removed	4

Mango Salsa

1	ripe mango, peeled and diced	1
2	green onions, finely chopped	2
¼ cup	chopped red bell pepper	50 mL
2 tbsp	chopped fresh cilantro	25 mL
2 tbsp	lime juice	25 mL

1. In a small bowl, whisk together lemon juice, olive oil, lemon zest, mustard and pepper. Place salmon in a shallow dish and pour marinade over fish. Marinate, refrigerated, for 20 minutes.

2. Arrange fillets on lightly greased broiler rack placed over oven pan. Convection bake in a preheated 400°F (200°C) convection toaster oven for 10 to 12 minutes, or until salmon is just cooked in center.

3. Meanwhile, to prepare salsa, in a medium bowl, combine mango, green onions, red pepper, cilantro and lime juice. Serve with salmon.

Halibut Provençal

Sauce

2 tbsp	olive oil	25 mL
1	small onion, chopped	1
2	cloves garlic, finely chopped	2
½ cup	dry white wine	125 mL
1 cup	chopped tomato	250 mL
1 tsp	grated orange zest	5 mL
½ tsp	dried thyme leaves	2 mL
½ tsp	salt	2 mL
½ tsp	black pepper	2 mL

Fish

1 tbsp	olive oil	15 mL
1 tbsp	lemon juice	15 mL
¼ tsp	salt	1 mL
¼ tsp	black pepper	1 mL
1½ lbs	halibut fillets, cut in 4 pieces	750 g
⅓ cup	pitted black olives	75 mL
2 tsp	capers	10 mL
2 tbsp	chopped fresh basil or parsley	25 mL

Makes 4 servings

Fish retains both flavor and moistness when topped with this sauce and cooked quickly in a convection toaster oven. If halibut is unavailable, try cod, snapper or tilapia. Serve with rice or couscous.

1. To make sauce, in a medium skillet, heat oil over medium-high heat. Add onion and garlic. Cook, stirring occasionally, for 3 minutes. Add wine, tomato, orange zest, thyme, salt and pepper. Bring to a boil, reduce heat and simmer for 8 minutes.

2. Meanwhile, lightly grease broiler rack and place over oven pan (add ¼ cup/50 mL water to pan). To prepare fish, in a shallow dish, combine olive oil, lemon juice, salt and pepper. Dip fish into marinade, then place on broiler rack.

3. Place rack under preheated broiler in top position of convection toaster oven. Leave door ajar. Broil for 6 to 8 minutes per side, or until fish flakes lightly with a fork (timing depends on thickness of fish). Place fish on a serving platter. Spoon sauce over fish and top with olives, capers and basil.

Roast Chicken with Orange and Sage

Makes 4 to 5 servings

A small chicken cooks to a beautiful golden brown in the convection toaster oven, and it is easy to prepare. Garnish with fresh orange sections and serve with a rice pilaf or mashed potatoes, or chill thoroughly and serve with potato salad.

1	3-lb (1.5 kg) chicken, patted dry	1
½ tsp	salt, divided	2 mL
½ tsp	black pepper, divided	2 mL
½	orange, cut in sections	½
4	cloves garlic, peeled and halved	4
3	sprigs fresh sage, or 1 tsp (5 mL) dried	3

1. Season inside of chicken with ¼ tsp (1 mL) salt and ¼ tsp (1 mL) pepper. Place orange sections, garlic and sage in cavity. Tuck chicken wing tips under back and tie legs together. Place breast side up on broiler rack set over oven pan. Sprinkle with remaining salt and pepper.

2. Convection bake in a preheated 350°F (180°C) convection toaster oven for 1 hour, or until juices run clear and a meat thermometer registers 180°F (82°C) when inserted into inner thigh.

3. Remove chicken from oven and cover with foil. Let stand for 15 minutes before carving.

Toasty Chicken Drumsticks

½ cup	apple juice or milk	125 mL
½ cup	cornflake crumbs	125 mL
½ cup	dry bread crumbs	125 mL
½ tsp	dried sage or savory leaves	2 mL
½ tsp	smoked paprika or chili powder	2 mL
½ tsp	salt	2 mL
6	chicken drumsticks, with or without skin	6

1. Pour apple juice into a shallow dish. In a separate shallow dish, combine cornflake crumbs, bread crumbs, sage, paprika and salt.

2. Roll drumsticks in apple juice and then roll in coating mixture, pressing in crumb mixture. (Prepare two or three drumsticks at a time.) Place on lightly greased foil-lined oven pan.

3. Convection bake in a preheated 350°F (180°C) convection toaster oven for 45 minutes, or until juices run clear. Turn once during cooking.

> **Smoked Paprika**
> This smoky spice is mainly produced in Spain. Look for it in food shops featuring Spanish or Italian specialties as well as some supermarkets. It is very full flavored, so use it sparingly at first. Store it at room temperature in a tightly covered container away from heat and humidity.

Makes 4 to 6 servings

A mixture of seasoned crumbs gives a crispy coating to chicken drumsticks, and dipping the chicken in a liquid first helps the crumbs adhere. Use buttermilk, thin yogurt, thinned mayonnaise or even tomato juice as a substitute for the apple juice.

Tandoori Chicken with Raita

Makes 4 servings

This is a very relaxed version of chicken tandoori, which is traditionally cooked in a hot tandoor oven. The yogurt and spice marinade tenderizes and flavors the chicken.

Raita is a cooling yogurt salad often served with spicy dishes. It can also be served as a spread or dip.

Make Ahead

Raita can be covered and refrigerated up to four hours before serving. Chicken is excellent cooked ahead and served chilled and sliced.

½ cup	unflavored yogurt	125 mL
2	cloves garlic, minced	2
2 tsp	chopped gingerroot	10 mL
2 tbsp	lemon juice	25 mL
½ tsp	paprika	2 mL
½ tsp	ground cumin	2 mL
½ tsp	ground coriander	2 mL
¼ tsp	ground cardamom or cinnamon	1 mL
¼ tsp	cayenne pepper	1 mL
4	6-oz (175 g) boneless, skinless chicken breasts	4

Raita

½	English cucumber, grated	½
½ tsp	salt	2 mL
¾ cup	unflavored yogurt	175 mL
½ cup	grated carrot	125 mL
½ tsp	granulated sugar	2 mL
¼ tsp	ground cumin	1 mL
2 tbsp	chopped fresh chives or green onion	25 mL
2 tbsp	chopped fresh mint	25 mL

1. To prepare chicken, in a small bowl, combine yogurt, garlic, ginger, lemon juice, paprika, cumin, coriander, cardamom and cayenne. Arrange chicken breasts in a single layer in an 8-inch (2 L) baking dish. Pour marinade over chicken and turn chicken to coat. Cover and refrigerate for 6 to 24 hours.

2. Arrange chicken breasts on lightly greased broiler rack set over oven pan. Convection bake in a preheated 350°F (180°C) convection toaster oven for 30 to 35 minutes, or until juices run clear.

3. Meanwhile, to prepare raita, combine grated cucumber with salt in a sieve placed over a bowl. Let stand for 25 minutes. Gently squeeze out excess moisture.

4. In a clean bowl, combine cucumber, yogurt, carrot, sugar, cumin, chives and mint. Taste and adjust seasonings if necessary. Serve with chicken.

Thai Pork Tenderloin

2	cloves garlic, minced	2
1 tbsp	chopped gingerroot	15 mL
2 tbsp	chopped fresh cilantro	25 mL
3 tbsp	hoisin sauce	45 mL
2 tbsp	lime juice or lemon juice	25 mL
1 tbsp	fish sauce or soy sauce	15 mL
1 tbsp	sesame oil	15 mL
2 tbsp	sweet Asian chili sauce	25 mL
2	pork tenderloins (about 12 oz/ 375 g each)	2

Makes 5 to 6 servings

An easy preparation for a tender, full-flavored pork tenderloin. Serve hot with steamed broccoli and rice or chill and slice thinly for sandwiches, salads or meat trays. For a less spicy version, reduce the sweet Asian chili sauce to 1 tbsp (15 mL).

1. In a small bowl, combine garlic, ginger, cilantro, hoisin, lime juice, fish sauce, sesame oil and chili sauce.

2. Arrange tenderloins in a single layer in a dish just large enough to hold pork. Pour sauce over meat, turning tenderloins to coat. Cover and refrigerate for 1 to 24 hours.

3. Arrange tenderloins with sauce on parchment-lined oven pan. Convection bake in a preheated 350°F (180°C) convection toaster oven for 25 to 30 minutes, or until juices run clear when tenderloin is pierced. Let stand for 5 minutes, then slice on diagonal.

Fish Sauce

Fish sauce is a thin, brown, salty liquid made from fermented or pickled fish. It is sold in large bottles and is used instead of salt in Thai cooking. If it is unavailable, use soy sauce.

Striploin Steak Roast with Green Sauce

Makes 3 to 4 servings

A thick striploin steak produces a small tender roast with the simplest of seasonings. Montreal steak spice is the secret ingredient. It is usually located in the spice/herb section of the supermarket, but you can also use your favorite seasoning mix. Green sauce (also called salsa verde) is a full-flavored condiment to serve alongside the carved steak.

Make Ahead

Green sauce can be covered and refrigerated up to a day ahead.

Green Sauce

½ cup	fresh parsley leaves	125 mL
3	green onions, coarsely chopped	3
1	slice white bread, crust removed, cubed	1
1 tbsp	red wine vinegar	15 mL
1	anchovy fillet, mashed, or 1 tsp (5 mL) anchovy paste	1
2 tsp	capers	10 mL
¼ cup	olive oil	50 mL
¼ tsp	salt	1 mL
¼ tsp	black pepper	1 mL

Roast

2	cloves garlic, minced	2
1 tbsp	lime juice or lemon juice	15 mL
1 tbsp	Worcestershire sauce	15 mL
1 tbsp	olive oil	15 mL
1	striploin steak (about 1 lb/500 g), 1½ inches (4 cm) thick	1
1 tbsp	Montreal steak spice	15 mL

1. To prepare sauce, chop parsley and green onions in a food processor. Add bread cubes, vinegar, anchovy and capers. Puree, then pour in olive oil and combine well. Season with salt and pepper.

2. For roast, combine garlic, lime juice, Worcestershire sauce and olive oil in a flat dish. Trim fat from steak. Dip both sides of steak into mixture, then roll steak in spice to coat. Place on broiler rack set over oven pan.

3. Convection bake in a preheated 375°F (190°C) convection toaster oven for 22 to 25 minutes, or until a meat thermometer registers 140°F (60°C) for medium-rare. Cover with foil. Let stand for 10 minutes before carving in thin slices. Serve with green sauce.

Homestyle Meatloaf

1 tbsp	olive oil	15 mL
1	onion, chopped	1
3	cloves garlic, finely chopped	3
1½ lbs	lean ground beef	750 g
1	egg	1
½ cup	dry bread crumbs	125 mL
½ cup	ketchup or chili sauce	125 mL
1 tbsp	horseradish	15 mL
1 tbsp	Worcestershire sauce	15 mL
1 tbsp	Dijon mustard	15 mL
½ tsp	dried sage leaves	2 mL
½ tsp	salt	2 mL
¼ tsp	black pepper	1 mL

Topping

¼ cup	ketchup	50 mL
1 tsp	horseradish	5 mL
1 tsp	Dijon mustard	5 mL

Makes 6 servings

This old standby is still a big favorite. Instead of ground beef you can use a combination of ground meats such as pork, veal, turkey or chicken. Serve leftovers in sandwiches.

1. In a small skillet, heat oil over medium-high heat. Add onion and garlic. Cook, stirring occasionally, for 3 minutes, or until softened.

2. In a large bowl, combine ground beef, egg, bread crumbs, ketchup, horseradish, Worcestershire, mustard, sage, salt, pepper and cooked onion mixture. Mix together thoroughly. Pack into an 8- by 4-inch (1.5 L) loaf pan.

3. For topping, in small bowl, combine ketchup, horseradish and mustard. Spread over meatloaf. Convection bake in a preheated 350°F (180°C) convection toaster oven for 60 to 70 minutes, or until a meat thermometer registers 170°F (77°C). Let stand for 5 minutes. Pour off any accumulated fat before serving.

Raisin and Rosemary Soda Bread

Makes one 9-inch (23 cm) loaf

Ireland's most popular bread bakes perfectly in the convection oven. For more even browning, turn the bread at half time. For a plain loaf, omit the rosemary and raisins.

2½ cups	all-purpose flour	625 mL
½ cup	whole wheat flour	125 mL
1 tsp	salt	5 mL
1 tsp	baking soda	5 mL
1 tbsp	chopped fresh rosemary, or 1½ tsp (7 mL) dried	15 mL
1 cup	golden raisins	250 mL
1¾ cups	buttermilk or unflavored yogurt	425 mL

1. In a large bowl, combine all-purpose flour, whole wheat flour, salt, baking soda, rosemary and raisins. Combine thoroughly.

2. Add buttermilk. Stir to combine but do not overmix (dough will be slightly sticky). Turn onto a floured surface. With floured hands, shape dough into a loaf about 9 inches (23 cm) long. Cut 5 diagonal slashes in top. Place on lightly floured oven pan.

3. Convection bake in a preheated 400°F (200°C) convection toaster oven for 20 minutes. Reduce heat to 350°F (180°C). Continue baking for 25 minutes, or until bread sounds hollow when tapped on bottom. Cool on a rack.

> ### Variations
> *Cheddar and Sun-dried Tomato Soda Bread:* Omit rosemary and raisins. Add 1 cup (250 mL) grated Cheddar cheese and 3 tbsp (45 mL) chopped dry or oil-packed sun-dried tomatoes.
>
> *Apricot Caraway Soda Bread:* Omit rosemary and raisins. Add ¾ cup (175 mL) diced dried apricots and 2 tsp (10 mL) caraway seeds.

Citrus Tea Bread

½ cup	butter, softened	125 mL
¾ cup	granulated sugar	175 mL
2	eggs	2
1 tbsp	grated lemon zest	15 mL
1 tbsp	grated orange zest	15 mL
1½ cups	all-purpose flour	375 mL
1 tsp	baking powder	5 mL
¼ tsp	salt	1 mL
½ cup	milk	125 mL
⅓ cup	confectioner's (icing) sugar	75 mL
3 tbsp	lemon juice	45 mL
3 tbsp	orange juice	45 mL

Makes one 8- by 4-inch (1.5 L) loaf

Simple and fresh tasting, this tea bread can be served plain or with fresh or stewed fruit. The bread freezes well, so serve half now, wrap the rest and freeze for up to six weeks.

1. In a large bowl, cream butter and sugar until light. Beat in eggs one at a time. Stir in lemon and orange zest.

2. In a separate bowl, combine flour, baking powder and salt. Add alternately to butter mixture with milk, making three liquid and two dry additions. Spoon into a greased and parchment-lined 8- by 4-inch (1.5 L) loaf pan.

3. Convection bake in a preheated 350°F (180°C) convection toaster oven for 45 minutes, or until a cake tester inserted in center comes out clean (rotate bread halfway through baking time).

4. Meanwhile, in a measuring cup, combine confectioner's sugar, lemon juice and orange juice. Stir to dissolve sugar. Using a skewer, pierce baked loaf in several places. Gradually spoon glaze over loaf. Cool loaf for 15 minutes before removing from pan. Cool completely on a rack.

Variation
Citrus Herb Bread: Add 2 tsp (10 mL) chopped fresh thyme, rosemary, lemon verbena or lavender flowers to batter with grated citrus zest.

Blueberry Almond Crisp

Makes 6 servings

Instead of using only blueberries, you can try a combination of fruits such as blueberries and peaches, blueberries and raspberries or raspberries and peaches. If you are using juicy fruits like peaches, stir in an additional 1 tbsp (15 mL) flour.
   Serve with Orange Yogurt Cheese.

4 cups	fresh or frozen blueberries	1 L
1 tbsp	all-purpose flour	15 mL
2 tsp	lemon juice	10 mL
½ tsp	almond extract	2 mL

Topping

1 cup	rolled oats (not instant)	250 mL
½ cup	packed brown sugar	125 mL
¼ cup	all-purpose flour	50 mL
¼ cup	sliced or slivered almonds	50 mL
¼ cup	butter, melted	50 mL

1. Arrange blueberries in a lightly greased 8-inch (2 L) square baking dish. Sprinkle berries with flour, lemon juice and almond extract. Stir to distribute flour.

2. For topping, in a bowl, combine rolled oats, sugar, flour and almonds. Stir in melted butter. Spread topping over fruit.

3. Convection bake in a preheated 350°F (180°C) convection toaster oven for 25 minutes, or until top is golden and blueberries are bubbling.

> ### Orange Yogurt Cheese
> Place 1 cup (250 mL) unflavored yogurt in a sieve lined with cheesecloth, coffee filter or paper towel and place sieve over a bowl (or use a yogurt strainer). Cover and refrigerate for 3 to 4 hours. Place drained yogurt in a bowl. Stir in 2 tbsp (25 mL) orange juice, 1 tsp (5 mL) grated orange zest and 1 tbsp (15 mL) granulated sugar. Cover and refrigerate until using. Makes about ½ cup (125 mL).

Baked Apples

4	apples (such as Northern Spy, Ida Red, Golden Delicious)	4
¼ cup	maple syrup	50 mL
¼ cup	apricot jam	50 mL
¼ cup	apple juice or water	50 mL
2 tbsp	lemon juice	25 mL
¼ tsp	ground nutmeg	1 mL

1. Core apples using an apple corer or melon ball scoop. Using a sharp knife, score peel about a third of the way down apples (this prevents apples from bursting). Arrange apples in a shallow baking pan that will hold juices.

2. In a small bowl, combine syrup, jam, apple juice, lemon juice and nutmeg. Spoon into center of apples, letting remainder drizzle over.

3. Convection bake in a preheated 375°F (190°C) convection toaster oven for 25 minutes. Spoon some glaze over apples. Rotate pan. Bake for another 20 to 25 minutes, or until apples are tender.

Makes 4 servings

Sometimes a forgotten dessert, baked apples are an appealing addition to any dessert table. If the apples are browning too much, reduce the oven temperature to 325°F (160°C) toward the end of the baking time. Serve warm with ice cream or flavored yogurt cheese (page 286).

Peach Brown Betty

Makes 4 to 5 servings

When peaches are in season, it is the time for an old-fashioned dessert like this one. Although peeled peaches are the norm, sometimes I just wash them and leave the peel on. Bread crumbs make a light crusty topping. (In some cookbooks, even stale cake crumbs are called for.) Just make sure the top does not get too dark (bread crumbs tend to brown more quickly than other crumb toppings).

5 cups	sliced peaches (about 8 or 9)	1.25 L
1/3 cup	granulated sugar	75 mL
2 tbsp	all-purpose flour	25 mL
2 tbsp	lemon juice	25 mL

Topping

1 cup	fresh bread crumbs	250 mL
3 tbsp	brown sugar	45 mL
2 tbsp	butter, melted	25 mL
1/4 tsp	ground allspice or cumin	1 mL

1. In a lightly greased shallow 6-cup (1.5 L) baking dish, combine peaches, granulated sugar, flour and lemon juice. Stir to mix in flour and sugar.

2. In a bowl, combine bread crumbs, brown sugar, melted butter and allspice. Sprinkle over peaches.

3. Convection bake in a preheated 325°F (160°C) convection toaster oven for 30 to 35 minutes, or until peaches are tender when tested with tip of a sharp knife, and top is golden.

Baked Rice Pudding

3	eggs	3
1¾ cups	milk	425 mL
¼ cup	packed brown sugar	50 mL
1 cup	cooked rice	250 mL
⅓ cup	dried blueberries, cranberries or golden raisins	75 mL
1 tsp	grated lemon or orange zest	5 mL
½ tsp	salt	2 mL
Pinch	ground nutmeg	Pinch

1. In a large bowl, beat eggs lightly. Add milk, sugar, rice, blueberries, lemon zest and salt. Combine thoroughly. Pour into a lightly greased 6-cup (1.5 L) shallow baking dish. Sprinkle with nutmeg.

2. Convection bake in a preheated 325°F (160°C) convection toaster oven for 35 to 40 minutes, or until a sharp knife inserted in center comes out clean. Let sit for 30 minutes before serving.

Makes 4 servings

A perfect way to use extra cooked rice, this pudding is satisfying without being too rich. If you have a sweet tooth, add up to 2 tbsp (25 mL) sugar. I like to serve this cold, cut in squares or triangles and accompanied by fresh fruit.

Make Ahead
Pudding can be prepared, covered and refrigerated for up to a day before serving.

Library and Archives Canada Cataloguing in Publication

Stephen, Linda
The convection oven bible / Linda Stephen.

Includes index.
ISBN-13: 978-0-7788-0154-2
ISBN-10: 0-7788-0154-3

1. Convection oven cookery. I. Title.

TX840.C65S843 2007   641.5'8   C2006-905906-3

Index